Peacebuilding and Post-War Transitions

This book asks how, and under what conditions, external–domestic inter-actions impact on peacebuilding outcomes during transitions to peace and democracy.

Why do so many peacebuilding interventions in post-war states result in stalled transitions despite heavy international support? This book suggests a new interaction-based explanation for this puzzle and proposes an 'analytical framework of peacebuilding interactions'. Based on eight cases of peacebuild-ing interactions, it demonstrates that the limited rationality of the actors involved in external–domestic interactions influenced the post-war transition results in Kosovo. Drawing on interviews and focus groups, the insights build on the process tracing of peacebuilding reforms in the area of Local Govern-ance and Police Reform, with a specific focus at the local level. Through an in-depth analysis of peacebuilding negotiations, this book shows how peace-builders' use of ad hoc interaction tactics – intended as heuristics to simplify decision-making in overly complex post-war environments – have the unin-tended effect of offering domestic actors additional leeway to prioritise their domestic agenda, often at the expense of achieving full democratisation. The resulting consequences of these actions mean that, even in highly resourced interventions, such as those implemented in Kosovo, stalled transitions become one of the most likely outcomes of the peacebuilding process.

This book will be of much interest to students of peacebuilding, war and conflict studies, European politics, security studies and IR in general.

Lisa Groß is a researcher at the German Institute for Development. She received her PhD from the Department of Politics and Public Administra-tion, University of Konstanz, Germany.

Routledge Studies in Peace and Conflict Resolution
Series Editors: Tom Woodhouse and Oliver Ramsbotham

Peacebuilding and Post-War Transitions

Assessing the impact of external–domestic interactions

Lisa Groß

Routledge
Taylor & Francis Group

LONDON AND NEW YORK

First published 2017
by Routledge
2 Park Square, Milton Park, Abingdon, Oxon OX14 4RN

and by Routledge
711 Third Avenue, New York, NY 10017

Routledge is an imprint of the Taylor & Francis Group, an informa business

British Library Cataloguing-in-Publication Data
A catalogue record for this book is available from the British Library

Library of Congress Cataloging-in-Publication Data
Names: Groß, Lisa, 1983– author.
Title: Peacebuilding and post-war transitions : assessing the impact of
external-domestic interactions / Lisa Groß.
Description: Abingdon, Oxon ; New York, NY : Routledge, 2017. |
Series: Routledge studies in peace and conflict resolution | Includes
bibliographical references and index.
Identifiers: LCCN 2016029985| ISBN 9781138210264 (hardback) |
ISBN 9781315455778 (ebook)
Subjects: LCSH: Peace-building. | Postwar reconstruction. |
Peace-building–Kosovo (Republic) | Postwar reconstruction.–Kosovo
(Republic)
Classification: LCC JZ5538 .G76 2017 | DDC 327.1/72–dc23
LC record available at https://lccn.loc.gov/2016029985

ISBN: 978-1-138-21026-4 (hbk)
ISBN: 978-1-315-45577-8 (ebk)

Typeset in Bembo
by Wearset Ltd, Boldon, Tyne and Wear

Contents

Acknowledgements

This book is the result of several years of research in Kosovo on the influence of peacebuilding on post-war transitions. I have learned a lot during this time and I hope to be able to share some of my insights with you while reading along.

Of course, a long research project such as this always depends on the support and the collaboration of the people around. I have received excellent academic support from Sonja Grimm, Gerald Schneider and Christoph Zürcher, who were never tired of giving me advice on how to develop my research idea and who encouraged me to think in different directions. Particular thanks goes to Sonja who has taken the time to read all my drafts and was never short of valuable advice. I have also profited from the valuable comments I received at conferences and I would like to thank the people who gave them, in particular, Séverine Autessere, Lothar Brock, Arnaud Kurze and Jelena Subotić.

The book draws its insights mainly from field research, which is barely possible without the support of insiders to the field in question. I am therefore deeply indebted to the friends I found in Kosovo, who shared their life stories with me and, equally important, their good taste for beautiful black Balkan humour. Without them, I would never have come to write the book as it stands now because it is only through the personal conversations that I started to make better sense of my observations. I am especially thankful to Admir, Ferid, Ljubiša and Mimoza for translating, moderating and helping me in all kinds of circumstances as well as to Adnan, Hanka and Shkumbin and all the youngsters of the youth centre in Bregore/Brdašce for making me feel welcome right from my arrival in Kosovo. I also owe much gratitude to my interview partners in Kosovo institutions and international organisations who were so kind to share their opinions and knowledge, sometimes even long after I had left the country. Without their readiness to spend their precious time with just another PhD student, I would not have been able to write the book. As I pledged anonymity, I cannot thank anyone in particular, but there were many whose support went beyond merely meeting up for a chat over a coffee and I am very grateful for this.

I am also obliged to several institutions that have significantly supported my research. The Heinrich-Böll Foundation funded the last years of my dissertation and offered inspiring opportunities for exchange with other stipends. And the University of Konstanz and the academic and non-academic staff has created an inspiring environment for this research.

Doing research would be much less fun if there was not the motivated crowd of fellow researchers and PhD students who are ready to offer support with anything they can – sharp thoughts, critical comments, office space or mensa meals. For this, my very special thanks go to Hanja Blendin, Sarah Riese, Joel Winckler, Constantin Ruhe and Lisbeth Zimmermann as well as to Aleksandar for his endless optimism and patience.

Finally, my gratitude goes to my parents Ursula and Wolfgang Groß and my sister Sophie for being who they are and for believing in me.

Abbreviations

AAK	Aleanca për Ardhmërinë e Kosovës/Alliance for the Future of Kosovo
AKR	Aleanca Kosova e Re/Alliance for New Kosovo
CC	Communities Committee
CEC	Commission of the European Communities
CEU	Council of the European Union
CSAT	Community Safety Action Team
CSP	Comprehensive Proposal for the Kosovo Status Settlement (Ahtisaari Plan)
DSS	Demokratska Stranka Srbije/Democratic Party of Serbia
DFID	Department for International Development
EU	European Union
EULEX	EU Rule of Law Mission in Kosovo
ICG	International Crisis Group
ICITAP	International Criminal Investigative Training Assistance Programme of the US State Department
ICO	International Civilian Office
ICTY	International Criminal Tribunal for the States of the Former Yugoslavia
IR	International Relations
JIAS	Joint Interim Administrative Structure of Kosovo
KFOR	Kosovo FORce
KP	Kosovo Police
KP	Koalicija Povratak/Coalition Return
LDD	Lidhja Demokratike e Dardanie/Democratic League of Dardania
LDK	Lidhja Demokratike e Kosovës/Democratic League of Kosovo
LLG	Law on Local Self-Government
LMT	Liaison Monitoring Team
LPSC	Local Public Safety Council
LUL	Law on the Use of Languages
MCSC	Municipal Community Safety Council

MLGA	Ministry of Local Government Administration
MMA	Monitoring, Mentoring and Advice by EULEX
MoF	Ministry of Finance
MONUSCO	United Nations Organization Stabilization Mission in the Democratic Republic of the Congo
NATO	North Atlantic Treaty Organisation
NGO	Non-Governmental Organisation
ODA	Official Development Aid
OECD-DAC	Organization for Economic Co-Operation and Development Development Assistance Committee
OSCE	Organisation for Security and Co-operation in Europe
PDK	Partia Demokratike e Kosovës/Democratic Party of Kosovo
PFC	Policy and Finance Committee
PISG	Provisional Institutions of Self-Government
RAE	Roma, Ashkali, Egyptian
SNV	Srpsko Nacionalno Veće/Serb National Council
SLS	Samostalna Liberalna Stranka/Independent Liberal Party
SPS	Socijalistička Partija Srbije/Socialist Party of Serbia
SRS	Srpska Radikalna Stranka/Serbian Radical Party
SRSG	Special Representative of the Secretary General
UÇK	Ushtria Çlirimtare e Kosovës/Kosovo Liberation Army
UN	United Nations
UNCIVPOL	UN Civilian Police
UNTAC	United Nations Transitional Authority in Cambodia
UNTAES	United Nations Transitional Administration for Eastern Slavonia
UNTAET	United Nations Transitional Administration in East Timor
UNHCR	United Nations High Commissioner for Refugees
UNMIK	United Nations Interim Administration Mission in Kosovo
UNSC	United Nations Security Council
USAID	United States Agency for International Development
ZIF	Zentrum für International Friedenseinsätze

1 Introduction

> [I] indicated that the UN was establishing a presence in Zabel/Šumarak and that it would appear to be in everyone's best interest if the UN team, which would probably not number more than five or six individuals, could be co-located with the Provisional Municipal Government. We were immediately offered all possible cooperation.
>
> *UNMIK Daily Report*, 21/08/1999, Zabel/Šumarak

On his first day in office on 21 August 1999, the UNMIK[1] Municipal Administrator from the quote above needed three things. First, he needed a good memory for names, as he was introduced immediately to several UÇK[2] members outside their headquarters as well as to the Municipal President and Vice-President and to the heads of the Departments of Administration, Economy and Finance, Social Issues, and Urbanization, among others. Second, he needed good organisational skills: Right after his introduction, he was presented with plans for (a) the reconstruction of the municipal hospital, (b) the search for 23 persons who had disappeared during the war and (c) a tuberculosis epidemic that had already infected 2000 individuals.[3] Third, he needed to have excellent negotiation skills – as UNMIK was in charge, at least theoretically – to administer the municipality and coordinate the above-mentioned projects with the above-mentioned actors. As a representative of the UN, he thus had to negotiate with domestic elites on a daily basis in order to gain cooperation for the peacebuilding goal to build peace and democracy.

The above situation exemplifies well how closely international and domestic actors are intertwined in post-conflict contexts and that peacebuilding entails manifold instances of day-to-day interaction between those intervening from outside to build peace and democracy and the domestic elites of the host country. Yet such day-to-day interaction processes have been largely absent from the study of peacebuilding, and what takes place inside a post-war country subjected to peacebuilding remains a 'black box' in many regards.[4] To shed new light on the inside of peacebuilding, this book examines the external–domestic interactions between peacebuilders and domestic actors and its impact on peacebuilding outcomes. The book seeks to answer the following questions: What really happens on the ground in peacebuilding? Who are the protagonists of peacebuilding, what are their goals, and how do they act to reach their goals? How, after all, is peacebuilding negotiated between peacebuilders and national and sub-national agents, and what are the results of such negotiations? In this manner, the book scrutinizes the inside of liberal peacebuilding with regard to the puzzle of why so many peacebuilding interventions – despite heavy international support – fail to facilitate the journey to peace and democracy. In fact, peacebuilding seems to be successful at ending wars and ensuring democratic openings, but full democratisation is seldom achieved (Doyle and Sambanis 2000, Paris 2004, Zürcher 2006). Of the 15 post-war countries with multidimensional peacebuilding missions[5] launched between 1989 and 2002,[6] only three have completed the transition to liberal democracies[7] – Croatia, El Salvador and Namibia. The majority of post-war countries – Haiti, Liberia, Mozambique, Sierra Leone, East Timor, Bosnia and Kosovo – show signs of stalled transition, indicating that though constituted as liberal democracies, the political and institutional practice differs widely from the Western democratic ideal. Some countries, such as Cambodia, have even turned into stable autocracies, or are still caught up in deadly conflict, as is the case in Afghanistan, the Democratic Republic of Congo and Somalia.

Peace and conflict researchers have come up with different explanations for the limited success of peacebuilding interventions in promoting peace and democracy. The most prominent standard explanations either emphasize the lack of international resources that restricts the potential of international actors to facilitate post-war democratisation (for example, Doyle/Sambanis 2000, Paris 2004), or underline the role of local resistance against externally introduced liberal norms and values (see, for example, Richmond 2009, Mac Ginty 2010). However, none of these standard explanations for peacebuilding success or failure have fully clarified the abundance of stalled transitions in peacebuilding. This book concentrates on a third, more recent explanatory approach that focuses on strategic interactions in peacebuilding as a promising route to better understanding peacebuilding outcomes (Barnett *et al.* 2014, Barnett and Zürcher 2008, Zürcher *et al.* 2013). So far, however, there is only limited systematic knowledge about what happens in a post-war state when international and domestic actors negotiate peacebuilding reforms.[8]

For that reason, the everyday interaction processes between international actors and domestic elites are investigated in greater depth to better understand how they might contribute to stalled post-war transitions. To do this, the book proposes an 'analytical framework of peacebuilding interactions' that helps systematically analyse how external–domestic interactions shape peacebuilding outcomes. The central argument of the book is that external–domestic interactions offer domestic elites opportunities to 'capture'[9] peacebuilding to further their own ends, which makes stalled transitions a more likely outcome of peacebuilding intervention. However, contrary to the small but growing literature on strategic interaction in post-conflict peacebuilding (Barnett *et al.* 2014, Barnett and Zürcher 2008, Zürcher *et al.* 2013), I do not assume that stalled transitions are entirely the result of strategic calculations on the part of the interacting counterparts. Instead, I argue that interactions are shaped by the *bounded rationality* of the actors involved and that leeway for reform capture often stems from ad hoc interaction tactics, which peacebuilders use as heuristics to simplify decision-making in a fast-moving and overly complex post-war environment. The study thus serves to theoretically and empirically enrich research on the role of interactions in peacebuilding.

Before presenting the analytical framework and argument more in depth, the most prominent explanations for peacebuilding and post-war transitions shall be briefly introduced.

Understanding post-war transitions

Standard explanations for post-war transitions

Why do so many post-war states end as stalled transitions despite extensive peacebuilding support? This puzzle has motivated many researchers in the field of peace and conflict studies in the past years. At the risk of over-simplification, I argue that two broad sets of explanations have dominated the debate: international capacity (or the lack thereof) and local resist-ance.[10] Both standard explanations have significantly contributed to our theoretical understanding of what determines peacebuilding success in establishing peace and democracy, how to conceptualise the phenomenon of stalled transitions, which type of interventions work and which do not. Because of this, they cannot be dismissed completely. However, as I will argue below, none of the approaches has managed to fully explain the various outcomes of post-war democratisation and so they exhibit important shortcomings.

The *international capacity* explanation sees international capacity as the main factor influencing post-war transitions to peace and democracy. It is the international side of peacebuilding that is at the centre of scholarly interest. Scholars of the international capacity approach argue that peace-building needs sufficient international engagement in terms of mandate, manpower and money to support transitions to peace and democracy (Doyle and Sambanis 2006, Krasner 2004, Paris 2004). Academics in this field search for the right mix of international capacity, instruments and programmes to support post-war transitions to democracy. In their seminal article, Doyle/ Sambanis (2000) argue that peacebuilding missions – in contrast to traditional observer or peacekeeping missions – are more successful in fostering post-war transitions to democracy because they are equipped with a broad mandate and a greater amount of manpower and financial resources to transform economic and state institutions (Doyle and Sambanis 2000). This strand of argument assumes that international capacity enables peacebuilders to coerce domestic elites into compliance or to level out the lack of domestic capacity for democratic institution building. Many authors support this claim (Diamond 2006, Dobbins 2007, Paris 2004). The puzzle is, however, that countries with relatively high international support either continue to be mired in conflict – as is seen in Afghanistan – or have failed to complete a transition to liberal democracy – as is seen in Bosnia and Herzegovina, East Timor and Kosovo.[11] At the same time, countries with relatively low international engagement such as El Salvador and Namibia have successfully transitioned into liberal democracies. The amount of international capacity deployed thus does not fully explain peacebuilding outcomes.[12] Furthermore, these studies tend to ignore that peacebuilders have to engage with domestic elites to reach their goals.

The *local resistance* explanation focuses on the role of local agency, local resistance and everyday politics to understand peacebuilding dynamics (Boege *et al.* 2009, Mac Ginty 2010, Richmond 2009, Richmond and Mitchell 2011a). This strand of literature argues that unequal power relations between peacebuilders and post-war societies produce domestic resistance against the liberal international norms promoted by peacebuilders, which might explain the limited success of peacebuilding in engineering liberal democracy (Campbell *et al.* 2011, Mac Ginty 2011, Newman *et al.* 2009, Richmond and Mitchell 2011b). Researchers denounce peacebuilding as a new form of imperialism (Chandler 2008) or neo-colonialism (Richmond 2010) that sparks local resistance in post-war states. Scholars engage with the various modes of local resistance emerging in response to post-war liberal norm promotion and differentiate between actions of resistance, partial cooperation, re-shaping, translation, co-option, modification, subversion and adoption, and investigate the merging of local (also called traditional or customary) and liberal norms and values in post-war states. Yet these studies tend to portray relations between international actors and domestic agents in an antagonistic manner, with imperialist peacebuilders being pitted against local agents. The numerous single case studies have not fully realised the promise to take local agents' preferences, strategies and resources seriously and to build a theoretical explanation for peacebuilding results that includes international as well as local factors.[13] Also, if peacebuilding inevitably sparks resistance against liberal international norms, how is it that there are successful examples of post-war transitions to liberal democracy?

The above-mentioned explanations explain part of the phenomenon of stalled post-war transition in the context of peacebuilding. Yet they fail in two regards: First, they do not provide a full explanation for the empirical puzzle of stalled post-war transitions. Second, the inside of peacebuilding remains a black box as both arguments fail to conceptually capture the role of day-to-day interactions between international and local actors for peacebuilding on the ground – the peacebuilders' daily routines of building peace and democracy are as much neglected as the domestic actors' manner of conducting politics. They thus fail to address relevant questions such as: How do peacebuilders gain domestic cooperation for their strategies and programmes, what power struggles take place between international and domestic actors to this end and what political dynamics evolve between different segments of the post-war society?

Only recently, a third explanation has emerged that investigates the abundance of stalled post-war transitions with a focus upon the interactive features of post-war politics (Barnett *et al.* 2014, Barnett and Zürcher 2008, Zürcher *et al.* 2013). These interaction-based explanations depart from static depictions of the post-war space and acknowledge the agency of both sides as well as the empirical reality of constant bargaining over reforms. In doing so, the explanations make an important contribution to both a better understanding of the inside of peacebuilding and a better understanding of the reasons for the abundance of stalled transitions in peacebuilding. Barnett and Zürcher (2008), for example, explain post-war transition outcomes through strategic bargaining between peacebuilders and domestic elites. The authors assume that peacebuilding outcomes will most likely consist of "a mix of reforms and consolidation of the status quo" (Barnett *et al.* 2014) due to the conditions at the outset of the bargaining situation. The question is, then, how this bargaining situation influences each side's choice of strategies and what peacebuilding results stem from these strategies. Three assumptions are central to the argument: First, peacebuilders and domestic elites have divergent goals in that peacebuilders are mainly interested in stability and liberalisation, and domestic elites are interested in maintaining political power (which liberal reforms threaten to undermine in some political systems) (Barnett and Zürcher 2008). Second, both sides are mutually dependent on each other in that peacebuilders need domestic cooperation to uphold stability and implement liberal reforms, while domestic elites need peacebuilders' resources to increase their power base (Barnett *et al.* 2014, Barnett and Zürcher 2008). Third, both sides are able to process all information available on the bargaining situation in order to strategically calculate the optimum outcome. Due to these strategic calculations, Barnett and Zürcher (2008) argue, both sides are willing to compromise on their initial goals and stalled transitions will be the most likely outcome of peacebuilding.

Yet there are still many open questions as to what the role of external–domestic interactions in post-war transitions to peace and democracy is; and why, and under what conditions, these interactions lead to a particular peacebuilding outcome. In-depth empirical studies on the process of external–domestic interplay in peacebuilding are still scarce, leading to an underdeveloped understanding of interactions in post-war spaces.[14]

This book aims to tap into this research gap by proposing an analytical framework of peacebuilding interactions to systematically describe, analyse and compare interaction processes. It thereby shows that external–domestic interactions are not a purely strategic exercise but shaped by bounded rationality and entail significant non-strategic elements that influence peacebuilding outcomes.

A new analytical framework of peacebuilding interactions

So how can we better understand external–domestic interactions in peacebuilding and its influence on peacebuilding outcomes? This book proposes an analytical framework of peacebuilding interactions with key categories that serve to illustrate and analyse external–domestic interactions in post-war transitions to peace and democracy. The analytical framework has been inductively developed based on fine-grained process tracing of external–domestic interactions. The goal was to understand what strategies external and domestic actors use to negotiate their positions and how the environment of interaction influences the course of peacebuilding reforms. The analytical framework is, thus, helpful in understanding what factors shape the external–domestic interplay, what kind of interaction patterns emerge, what causal links exist between external–domestic interactions and peacebuilding outcomes, and how these might help to explain incomplete transition processes.

The analytical framework of peacebuilding interactions is organised around a set of categories presented below: (1) international ad hoc tactics such as selectivity, prioritisation and leverage; (2) domestic responses of cooperation, foot-dragging, modification or resistance; (3) the environment of interaction that influences domestic adoption costs and (4) a set of possible peacebuilding outcomes.

1   The *international ad hoc tactics of selectivity, prioritisation and leverage* have to be understood as heuristics for peacebuilders to navigate complex and challenging post-war settings. These ad hoc tactics are of a non-strategic nature and offer various opportunities for reform capture. *Selectivity* describes an interaction tactic where peacebuilders tend to select only a sub-set of rules from a reform initiative when negotiating reform implementation. Selectivity offers domestic actors leeway to ignore the non-selected rules at no cost and further leeway for reform capture at a low cost. Only if peacebuilders manage to cover the total set of rules during an interaction process, an outcome of full implementation is possible. *Prioritisation* describes a situation in which a reform is raised to the top of the international agenda. Then peacebuilders are less inclined to tolerate non-compliance and vehemently insist on the implementation of at least a *minimum set of rules*. Prioritisation thus makes no implementation a less likely outcome. *Leverage* describes the ability of peacebuilders to alter domestic actors' calculation of (non-)adoption costs through the use of higher or lower leverage norm promotion instruments. If low leverage is used, domestic actors gain further leeway to capture reforms at a low cost. High leverage makes

no implementation a less likely outcome. The degree of implementation thus depends on a combination of selectivity, prioritisation and leverage in a given environment.

2   *Domestic responses* to international demands for rule implementation can take the form of cooperation, foot-dragging, modification and resistance. *Cooperation* means that domestic actors fully follow international demands. *Foot-dragging* implies that domestic actors show low commitment to international demands and invest insufficient time, financial resources or human resources. *Modification* means that domestic actors substantially depart from peacebuilders' intentions for their implementation of a reform. *Resistance* refers to outright refusal to follow international demands.

3   The *environment of interaction* can be enabling or constraining for peacebuilders' reform goals and implies differences in adoption costs for domestic elites with regard to a peacebuilding reform. In an enabling environment of interaction, domestic elites are willing to cooperate with the reform demands of peacebuilders, as domestic adoption costs are low. In a constraining environment of interaction, domestic elites might prefer to respond with strategies of foot-dragging, modification or even resistance, as domestic adoption costs are considerably higher.

4   There are three possible *peacebuilding outcomes* for an external–domestic interaction: full implementation, captured implementation or no implementation. *Full implementation* means that the total set of rules of a reform is implemented the way peacebuilders intended. *Captured implementation* means that the total set or sub-set of rules of the reform are implemented in a way that accommodates domestic priorities while diverting from peacebuilders' original intents. *No implementation* means that none of the rules of the reform are implemented.

Based on this analytical framework of peacebuilding interactions, I show that international capacity is less relevant to the transition process than assumed by the literature because peacebuilders do not necessarily make use of high international capacity even if they are theoretically equipped with it. Additionally, I show that – although local resistance is often an important reason for reform failure – reform failure is not a necessary outcome of local resistance. Lastly, I show that current research on peacebuilding as a strategic interaction has focused too narrowly on strategic calculations as an explanatory factor for why interaction matters, neglecting the role of bounded rationality in the interaction.

Main argument

The main argument of this book is that external–domestic interactions do matter for peacebuilding outcomes, also due to non-strategic aspects of the external–domestic interaction. Peacebuilders are overwhelmed with the fast-changing and overly complex post-war environment they find themselves in. This challenges peacebuilders' ability to process all available information and to calculate optimum strategies when negotiating the implementation of peacebuilding reforms. Under these cognitive constraints, peacebuilders act with bounded rationality and resort to ad hoc interaction tactics as a repertoire of heuristics for simplifying decision-making. External–domestic interactions are thus shaped by bounded rationality rather than merely strategic calculations.

External–domestic interactions are furthermore a necessary condition for reform implementation because domestic actors only start to act after they have been advised by peacebuilders to do so: If one follows the implementation of externally induced peacebuilding reforms in Kosovo carefully, it quickly becomes apparent that peacebuilding reforms are seldom implemented immediately after they have been legally adopted. In most cases, international initiative by peacebuilders is needed to motivate the domestic side to take action in reform implementation.

The ad hoc interaction tactics of prioritisation, selectivity and leverage, which represent peacebuilders' coping strategies for situations of complexity, offer domestic elites leeway to capture reforms and thus make an outcome of stalled transition more likely. The degree of implementation is dependent on the combination of interaction tactics used in the process of external–domestic interaction in a given environment. If selectivity is high, full implementation of the reform is less likely. If prioritization is high, no implementation is less likely. The same goes for leverage: If leverage is high, no implementation becomes less likely. It is even possible to deduct testable generalisations over the role of selectivity, prioritisation and leverage in peacebuilding outcomes. For example, full implementation is more likely if no selectivity occurs over time. Captured implementation is more likely if selectivity and prioritisation or leverage occur. No implementation is more likely if neither prioritisation nor leverage occurs. The case studies in this book exemplify my claims.

Definitions

Peacebuilding

The practice of *peacebuilding* is essentially guided by the liberal peace paradigm – the idea of building peace through democracy and a market economy. Paris (1997), the first to point out that peace missions are based on the concept of liberal peace, sees the central tenet of this paradigm in "the assumption that the surest foundation for peace, both within and between states, is market democracy, that is, liberal democratic polity and a market-oriented economy".[15] The democratic peace proposition that democracies are less likely to go to war with each other, first discussed by Kant in *Perpetual Peace* (Kant 1984), is used as a powerful argument to promote democracy in post-conflict societies. The goal of peacebuilding is the transformation of post-war states into liberal democracies with free and fair elections, institutional checks and balances, human and political rights, rule of law, transparent and accountable institutions, opportunities for citizen participation, and market economies with independent banking systems, private businesses and protection of private property (Paris 1997).

Contemporary peacebuilding uses a multi-dimensional approach to rebuilding war-shattered states. Boutros-Ghali's ground-breaking 1992 report, *An Agenda for Peace*, defines peacebuilding as "action to identify and support structures which will tend to strengthen and solidify peace in order to avoid relapse into conflict" (UN 1992). This marked a significant turn in international peacekeeping towards engaging with the inner workings of a state by taking on reforms in the economic, political and social sphere. Post-conflict states not only have to disarm, reform the security sector and organise elections, they are also encouraged to reform their institutions and the economy according to liberal principles, and to build capable, accountable and responsive structures in which power is contested non-violently. Today's peacebuilding components, programs and projects therefore deal with diverse activities in the areas of election organisation, political party support and institution building based on the principles of democracy, human rights and rule of law (Zeeuw and Kumar 2006). All activities share the liberal peace assumption that democracy, rule of law and economic liberalization will lead to sustainable peace (Barnett 2007).

Stalled transition

Stalled transition describes a transition from war-to-democracy and/or authoritarianism-to-democracy that did not result in fully-fledged liberal democratic statehood but came to a standstill on the way. A *fully-fledged liberal democracy* would be a political system that satisfies at least the basic definition of liberal democracy: free and fair elections, a multi-party system, political rights and civil liberties, as well as institutional checks and balances. This aligns in part with Dahl (1971), who sees democracy as a political system with free and fair elections and as a multi-party system that guarantees political rights and civil liberties to enable its citizens to formulate and signify preferences.

A stalled transition refers to a situation in which the legal framework of state institutions conforms largely to the definition of liberal democracy presented above, but the actual practice differs widely. March and Olsen speak of a de-coupling of formal institutional ideals and actual behaviour that takes place in such situations (March and Olsen 2008). Such stalled transitions can be observed in many post-conflict countries (Grimm 2008, Grimm and Merkel 2008, Zürcher *et al.* 2009) and manifest themselves in the co-existence and sometimes clash of liberal elements with illiberal, traditional and customary norms, institutions and practices (Belloni 2012). Countries in a state of stalled transition are not necessarily in a transitory phase between democracy and autocracy (Carothers 2002) but "are characterised by a mixture of institutional traits typical of both these regimes" (Cassani 2013) or by an interlocking of formal democratic institutions and traditional informal practices (Morlino 2008, Zinecker 2009).

Research design and methodology

Methodologically, the book is based on an inductive, qualitative, local-level study that compares external–domestic interaction processes over four reform initiatives in the two Kosovo municipalities of Zabel/Šumarak and Bregore/Brdašce.[16] Kosovo is a particularly interesting case for studying interactions in peacebuilding as it hosts one of the most intrusive peacebuilding missions in the history of the UN in terms of mandate, troops and financial assistance per capita.[17] I was especially interested in high international capacity interventions because the assumption that there is a direct relationship between peacebuilding success and the level of international capacity has powerfully shaped the peacebuilding discourses in academia and in practice. According to the international capacity explanation, Kosovo would represent a promising case for a successful democratisation. Yet Kosovo shows only relatively modest success in transforming into a full-fledged liberal democracy. Kosovo is rated only as 'partly free' by Freedom House (Freedom House 2014) and reports the lowest economic development in the region (Peci *et al.* 2010). This is why studying interactions in Kosovo is of particular interest to those wanting to know more about the limited success of peacebuilding.

The inductive development of the analytical framework is based on fine-grained process tracing of external–domestic interactions at the sub-national level in two Kosovo municipalities. The case studies are situated at the level of individual reform initiatives. I presumed that an interaction-based argument would have to hold up against the two standard explanations to prove its theoretical relevance. The case selection is therefore based on variance with regard to the level of capacity and the level of resistance of peacebuilding reforms to allow for (brief) theory testing of the standard explanations: The high capacity explanation would expect reforms with high capacity to result in full implementation, while in the case of reforms with low capacity, a full implementation outcome would become less likely. The local resistance explanation would expect reforms promoting democracy (weak resistance) to result in full implementation, while reforms promoting minority rights (strong resistance) would result in no implementation. I have selected one high capacity policy field – police reform – and one low capacity policy field – local governance reform.[18] In the low capacity field of local governance, I investigated the democracy promoting reform of Participatory Budget Planning (weak resistance) and the minority rights promoting Communities Committees reform (strong resistance). In the high capacity field of police reform, I selected the democracy promoting reform of Municipal Community Safety

Councils (MSCS) (weak resistance) and the minority rights promoting reform of Minority Community Policing (strong resistance).[19] I sought to hold constant those context conditions usually considered relevant for peacebuilding success.[20] Table 1.1 shows the case selection.

The design enabled me to check the extent to which standard explanations can actually account for the peacebuilding outcome. Given that neither the capacity argument nor the local resistance argument could provide consistent explanations for the outcomes of my case studies, there is a need for alternative explanations such as offered by current interaction-based arguments.

To operationalise the peacebuilding outcome, I differentiate between full implementation, captured implementation and no implementation and divide reform outcomes into a formal dimension, practice dimension and content dimension. The middle ground category of captured implementation leans on Barnett, Fang and Zürcher's (2014) description of captured peacebuilding as a situation in which local elites reduce peacebuilding to an instrument of their priorities, be it for socio-economic development, political power or the Kosovo status. The advantage of a qualitative micro-level study is that it allows for a nuanced picture of whether implementation takes place according to peacebuilders' intentions or is captured for domestic priorities. The *formal dimension* refers to the formal establishment of an institution, office or group. The *practice dimension* refers to the functionality of the reform according to the rules regarding practices, such as number of meetings, accountability and reporting rules, etc. The *content dimension* focuses on the meaning and purpose given to the reform by those who implement it.

The data was gathered during three research trips over a total of four months in Kosovo between May 2012 and December 2013. Each time, I divided my stay between the two municipalities, Bregore/Brdašce and Zabel/ Šumarak, and the capital, Prishtina. The empirical data for the process tracing is derived from 91 interviews, seven focus groups and analysis of primary documents and secondary literature. I conducted 91 interviews: 53 interviews with domestic actors, 38 interviews with peacebuilding organisations, 27 of which were held with international staff and 11 of which were held with

Table 1.1 Case selection of peacebuilding reforms following the standard explanations

	STRONG SUPPORT *Democracy*	WEAK SUPPORT *Minority rights*
LOW CAPACITY *Local governance*	Participatory Budget Planning	Communities Committee
HIGH CAPACITY *Police*	Municipal Community Safety Council	Minority Community Policing

Source: own compilation.

national staff. Focus group discussions were used to gain a better understanding of the level of resistance against an international norm and the meaning that the local population attached to democracy and minority rights. I held seven focus group discussions with 52 Kosovo Albanians and Kosovo Serbs living in the two municipalities. For document analysis, the primary documents used include, amongst others, the meeting minutes of the Municipal Assemblies, Municipal Community Safety Councils and Community Committees as well as UNMIK daily reports, Municipal Assembly monitoring reports by the Organisation for Security and Co-operation in Europe (OSCE), progress reports by the OSCE or the European Union (EU), policy papers and project reports. I am aware that a study at the level of reform initiatives in one post-conflict state does not allow for the drawing of generalisations about a broader universe of post-conflict states. I am still confident that my local-level approach allows drawing broader conclusions on the logic of post-war transitions beyond particular reforms initiatives. I thereby follow Barnett *et al.* (2014), who argue that it "is the aggregate outcome of negotiations across all these policy areas ... that in the end determines the kind of state that evolves".

Overview of the book

Chapter 2 reviews the current standard explanations for stalled post-war transitions to peace and democracy. The first part explores the two most prominent standard explanations: international capacity and local resistance. I argue that neither approach fully explains the empirical puzzle, nor do they fail to conceptually integrate the role of external–domestic interactions in peacebuilding results. In the second part, recent interaction-based approaches are presented and remaining research gaps discussed. I argue that while strategic interaction explanations offer a convincing argument for how interactions might impact peacebuilding outcomes – particularly how they might produce stalled transitions – these accounts still lack in-depth empirical studies that carve out causal mechanisms linking the interaction process with peacebuilding outcomes.

Chapter 3 develops the analytical framework of peacebuilding interactions according to which the negotiation of peacebuilding is analysed in the case studies. Carved out from inductive analysis, it offers a road to a detailed description of negotiation processes and helps to clarify how interactions facilitate stalled post-war transitions. Empirical evidence from field research serves to illustrate the argument.

Chapter 4 introduces the reader into the everyday life of post-war Kosovo, covering the conflict background, the different international and local actors that negotiate peacebuilding reforms on the ground, and aspects of everyday life in Kosovo such as the struggle for survival, aspirations for freedom and a better life, and the political question of the Kosovo status. A better understanding of these aspects of Kosovo everyday life provides valuable insights into the motivations of domestic actors when interacting with their international counterparts and into how and why reform capture takes place. It is from these empirical observations that the analytical framework of peacebuilding interactions gains traction.

Chapter 5 and Chapter 6 are dedicated to case studies in the policy fields of local governance and police. Chapter 5 deals with the low international capacity policy field of local governance. The peacebuilding reforms discussed here are Participatory Budget Planning and Communities Committees. Chapter 6 presents the high international capacity policy field of police reform. The peacebuilding reforms studied are Municipal Community Safety Councils and Minority Community Policing. The case studies all follow a specific structure: First, the reader is introduced to the overall goal of the reform initiative. Then, the operationalisation of the peacebuilding outcome for the particular reform initiative is presented. The use of the ad hoc interaction tactics of prioritisation, selectivity and leverage is discussed for each reform initiative. I distinguish three time periods in every reform initiative, delineated by the particular sub-set of rules that the peacebuilders selected. Then, the interaction process between peacebuilders and municipal elites is traced in detail for each municipality. At the end, the key findings on the impact of the external–domestic interaction on the peacebuilding outcome are summarized.

Chapter 7 compares the results of the case studies in order to draw conclusions about the role of external–domestic interactions in capturing peacebuilding reforms in Kosovo. The discussion is structured according to key categories of the analytical framework: First, all peacebuilding outcomes are compared, showing that none of the standard explanations were able to fully predict them. Then, to showcase that non-strategic interactions might offer a viable alternative explanation, the role of prioritisation, selectivity and leverage is discussed in detail and an analysis of how these ultimately influenced the peacebuilding outcome in a given environment is provided.

Chapter 8 presents the general conclusions of the book and discusses the implications for peacebuilding practice.

Notes

1 UNMIK is the acronym for the United Nations Interim Mission in Kosovo. UNMIK Administrators were deployed in every Kosovo municipality to supervise the Municipal Administration.
2 UÇK is the acronym for the Albanian Ushtria Çlirimtare e Kosovës (Kosovo Liberation Army).
3 UNMIK Daily Report, 21/08/1999, Zabel/Šumarak.
4 For an exception see studies by Barnett and Zürcher (2008), Zürcher *et al.* (2013), Barnett *et al.* (2014), Autesserre (2009).
5 Multidimensional peacebuilding missions have a mandate to support democratisation,

while traditional observer or peacekeeping missions do not (Doyle and Sambanis 2000).

6 I restrict my sample to multidimensional peacebuilding interventions between 1989 and 2002 because I am interested in the long-term effects of interventions (ten years after the start of mission). Please see Appendix 1 for all peacebuilding missions launched between 1989 and 2002.

7 All estimations of the quality of liberal democracy are based on the Freedom House Freedom in the World Index 2014. For a critique of the Freedom House Index see Casper and Tufis (2002).

8 For sure, studies on interactions in post-war context already exist. In Kosovo, for example, interactions have been studied by Zaum (2007), Narten (2009) or Tansey (2009). However, they have not been interested in the concrete characteristics of an interaction process that lead to a particular peacebuilding outcome, as this book does.

9 'Capture' refers here to the implementation of liberal peacebuilding reforms in a way that accommodates domestic priorities while diverting from peacebuilders' original intents. It is not intended to portray domestic behaviour negatively. It seeks to express that domestic elites consciously set priorities and, as a result, choose to implement peacebuilding in a way that sometimes diverts from international actors' original intentions.

10 The literature cannot, of course, be reduced to these two standard explanations. Further explanatory approaches examine, for example, the role of sequencing of international peacebuilding activities (Fukuyama 2005) or the management and coordination of peacebuilding missions (Benner and Rotmann 2008).

11 See Zürcher (2006) for international capacities employed in peacebuilding between 1989 and 2002 and Freedom House (2014) for the quality of democracy.

12 Zürcher (2006, 2013) makes a similar argument in two separate books based on the analysis of 17 and nine peacebuilding missions, respectively.

13 The article of Mac Ginty (2010) makes conceptual advances in this direction although it lacks systematic empirical evidence.

14 *The Peacebuilders Contract* (Barnett and Zürcher 2008) provides two illustrative case studies on Afghanistan and Tajikistan. *Compromised Peacebuilding* (Barnett et al. 2014) calculates peacebuilding outcomes, using empirical material for illustrative purposes. *Costly Democracy* (Zürcher et al. 2013) offers snapshots of nine empirical case studies that illustrate how strategic interactions explain otherwise unexpected peacebuilding outcomes, but the book lacks a systematic process tracing.

15 Paris (1997) first coined the term 'liberal internationalism', and later introduced the term 'liberal peace', while essentially describing the same underpinning of the liberal logic of reconstruction. The term 'liberal peace' has echoed widely in the peacebuilding community and is used to refer to (and criticise) the goals of peacebuilding (Campbell et al. 2011, Chandler 2006, Mac Ginty and Richmond 2009, Newman et al. 2009).

16 I have anonymised the names of the two Kosovo municipalities to protect interviewees.

17 Please refer to Appendix 1 for an overview.

18 The operationalisation of the level of international capacity is as follows: *High international capacity* requires that international actors hold a supervisory mandate for executive, judicative, legislative or administrative tasks *and* that the policy field receives financial investment per capita above average compared to other policy fields. *Low international capacity* requires that international actors do not hold a

supervisory mandate in any area *and* that the policy field receives an investment of financial resources per capita below the average compared to other policy fields. Please see Appendix 2 for an overview of international capacity vested per policy field in the case of Kosovo.

19 The operationalisation of the level of resistance is based on focus group discussions and is as follows: *Weak local resistance* refers to a situation in which citizen support is high, meaning that the majority of statements by citizens about an international norm were positive. This was the case with the norm of democracy. *Strong local resistance* refers to a situation in which citizen support is low and the majority of citizens' statements are negative. This was the case with the norm of minority rights. Please see Appendix 3 for an overview.

20 The two communities are similar with regard to context variables that researchers find influential in post-conflict transitions to democracy: (1) the level of socio-economic development (Przeworski and Limongi 1997), (2) legacies of violent conflict (Doyle and Sambanis 2000), (3) former experience with democracy (Merkel 2010), (4) pre-existing social, ethnical and religious cleavages (Petrovic 2008), (5) the strength of civil society (Tusalem 2007) and (6) the level of the capacity to govern by state institutions (Rotberg 2004). Zabel/Šumarak and Bregore/Brdašce, the two municipalities studied, are average Kosovo Albanian majority municipalities that could be representative of most of Kosovo outside of Prishtina. Both are middle-sized municipalities, their main economic sector is agricultural production, and they have Serbian minority populations and some Roma living there.

References

Acharya, Amitav. (2004). How Ideas Spread. Whose Norms Matter? Norm Localization and Institutional Change in Asian Regionalism. *International Organization*, 58 (2), 239–275.

Autesserre, Séverine. (2009). Hobbes and the Congo. Frames, Local Violence, and International Intervention. *International Organization*, 63 (2), 249–280.

Barnett, Michael. (2007). Peacebuilding. What Is in a Name? *Global Governance*, 13 (1), 35–58.

Barnett, Michael, Fang, Songying and Zürcher, Christoph. (2014). Compromised Peacebuilding. *International Studies Quarterly*, Online First, 1–13.

Barnett, Michael and Zürcher, Christoph. (2008). The Peacebuilder's Contract. How External State-Building Reinforces Weak Statehood. In: Paris, R. and Sisk, T. D. (eds), *The Dilemmas of Statebuilding. Confronting the Contradictions of Postwar Peace Operations.* Abingdon: Routledge, 23–52.

Belloni, Roberto. (2012). Hybrid Peace Governance. Its Emergence and Significance. *Global Governance*, 18, 21–38.

Benner, Thorsten and Rotmann, Philipp. (2008). Learning to Learn? UN Peacebuilding and the Challenges of Building a Learning Organization. *Journal of Intervention and Statebuilding*, 2 (1), 43–62.

Boege, Volker, Brown, Anne, Clements, Kevin and Nolan, Anna. (2009). Building Peace and Political Community in Hybrid Political Orders. *International Peacekeeping*, 16 (5), 599–615.

Burnell, Peter. (2007). From Evaluating Democracy Assistance to Appraising Democracy Promotion. *Political Studies*, 56 (2), 414–434.

Campbell, Susanna, Chandler, David and Sabaratnam, Meera (eds). (2011). *A Liberal Peace? The Problems and Practices of Peacebuilding*. London: Zed.

Carothers, Thomas. (2002). The End of the Transition Paradigm. *Journal of Democracy*, 13 (1), 5–21.

Casper, Gretchen and Tufis, Claudiu. (2002). Correlation versus Interchangeability. The Limited Robustness of Empirical Findings on Democracy Using Highly Correlated Datasets. *Political Analysis*, 11 (2), 1–11.

Cassani, Andrea. (2013). Hybrid What? Partial Consensus and Persistent Divergences in the Analysis of Hybrid Regimes. *International Political Science Review*, Online First, 1–17.

Chandler, David. (2006). *Empire in Denial. The Politics of State-Building*. Pluto Press.

Chandler, David. (2008). Post-Conflict Statebuilding. Governance without Government. In: Pugh, M. (ed.) *Whose Peace? Critical Perspectives on the Political Economy of Peacebuilding*. Basingstoke: Palgrave, 337–356.

Dahl, Robert A. (1971). *Polyarchy. Participation and Opposition*. New Haven: Yale University Press.

Diamond, Larry. (2006). Promoting Democracy in Post-Conflict and Failed States. Lessons and Challenges. *Taiwan Journal of Democracy*, 2 (2), 93–116.

Dobbins, James. (2007). *The Beginner's Guide to Nation-Building*. Santa Monica, CA.

Doyle, Michael W. and Sambanis, Nicholas. (2000). International Peacebuilding. A Theoretical and Quantitative Analysis. *American Political Science Review*, 94 (4), 779–801.

Doyle, Michael W. and Sambanis, Nicholas. (2006). *Making War and Building Peace. United Nations Peace Operations*. Princeton: Princeton University Press.

Finkel, Steven E., Pérez-Liñán, Anibal and Seligson, Mitchell A. (2007). The Effects of U.S. Foreign Assistance to Democracy Building, 1999–2007. *World Politics*, 59 (3), 404–439.

Freedom House. (2014). Freedom in the World 2013 [Online]. Available at: http://freedomhouse.com/kosovo [accessed 04/03/2014].

Fukuyama, Francis. (2005). "Stateness" First. *Journal of Democracy*, 16 (1), 84–88.

Grimm, Sonja. (2008). External Democratization after War. *Success and Failure. Democratization*, 15 (3), 525–549.

Grimm, Sonja and Merkel, Wolfgang (eds). (2008). *War and Democratization. Legality, Legitimacy and Effectiveness*. London: Routledge.

Kant, Immanuel. (1984). *Zum Ewigen Frieden. Ein philosophischer Entwurf*. Reclam.

Krasner, Stephen. (2004). Sharing Sovereignty. New Institutions for Collapsed and Failing States. *International Security*, 29 (2), 85–120.

Mac Ginty, Roger. (2010). Hybrid Peace. The Interaction Between Top-Down and Bottom-Up Peace. *Security Dialogue*, 41 (4), 391–412.

Mac Ginty, Roger. (2011). *International Peacebuilding and Local Resistance. Hybrid Forms of Peace*. Basingstoke: Palgrave Macmillan.

Mac Ginty, Roger and Richmond, Oliver P. (eds). (2009). *The Liberal Peace and Post-War Reconstruction*. Abingdon: Routledge.

March, James G. and Olsen, Johan P. (2008). The Logic of Appropriateness. In: Moran, M., Rein, M. and Goodin, R. (eds), *The Oxford Handbook of Public Policy*. 689–708.

Merkel, Wolfgang. (2010). *Systemtransformation. Eine Einführung in die Theorie und Empirie der Transformationsforschung*. Wiesbaden: VS Verlag für Sozialwissenschaften.

Morlino, Leonardo. (2008). *Hybrid Regimes or Regimes in Transition?* Madrid.

Narten, Jens. (2009). The Dilemmas of Promoting 'Local Ownership'. The Case of Postwar Kosovo. In: Sisk, T. D. (ed.) *The Dilemmas of Statebuilding.* New York: Routledge, 252–284.

Newman, Edward, Paris, Roland and Richmond, Oliver (eds). (2009). *New Perspectives on Liberal Peacebuilding.* Tokyo: United Nations University Press.

Paris, Roland. (1997). Peacebuilding and the Limits of Liberal Internationalism. *International Security,* 22 (2), 54–89.

Paris, Roland. (2004). *At War's End. Building Peace after Civil Conflict.* Cambridge: Cambridge University Press.

Petrovic, Milenko. (2008). The Role of Geography and History in Determining the Slower Progress of Post-Communist Transition in the Balkans. *Communist and Post-Communist Studies,* 41 (3), 123–145.

Przeworski, Adam and Limongi, Fernando. (1997). Modernization. Theories and Facts. *World Politics,* 49 (02), 155–183.

Richmond, Oliver. (2009). Becoming Liberal, Unbecoming Liberalism. Liberal-Local Hybridity via the Everyday as a Response to the Paradoxes of Liberal Peacebuilding. *Journal of Intervention and Statebuilding,* 3 (3), 324–344.

Richmond, Oliver. (2010). Resistance and the Post-Liberal Peace. *Millennium – Journal of International Studies,* 38 (3), 665–692.

Richmond, Oliver and Mitchell, Audra. (2011a). Peacebuilding and Critical Forms of Agency. From Resistance to Subsistence. *Alternatives,* 36 (4), 326–344.

Richmond, Oliver and Mitchell, Audra (eds). (2011b). *Hybrid Forms of Peace. From the 'Everyday' to Post-Liberalism.* Basingstoke: Palgrave.

Rotberg, Robert I. (ed.) (2004). *When States Fail. Causes and Consequences.* Princeton/Oxford: Princeton University Press.

Schimmelfennig, Frank. (2008). EU Political Accession Conditionality after the 2004 Enlargement. Consistency and Effectiveness. *Journal of European Public Policy,* 15 (6), 918–937.

Sedelmeier, Ulrich. (2011). Europeanisation in New Member and Candidate States. *Living Reviews in European Governance,* 6 (1), 5–52.

Tansey, Oisín. (2009). *Regime-Building. Democratization and International Administration.* New York: Oxford University Press.

Tusalem, Rollin F. (2007). A Boon or a Bane? The Role of Civil Society in Third- and Fourth-Wave Democracies. *International Political Science Review,* 28 (3), 361–386.

UN. (1992). An Agenda for Peace. Preventive Diplomacy, Peacemaking, and Peace-Keeping. Report of the Secretary-General Pursuant to the Statement Adopted by the Summit Meeting of the Security Council on 31 January 1992. In: United Nations Documents (ed.). New York.

Zaum, Dominik. (2007). *The Sovereignty Paradox. The Norms and Politics of International Statebuilding.* Oxford: Oxford University Press.

Zeeuw, Jereon de and Kumar, Krishna (eds). (2006). *Promoting Democracy in Post-Conflict Societies.* Boulder: Lynne Rienner.

Zinecker, Heidrun. (2009). Regime-Hybridity in Developing Countries. Achievements and Limitations of New Research on Transitions. *International Studies Review,* 11, 302–331.

Zürcher, Christoph. (2006). *Is More Better? Evaluating External-Led State Building After 1989.* Stanford: Stanford University Press.

Zürcher, Christoph, Manning, Carrie, Evenson, Kristie D., Riese, Sarah and Roehner, Nora. (2013). *Costly Democracy. Peacebuilding and Democratization after War.* Stanford: Stanford University Press.

Zürcher, Christoph, Röhner, Nora and Riese, Sarah. (2009). External Democracy Promotion in Post-Conflict Zones. Evidence from Case Studies. *Taiwan Journal of Democracy*, 5 (1), 241–259.

2 Explaining post-war transitions in peacebuilding

Why do so many post-war states fail to successfully transition to peace and democracy despite powerful support by peacebuilding missions? The most prominent standard explanations for the success or failure of peacebuilding *international capacities* and *local resistance*. There are, of course, a range of other explanations for the success or failure of peacebuilding, such as the sequencing of peacebuilding measures (Fukuyama 2005), the management and coordination of peacebuilding missions (Benner and Rotmann 2008) or the domestic context conditions of socio-economic development, history of democracy or depth of conflict (Fortna 2008). The reason I chose to focus on the explanations above is that they can be seen as two influential antipodes in the peacebuilding debate – one concentrating on the international side, the other on the local side. The emerging interaction-based approach discussed subsequently in this chapter can then be seen as a synthesis of elements from both. The above-mentioned standard explanations have also guided my case selection, as was explained in the introduction.

The *international capacity* explanation emphasizes the strength vested with the peacebuilders to enforce their liberal vision of the post-war state (Dobbins *et al.* 2005, Doyle and Sambanis 2000, Paris 2004), while the *local resistance* explanation focuses on the domestic side that aims to jeopardize (Stedman 1997) or subvert the peacebuilding agenda (Mac Ginty 2011, Richmond 2010, 2011b). Yet neither of these explanations fully explains the abundance of stalled transitions in peacebuilding contexts: The international capacity explanation fails to account for highly intrusive peacebuilding missions with stalled transitions in countries such as Afghanistan, Bosnia and Herzegovina and Kosovo, and the local resistance explanation fails to account for those post-war states that have completed a transition to liberal democracy such as Croatia. And neither explanation acknowledges the established finding in transition research that democratisation is always an outcome of the strategic negotiations *between* and decision-making *of* politically relevant actors (Merkel 2010, Przeworski 1991). This, in turn, is the strength of recent contributions that put a stronger focus on the role of external–domestic interactions in post-war contexts. After an in-depth examination of these explanations, I explain how this book aims to empirically and theoretically contribute to the debate on stalled post-war transitions, particularly to interaction-based approaches.

Explaining post-war transitions I: international capacity

International capacity – or the lack thereof – remains the most prominent explanation in the debate over the success or failure of peacebuilding missions. The central argument is that high international capacity (in terms of mandate, financial resources and personnel) is needed for the success of peacebuilding interventions in establishing peace and democracy (Diamond 2006, Dobbins 2003, 2007, Doyle and Sambanis 2000, 2006, Paris 2004). Peacebuilding is portrayed as an intrusive endeavour in which "intervening authorities first dismantle an existing state apparatus and then build a new one, in the process consciously disempowering some elements of society and empowering others" (Dobbins 2007). Therefore, a strong international mandate and the investment of sufficient resources – money, personnel and time – are held to be critical for this undertaking because they allow peacebuilders to coerce domestic elites into compliance and they compensate for insufficient resources and skills (Dobbins *et al.* 2005, Doyle and Sambanis 2000, Paris 2004). The core tenet of this approach is that *the higher the level of international capacity is, the more likely a transition to peace and democracy is.*

A main concern of scholars in this field is how the UN and other international actors can improve their record in building peace and democracy. Whether peacebuilding missions should follow a sequencing strategy of 'Security First' (Marten 2004), 'Institutionalisation First' (Paris 2005), 'Stateness First' (Fukuyama 2004), or 'Civil Society First' (Lederach 1997) is highly debated. Donor coordination and mission management are also scrutinized, as poor coordination between civil and military components or donor agencies is regarded as part of the problem (Benner and Rotmann 2008). Aside from these more general concerns, there exist countless studies on the most efficient set-up of peacebuilding reform programmes in the fields of security sector reform, transitional justice and rule of law. The problem-solving rationale prevalent in this strand of peacebuilding literature is based on the firm belief that peacebuilders only have to 'get it right', as the quote below exemplifies:

> Each nation to be rebuilt may be unique, but the nation-builder has only a limited range of instruments on which to rely. These are largely the same from one operation to the next. This guide describes how such contingents are best recruited and organized, how much of each will be required, how long they will be needed, and how they have been best employed in prior operations.
>
> (Dobbins 2007: vii)

There are, of course, good reasons to believe that a high level of international capacity will ensure peacebuilding success to foster peace and democracy.

First, well-staffed and well-resourced peacebuilding missions provide a credible third party security guarantee for the former warring parties (Doyle and Sambanis 2000, Paris and Sisk 2007b). Second, sufficient international capacity offers peacebuilders the means to coerce less committed domestic actors into compliance with the conditions set out in the mission mandate (Paris 2004). Lastly, sufficient international financial resources can compensate for the lack of local capacities on the ground (Doyle and Sambanis 2000).

Doyle and Sambanis (2000), in their elaborate study on the success of UN peacekeeping after civil wars, were amongst the first and most prominent proponents of increasing the international capacity of peace missions in terms of mandate and resources. The authors made a plea for widening UN mission mandates to multidimensional peacebuilding missions that would encompass an explicit mandate for democracy promotion and provide a high number of troops and financial resources to support the peace process. This claim was based on their findings that multidimensional peacebuilding missions in particular make a positive contribution to the democratisation of post-conflict states (Doyle and Sambanis 2000).[1] If one differentiates according to type of UN mission, the study shows that only multidimensional UN peacebuilding missions significantly and positively correlate with strict peace-building success – meaning the absence of violence and war *and* the establishment of liberal democracy (Doyle and Sambanis 2000). The authors conclude:

> We expect these missions that combine nonpassivity in the implementation of the mandate with high levels of resources and technical capacity needed to rebuild political institutions to have a strong effect.
>
> (Doyle and Sambanis 2006)

The positive impact of peace interventions on peace and democracy has been confirmed by several quantitative studies (Doyle and Sambanis 2006, Fortna 2008, Pickering and Peceny 2006), although some also shed doubts on this optimistic picture. Bueno de Mesquita and Downs (2006), for example, find a negative relationship between military interventions and democratisation after 10 to 20 years. Fortna (2008) also finds no significant correlation between the type of peacekeeping[2] and democratic progress and concludes that "peacekeeping may help foster democratisation in the short term but tends to undermine it over the long term" (Fortna 2008). And Zürcher's (2006) comparative study of 17 UN peacebuilding interventions similarly notes that UN peacebuilding missions experienced the greatest success in terms of the absence of war, but were least successful in terms of democratisation.

Despite these discrepancies in findings, the surge of studies that ask for an investment in greater international capacities has not diminished. A RAND study on US nation-building, for example, states "[. . .] that the most important determinant of success is the level of effort – measured in time, manpower, and money" (Dobbins 2003). Ruggeri *et al.* (2012) find that the troop size of the mission matters as "rebel groups and local governments are more willing to cooperate with larger UN missions".

In his 2004 book, *At War's End*, Paris (2004) goes even further and argues that even more international capacity is needed in the form of far-reaching international mandates for transitional administrations if peacebuilding is to achieve its objectives of liberal democracy and market economy, because the objectives of liberal peacebuilding are inherently competitive and conflictive processes and could possibly harm on-going re-construction activities by stirring up violence between competing factions:

> Peacebuilders should continue to seek to transform war-shattered states into liberal market democracies, but with a different technique – by constructing the foundations of effective political and economic institutions *before* the introduction of electoral democracy and market-oriented adjustment policies, a strategy that I call Institutionalization Before Liberalization (IBL).
>
> (Paris 2004)

Paris asks for an interim administration with executive, legislative and judicative powers to be installed until viable domestic state institutions are built. The (re-)turn to democracy would then take place step by step with local elections first and national elections deferred until the political conditions are more suitable (Paris 2004).[3] This is exactly the strategy the international community in Kosovo had chosen.

Paris's conclusions widely resonated in the scholarly community and an increasing number of scholars turned to the idea of supervision in the form of trusteeships, interim administrations or shared sovereignty to achieve the goals of liberal peacebuilding. Supervision could be the road to success, these scholars felt, if equipped with the right amount of human and financial resources. Krasner (2004, 2005) proposed the principle of shared sovereignty to "encourage the development of well-functioning polities that provide security, social services, and opportunities for economically remunerative work" (Krasner 2005). Fearon and Laitin (2004) demanded that critical cases of state failure be put under the control of international institutions in the form of neotrusteeship-arrangements. Schneckener (2006) recommended international policy tools ranging from stabilisation to the (re-)construction of completely new state structures.[4] Caplan (2002) also demanded supervision in order for peacebuilders to build up liberal democracies and market economies:

> While it may not always be necessary for administrators to exercise full authority (and they should seek to devolve as much responsibility to the local population as feasible), without such authority they are more likely to be obstructed by local actors in their efforts to achieve the aims of their mandates.
>
> (Caplan 2002)

The empirical proof for the appropriateness of such far-reaching measures has, however, been absent so far. Even the most heavily supervised UN administrations in Kosovo and East Timor, or quasi-protectorates such as Bosnia and Herzegovina, do not fare better in terms of democratic quality than other states where peacebuilding fosters post-conflict democratisation with less wide-ranging means (Zürcher 2007). Lastly, empirical case studies on intrusive international intervention in countries such as Bosnia and Herzegovina (Knaus and Martin 2003), East Timor (Beauvais 2001) or Kosovo (Chesterman 2001, Tansey 2009, Zaum 2007) put into question the supervisors' impact on liberal norm promotion and institution building.[5] What is more, intrusive undertakings such as international administrations are not without practical difficulties (Caplan 2002, 2005, Chesterman 2004, 2005, Tansey 2009). There are several challenges during the implementation of high capacity peacebuilding missions: Strategic mission planning requires the inclusion of local parties although these might not share the peacebuilders' goals (Caplan 2002); mission management relies on international agencies to 'get things done' instead of investing in the capacity building of local actors (Caplan 2004); international actors tend to rule by degree in case they cannot gain support from local actors (Caplan 2002); and there are no accountability structures that would hold international administrators accountable for wrongdoing (Caplan 2006). After all, international administrations are a deeply political undertaking with which peacebuilders become entangled when supporting peace and democracy:

> In reality, the two spheres [international administration and politics] represent inextricably related areas of activity. Civil administration inevitably entails policy decisions, many of them political in nature, which require choices to be made that may reflect fundamentally different or even competing goals and values.
>
> (Caplan 2005)

Given these practical challenges, the use of high international capacity has also stirred ethical concerns. Some argue that an imposed democratisation strategy would deny local ownership and prevent home-grown democracy (Chandler 1999). Too much engagement could foster a culture of dependency on aid and expert consultancy and might keep authoritarian elites in place instead of providing space for democratic elite change (Jarstad and Sisk 2008b, Suhrke 2006). Failure to devolve responsibility could create dissatisfaction in the local population, endanger local-international cooperation, and inhibit domestic actors from developing own democratic practice and procedures (Caplan 2005, Chesterman 2004). The legitimacy of international supervision is thus easily put into question (Jarstad and Sisk 2008a, Paris and Sisk 2007a, 2009).

The problem with the international capacity explanation is that it concentrates too strictly on international activities in post-war transitions and rarely takes stock of its own limitations in peacebuilding in post-war settings.

Studies that centre on international capacities tend to ignore the important role of domestic context or domestic agency and neglect the fact that peace-builders have to negotiate the envisioned reform programme with the domestic side in order to gain consent. The approach seems to be conceptually incapable of integrating the empirical reality of external–domestic inter-action in instances of post-war norm promotion. The neglect of domestic agency, interests and power struggles between internationals and locals – as well as within domestic parties – evokes the erroneous belief that inter-national actors could be in complete control of domestic transition processes. Yet the stalled transitions of high capacity interventions in Afghanistan, Iraq, Bosnia and Herzegovina and Kosovo show that they are not.

Explaining post-war transitions II: local resistance

The second standard explanation for the abundance of stalled post-war trans-itions in peacebuilding is local resistance. Stalled transitions are seen as the result of local opposition against unequal power vested in peacebuilding missions and the international spread of liberal norms, which either do not reso-nate with local needs or endanger the position of power holders (Mac Ginty 2011, Richmond 2010, 2011b, Stedman 1997). Local resistance as an explana-tion for the failure of peacebuilding can be found in the mainstream peace-building publications (Paris 2004, Stedman 1997) as well as in critical peacebuilding scholarship (Mac Ginty 2011, Richmond 2010). While main-stream peacebuilding tends to portray local resistance as the illegitimate act of authoritarian and corrupt post-war elites, critical peacebuilding depicts local resistance as a legitimate act of opposition against an imperialist (Chandler 2006), neo-liberal (Duffield 2007), neo-colonial (Richmond 2011b), or other-wise illegitimate peacebuilding regime. Critical scholars thus reflect upon the uncritical appraisal of the patronizing practices of international administrations and the universalist approach taken with regard to the promotion of liberal norms and values. The core tenet of this line of thinking is that *the stronger the level of local resistance is, the less likely a transition to peace and democracy is.*

As an antipode to the international capacity explanation, scholarship dealing with local resistance emphasizes the agency of local actors in peace-building interventions. The contribution of critical peacebuilding studies is of particular importance as scholars re-introduce domestic actors as subjects in the peacebuilding discourse and turn the focus on the role of local agency in the everyday. The interactive character of peacebuilding thus becomes more visible as constant interaction, negotiation and bargaining between outside actors and local elites, civil society and the broader population is acknow-ledged, although not systematically investigated.

There are, however, different interpretations of why and where local resistance occurs. Mainstream peacebuilding scholars focus at the elite level and see peacebuilding as jeopardised by 'spoilers' of the peace process who have much to lose but little to gain from transitions to peace and democracy

(Stedman 1997). The main problem, authors argue, is the domestic 'unwill-ingness to reform' of presumably un-democratic political elites who oppose the opening of the political or economic sphere in an attempt to maintain their tight grip on state power. Peacebuilding initiatives would threaten the power, worldview, or interests of these so-called spoilers (Menkhaus 2006, Stedman 1997). Domestic elites are assumed to have low interests in support-ing democratic norms because compliance with international standards of democracy, human rights or rule of law possibly weakens the power position of the incumbent power holders (Zürcher 2011). Similar arguments exist in democracy promotion research, where stalled democratisation is interpreted as "deeply embedded resistance to any change" from autocratic leaders that cling to their power (Carothers 2004). Hence, domestic actors are primarily dealt with as spoilers of peace processes that need to be contained by inter-nationals (Paris 2004, Stedman 1997), and international actors are called to manage these spoilers and provide security guarantees (Walter 2002).

Critical peacebuilding scholars, in contrast, investigate local resistance more broadly, including political elites, civil society and the post-war population at large (Kappler and Richmond 2011, Mac Ginty 2011, Richmond 2010, 2011b, Richmond and Mitchell 2011b). Drawing on a Foucauldian notion of power, critical scholars argue that everywhere there is power, there is resist-ance (Richmond 2010). As peacebuilding interventions are based on unequal power relations between local actors and interveners, they are portrayed as inherently political undertakings relating to competing ideas, political contes-tation and power (Jabri 2007). The critical scholars' interpretation of domestic motivations for resistance differs sharply from mainstream peacebuilding scholars: Resistance is assumed to be directed at the authority of or domina-tion by international peacebuilders as well as their ideals of a liberal demo-cratic state that does not resonate with local needs (Richmond 2010). The reason domestic actors react with resistance against the build-up of formal liberal-democratic state institutions is that international organisations tend to rely on top down approaches and focus on state institutions, state bureaucracy and state elites instead of bottom up approaches that resonate with the 'everyday' of people (Richmond 2010). Local resistance can be directed against a multitude of things: against liberal values, pluralism, rights-based approaches, universality, individualism and free markets as well as against modernisation, central state power and state sovereignty (Richmond 2010). The concern that the liberal peacebuilding package is not appropriate for post-war societies because it does not connect with local traditions, values and beliefs is also shared beyond the critical peacebuilding camp: Pouligny (2005), for example, criticises how peacebuilding "leads to a de facto exclu-sion of the so-called traditional arrangements existing in the society" and ignores how "traditional ways of organizing may participate in a local experi-ment of 'democracy'". Hohe (2002) attributes the limited success of peace-building in East Timor to the failure to connect to "local social structures of political authority and legitimacy – that is, the local paradigms". Similarly to mainstream scholars, critical scholars portray the behaviour of domestic actors as opposing liberal democratic values, although this time it is accepted as a legitimate response to illegitimate international domination.

In the eyes of critical peacebuilding scholars, local resistance is apparent in many ways, usually in the sphere of the 'everyday', outside of formal state institutions (Richmond 2010, 2011a, Roberts 2011). Researchers describe diverse modes of local resistance such as resistance, re-shaping, responding or subsistence (Richmond and Mitchell 2011a); "resistance, cooption, appropriation, ignorance or modification" (Richmond 2010); "outright resistance, or more subtle resistance such as non-cooperation or partial cooperation" (Mac Ginty 2010); or resistance, subversion and exploitation (Mac Ginty 2011). Kappler and Richmond (2011) differentiate more systematically between forms of resistance in the civil society in Bosnia and Herzegovina: (a) resistance to liberal peace project, (b) translation of liberal peace project, (c) adoption, while maintaining a connection to the local sphere. Most of these terms, however, are seldom defined or used in a coherent manner, and some of the described domestic behaviour begs the question of whether it is indeed directed against the liberal peacebuilding project or simply points to limitations in capacity on the domestic side.

The problem with the local resistance explanation is that its focus on local resistance fails to explain why some peacebuilding missions are successful in supporting the transition to democracy despite the unequal power relations assumed to unequivocally provoke resistance. Cases such as Croatia, where influential political elites showed intrinsic commitment to the liberal democratic agenda, remain un-reflected in this approach. The local resistance argument is indeed in danger of falling prey to the reduction of domestic agency to resistance: Domestic opposition is either depicted as illegitimate acts to stay in power by using illiberal means (mainstream scholarship) or portrayed as legitimate, locally rooted signs of rebellion against an externally imposed set of governance (critical scholarship). In doing so, the depiction of domestic agency remains normative and ignores the complexity of domestic behaviour in peacebuilding by ruling out the possibility of local support and cooperation in the liberal peace. There is no room for the notion that some domestic actors might share liberal norms and values or welcome peacebuilding as part of a development agenda for their country. Neither is there acknowledgement that acts of resistance by political elites in a democratizing county might point to different opinions on *how* and *to what extent* these ideas should be put into practice, but not to opposition to the fundamental principles.

The limitations of standard explanations

There is the sense that both explanations – international capacity and local resistance – fail to grasp important aspects of post-war transition processes under international tutelage and are therefore limited in their explanatory potential. The international capacity argument does not succeed in explaining why the high international capacity peacebuilding missions in East Timor or Kosovo failed to coerce and support the transition to full-fledged democracy. Most scholarly accounts in this field evoke the erroneous belief that peace-builders are in complete control of post-war politics. The focus on the inter-national side of peacebuilding in combination with the problem-solving approach of most studies leads to a preoccupation with the 'right use' of international instruments and strategies, while ignoring the role of domestic agency and external–domestic encounters in post-war states. This neglect of domestic agency and power struggles between various political players pro-duces an inherently static picture of post-conflict transitions and leaves domestic interests, strategies and internal power struggles out of the scholarly discourse. In so doing, it fails to integrate the view of those that are expected to 'democratize' and obfuscates the enormity of the task that peacebuilding as social engineering sets out to achieve.

The local resistance argument, on the other hand, fails to explain why there are post-war transitions to democracy at all, given that peacebuilding is assumed to necessarily provoke resistance to international norms and values. It also lacks an explanation for why and when different modes of resistance emerge and whether these might be related to the type of international norms promoted or the international capacity deployed.

The following section presents the third explanatory approach that can be seen as a middle ground between those studies concentrating on the inter-national contribution to post-war transitions and those concentrating on the local response to international intervention. The central task here is to find an appropriate conceptual framework for global-local encounters in peacebuild-ing and to determine how this might contribute to a causal explanation of stalled post-war transitions.

Explaining post-war transitions III: external–domestic interactions

Studies on the encounters of peacebuilders and local actors in international interventions have seen considerable growth in recent years. A certain unease with the early 2000s blueprint prescriptions of 'liberal peace' and the common portrayal of post-war elites and societies as deficient democracies that have to be civilised (Paris 2002) or educated (Gheciu 2005), rather than being per-ceived as political systems in their own right (Boege *et al.* 2009), certainly contributed to this trend. But the closer examination of the empirical reality in post-war states also facilitated this development: The look inside post-war states made researchers realise that peacebuilding permeates all stages of the political process, that it is often difficult to disentangle external and domestic actors and that new forms of governance emerge. Kosovo is a prime example of the close entanglement of the international and local spheres: External actors write policy proposals, sit as advisors in ministries and municipal offices, or monitor parliamentary debates and municipal board meetings. They follow the implementation of new policies and even develop benchmarking systems to evaluate policy performance. In addition, peacebuilders hold numerous informal head-to-head meetings with key political figures to clarify standpoints and exchange information. The various stages of policy making are thus not only shaped by the domestic government, legislature, political parties and bureaucracy, but also by international organisations and agencies on the ground. As a result, it can be quite challenging to conceptually differentiate between the outsider and insider in post-war transitions (Leininger 2010), even geographically: External players may hold an office next to the government building of interest or are even provided with office space within the domestic institution. In Kosovo, for example, the coordinator of an EU twinning programme keeps an office in the Kosovo Ministry of Local Government Administration, and the EU Rule of Law Mission is provided with offices in the respective police stations. Similarly, the domestic side penetrates the international sphere: International peacebuilding organisations recruit 'national staff', who are endowed with tasks of ever-growing responsibility the longer a mission stays on the ground, or even hire citizens of the post-war state as 'international staff'. While this blending of external and domestic sides in political processes is a social reality, it remains important to examine the back and forth between actors working for international peacebuilding organisations and those situated in domestic institutions.

Given the multiple points of contact between peacebuilders and local actors in post-conflict settings, the question arises as to what role these external–domestic interactions play in the success or failure of peacebuilding in general and in the implementation of peacebuilding reforms in particular. Only in the past years, however, has this question begun to play a more important role in the scholarly debate on the impact of peacebuilding on post-war transitions. Scholars have started to search for conceptualisations that better grasp the multiple points of contact between interveners and local actors and that make local agency visible in the scholarly discourse again (Richmond 2010, Richmond 2011b). The recent interaction-focused studies ask how interventions affect political institutions, actors and post-war societies at large and how different norms, values or perceptions are negotiated between interveners and representatives of the post-war state (Barnett and Zürcher 2008, Björkdahl and Höglund 2013, Jarstad and Belloni 2012, Mac Ginty 2011, Millar *et al.* 2013, Richmond 2009). These studies contribute to knowledge in three areas: (1) They uncover that the goals of liberal peacebuilding do not necessarily correspond to the interests, customs, or needs of the local post-war population; (2) they criticise unequal power relations inherent in the peacebuilding enterprise and put into question the legitimacy of international intervention practices; (3) they offer different conceptualisations of peacebuilding outcomes that avoid portraying the post-war state as deficient compared to Western liberal democracies.

The most prominent concepts for capturing global-local encounters in post-war settings are *hybridity* (Belloni 2012, Mac Ginty 2011, Richmond 2009), *friction* (Björkdahl and Höglund 2013, Millar *et al.* 2013), *strategic interaction* (Barnett and Zürcher 2008), *peacebuilding frames* (Autesserre 2009, Autesserre 2010) and *Interventionskultur* (Bonacker *et al.* 2010). *Hybridity*, a term used by Richmond (2009), Mac Ginty (2011), Belloni (2012) and many others, refers to "the coexistence and interaction of the international and the local, of liberal and illiberal norms, institutions, and actors" (Belloni 2012) in post-war states. *Friction* describes the "unpredictable and unexpected nature" of peacebuilding interactions between international and local actors (Millar *et al.* 2013). *Strategic interaction* (Barnett and Zürcher 2008) asks from a bargaining perspective how peacebuilders and domestic actors negotiate their interests and how this explains stalled transitions. *Peacebuilding frames* explain the international failure to build peace (Autesserre 2009, 2010) by analysing the relationship between local violence and peacebuilding activities in DRC. *Interventionskultur* (Bonacker *et al.* 2010) deals with the global-local interface from a sociological perspective and investigates how interventions shape inner dynamics of post-war societies ('societies of intervention'). Still, contributions in the field of hybridity or friction offer largely descriptive accounts of the myriad interactions in peacebuilding, while peacebuilding frames or *Interventionskultur* focus on transitions from war-to-peace or sociological micro-encounters. The question of how to explain a post-war transition to democracy is not addressed systematically.

Research on strategic interactions is most explicit in addressing the question of how global-local encounters influence post-war transitions in peacebuilding contexts (Barnett *et al.* 2014, Barnett and Zürcher 2008, Zürcher *et al.* 2013). This is why I will dedicate the remainder of this chapter to this approach and later explain how this book empirically and theoretically contributes to this line of thinking. Research on interactions in peacebuilding characterizes interaction as strategic, seeing peacebuilders and domestic elites as rational, goal-oriented and mutually dependent actors who anticipate the reaction of their counterpart to reach their optimum outcome (see for example Barnett *et al.*, 2014: 4). Due to the divergent goals of peacebuilders and domestic elites, both sides are assumed to strategically agree to a compromise, with a stalled transition being the best outcome either side can get (Barnett/Fang/Zürcher, 2014). Peacebuilding is understood as:

> Politics of strategic interaction in which different actors with different preferences are in a condition of mutual dependence and are constantly attempting to strategize and maximize their payoffs under a set of constraints.
>
> (Barnett *et al.* 2014)

Strategic interaction as a concept takes centre stage in *The Peacebuilders Contract* (Barnett and Zürcher 2008), *Costly Democracy* (Zürcher *et al.* 2013) and *Compromised Peacebuilding* (Barnett *et al.* 2014). *The Peacebuilders Contract* sets out the assumptions of 'peacebuilding as a bargaining game'. *Compromised Peacebuilding* also does the maths of the bargaining model and *Costly Democracy* is an empirically grounded book based on a structured, focused comparison of nine case studies of interventions. The authors understand peacebuilding as an (almost) endless series of repeated interactions between strategic actors over peacebuilding mandates, policies and reform initiatives. Negotiations take place between three sorts of actors: the international peacebuilders, the national elites and the sub-national or rural elites (Barnett and Zürcher 2008). Each side has different preferences, but peacebuilders and national elites tend to be willing to negotiate a compromise in order to gain the cooperation of the other side to reach their own strategic objectives (Barnett and Zürcher 2008). This often results in peacebuilders and national elites pursuing "their collective interest in stability and symbolic peacebuilding, creating the appearance of democratic change while leaving largely in tact existing state-society relations" (Barnett and Zürcher 2008). Peacebuilders, then, prefer a second-best solution, making stalled transitions more likely.

Peacebuilding as strategic interaction rests on several assumptions to explain stalled transitions in post-war contexts: First, peacebuilders and domestic elites are goal-oriented actors that pursue diverging goals (Barnett *et al.* 2014, Barnett and Zürcher 2008).[6] Second, peacebuilders and domestic elites need each other to achieve at least part of these goals (Barnett and Zürcher 2008). Third, peacebuilding reforms incur adoption costs on domestic elites, but to different extents, depending on a range of factors (Zürcher *et al.* 2013). Fourth, all actors involved have complete information regarding the ideal points of the other actors and their willingness to commit to any agreement (Barnett *et al.* 2014). Because peacebuilding operations are typically launched when the fighting has stopped, the bargaining game unfolds against the backdrop of a cease-fire agreement that has been accepted by the key parties on the ground.

Each of these assumptions is discussed in the following paragraphs.

Diverging goals between international and domestic actors are key to understanding the logic of external–domestic bargaining in peacebuilding. Barnett and Zürcher (2008: 3) assume that peacebuilders are interested in *stability* and *liberalisation*, while domestic elites are interested in maintaining *power*. This is why negotiations are necessary. Stability, meaning the absence of war and a stable partner in the capital, is the primary goal of peacebuilders because it is an important precondition for the security of the peacebuilders and their ability to pursue reforms. The implementation of liberal democratic reforms, then, represents only the second priority (Barnett and Zürcher 2008). Domestic elites, on the other hand, are interested in maintaining political power and dominance over potential rivals. In *Costly Democracy*, Zürcher *et al.* (2013) further broaden their definition of domestic goals, including in them domestic elites' interest in physical security and primary political objectives, and sub-national elites' interest in local power and autonomy from the central state (Barnett *et al.* 2014, Barnett and Zürcher 2008).

The mutual dependencies of peacebuilders and domestic actors are further important factors in the interaction process, as both sides need each other for cooperation, Barnett and Zürcher (2008, 2014) argue. Peacebuilders, on the one hand, need the cooperation of the domestic elites in order to reach their goals of maintaining stability and implementing liberalisation reforms. Additionally, peacebuilding missions are based on consent, and international actors are therefore expected to cooperate with domestic elites (Barnett and Zürcher 2008). Domestic elites, on the other hand, cooperate because they need the financial resources offered by peacebuilders, which could be used to further broaden their local power base (Barnett and Zürcher 2008). Further reasons for cooperation might be the domestic elites' need of the international community's consent on political projects such as independent statehood – as in Kosovo, East Timor or Namibia (Zürcher *et al.* 2013).

The *domestic adoption costs* of peacebuilding reforms can be increased or decreased by peacebuilders' strategies, which is why interactions are so important to the desired outcome of peacebuilding. In *Costly Democracy*, Zürcher *et al.* (2013) argue:

> Domestic political actors calculate adoption costs based on the degree to which the terms of the peace settlement and the content of the peace-building package will affect their physical security and the achievement of their primary political objectives.
>
> (Zürcher *et al.* 2013)

The preferences of domestic elites are thus "to a great extent shaped by the costs they incur in adopting democracy, as well as the leverage that peacebuilders can muster to increase the costs of nonadoption" (Zürcher *et al.* 2013).

Complete information on the goals and constraints of the interacting counterpart is a precondition of a strategic interaction process in order for both sides to be able to calculate the optimum outcome. Barnett, Zürcher and Fang (2014) assume that all actors involved have complete information regarding the ideal points of the other actors as well as the willingness to commit to any agreement. The authors argue that "[t]he claim that actors have a general understanding of each other's ideal points – the kind of state each wants – is reasonable given their intimate knowledge of each other during this process" (ibid.).

The outcome of such strategic interaction is that peacebuilders and domestic elites agree on a compromise, which could, according to Barnett and Zürcher (2008), have four possible outcomes: cooperative peacebuilding, co-optive peacebuilding, captured peacebuilding, or conflictive peacebuilding.[7]

To investigate strategic interaction in peacebuilding provides valuable new insights into democratization processes after war because it accounts for the various instances of external–domestic interactions as they take place in the empirical world of peacebuilding. In this way, the authors go beyond structural accounts that underline international capacity or context conditions and stress the critical role of interactions between different sorts of actors. Yet there are still many open questions about why, and under what conditions, external–domestic interactions lead to a particular peacebuilding outcome.

Remaining research gaps

The existing research on external–domestic interaction in peacebuilding focuses on the national level and emphasizes the rational and strategic considerations in an interaction process, drawing on case studies of negotiations over policy proposals (Zürcher *et al.* 2013) or theoretical modelling (Barnett *et al.* 2014) at national level. With a view to complement existing research, this book investigates external–domestic interactions from a different angle than previous studies by focusing on the *interaction process*, the *local level* and the *reform implementation* stage.

The argument of the book is that at the local level, external–domestic interactions facilitate stalled transitions not only due to strategic considerations, but also due to the bounded rationality inherent in interactions. 'Bounded rationality' describes a situation in which actors, albeit intending to be rational, make decisions under cognitive constraints, which does not allow them to process the complete information available (Gigerenzer and Selten 2002, Kahnemann 2011, Simon 1956). It is the change of perspective on process, local level and implementation that allowed for the detection of bounded rationality in interaction processes.

Why are process, local level and implementation important at all? First, a focus on the interaction *process* allows tracing how day-to-day interactions between internationals and domestic elites evolve over time. This might yield important insights into the mechanisms of how interactions influence peacebuilding outcomes. In that regard this study is one of the few systematic, structured comparisons that uses detailed process tracing to study interaction and intervention outcomes.[8] The use of an inductive approach to the development of empirically grounded categories to describe an external–domestic interaction process allows for a systematic and comparative process-tracing of external–domestic interactions as well as the identification of interaction patterns. Second, numerous studies reveal that post-war transitions fail due to the disconnect between a predominantly democratic legal framework and diverging practices (Zürcher *et al.* 2009). If one follows the external–domestic interaction over peacebuilding reforms closely, there is an obvious discrepancy between negotiations (1) at the stage of policy formulation leading to legal adoption and (2) at the stage of enforcement during policy implementation (Fearon 1998). Yet most studies on external–domestic interactions in peacebuilding concentrate on the policy formulation stage, but leave out how reform implementation is negotiated.[9] Unique within the literature, this book follows interaction both at the local level and throughout implementation. The *local level* and the *reform implementation* stage are crucial, as this is where reforms are put into practice and make a difference in the daily lives of the population. The local level is where peacebuilders monitor, negotiate and enforce peacebuilding practice, and implementation is the crucial point when peacebuilding reforms evolve from 'paper to practice'. While most articles are about whether international norms are transferred into national legislation and institutional design, the second stage – implementation – is much less frequently studied. Authors who take a look at implementation come to less optimistic judgements about external influences on democratisation as it is far easier to formally adopt a reform than to actually change behaviour (Lavenex and Schimmelfennig 2011).

In the following chapter, I propose an analytical framework of peacebuilding interactions that allows the capturing of strategic as well as non-strategic elements of an interaction process and provides for a more adequate understanding of the functioning of interactions in post-war transitions to peace and democracy.

Notes

1 Doyle and Sambanis (2000: 781) distinguish between monitoring and observer missions, traditional peacekeeping, multidimensional peacebuilding and peace enforcement missions.
2 Fortna differentiates between no peacekeeping (PK), no UN PK and UN PK as well as between types of the UN PK: observer mission, interpositional, multidimensional or enforcement mission.
3 Recently, Paris has taken a more critical stance (for example Paris and Sisk 2009).
4 To be precise, Schneckener, Krasner, Fearon and Laitin write about the take on fragile or failing states. These, however, overlap to a great extent with countries emerging from war.
5 For a comprehensive but critical account of the democratisation process of all three interventions, please see Tansey (2009).
6 In the later version of *The Peacebuilders Contract* by Barnett, Fang and Zürcher (2014: 9, forthcoming), the authors also account for the fact that there might be different degrees of preference in correspondence between peacebuilders and domestic elites.
7 Barnett and Zürcher treat these interactions as outcomes.
8 The argument by Barnett, Fang and Zürcher (2014, 2008) on interactions and post-war transition is based on theoretical models. Only Zürcher *et al.* (2013) provides systematic, empirical comparisons of interactions, although limited to the national level and policy formulation, and without chronological process-tracing.
9 *Costly Democracy* presents examples of interactions over basic terms of peacebuilding, such as the Bonn Agreement for Afghanistan (Zürcher *et al.* 2013) or Kosovo independence (Zürcher *et al.* 2013). Yet the mere adoption of international norms does not necessarily lead to domestic change, as transitions seem to get stuck at the implementation stage.

References

Autesserre, Severine. (2009). Hobbes and the Congo. Frames, Local Violence, and International Intervention. *International Organization*, 63 (2), 249–280.
Autesserre, Severine. (2010). *The Trouble with the Congo. Local Violence and the Failure of International Peacebuilding*. Cambridge: Cambridge University Press.

Barnett, Michael, Fang, Songying and Zürcher, Christoph. (2014). Compromised Peacebuilding. *International Studies Quarterly*, Online First, 1–13.

Barnett, Michael and Zürcher, Christoph. (2008). The Peacebuilder's Contract. How External State-Building Reinforces Weak Statehood. In: Paris, R. and Sisk, T. D. (eds), *The Dilemmas of Statebuilding. Confronting the Contradictions of Postwar Peace Operations*. Abingdon: Routledge, 23–52.

Beauvais, Joel C. (2001). Benevolent Despotism. A Critique of U.N. State-Building in East Timor. *International Law and Politics*, 33 (4), 1101–1178.

Belloni, Roberto. (2012). Hybrid Peace Governance. Its Emergence and Significance. *Global Governance*, 18, 21–38.

Benner, Thorsten and Rotmann, Philipp. (2008). Learning to Learn? UN Peacebuilding and the Challenges of Building a Learning Organization. *Journal of Intervention and Statebuilding*, 2 (1), 43–62.

Björkdahl, Annika and Höglund, Kristine. (2013). Precarious Peacebuilding. Friction in Global–Local Encounters. *Peacebuilding*, 1 (3), 289–299.

Boege, Volker, Brown, Anne, Clements, Kevin and Nolan, Anna. (2009). Building Peace and Political Community in Hybrid Political Orders. *International Peacekeeping*, 16 (5), 599–615.

Bonacker, Thorsten, Daxner, Michael, Free, Jan and Zürcher, Christoph (eds). (2010). Interventionskultur. Zur Soziologie von Interventionsgesellschaften. Wiesbaden: VS Verlag für Sozialwissenschaften.

Bueno de Mesquita, Bruce and Downs, George W. (2006). Intervention and Democracy. *International Organization*, 60 (3), 627–650.

Caplan, Richard. (2002). *A New Trusteeship? The International Administration of War-Torn Societies*. Oxford: Oxford University Press.

Caplan, Richard. (2004). Partner or Patron? International Civil Administration and Local Capacity Building. *International Peacekeeping*, 11 (2), 229–247.

Caplan, Richard. (2005). *International Governance of War-Torn Societies. Rule and Reconstruction*. Oxford: Oxford University Press.

Caplan, Richard. (2006). Who Guards the Guardians? International Accountability in Bosnia. In: Chandler, D. (ed.) *Peace without Politics? Ten Years of International State-Building in Bosnia*. London: Routledge, 157–170.

Carothers, Thomas. (2004). *Critical Mission. Essays on Democracy Promotion*. Washington DC: Carnegie Endowment for International Peace.

Chandler, David. (1999). *Bosnia. Faking Democracy after Dayton*. London: Pluto Press.

Chandler, David. (2006). *Empire in Denial. The Politics of State-Building*. Pluto Press.

Chesterman, Simon. (2001). *Kosovo in Limbo. State-Building and 'Substantial Autonomy'*. New York.

Chesterman, Simon. (2004). *You the People. The United Nations, Transitional Administration and State-Building*. Oxford: Oxford University Press.

Chesterman, Simon. (2005). Transitional Administration, State-Building and the United Nations. In: Chesterman, S., Ignatieff, M. and Thakur, R. (eds), *Making States Work. State Failure and the Crisis of Governance*. New York: United Nations University Press, 339–358.

Diamond, Larry. (2006). Promoting Democracy in Post-Conflict and Failed States. Lessons and Challenges. *Taiwan Journal of Democracy*, 2 (2), 93–116.

Dobbins, James. (2003). *America's Role in Nation-Building. From Germany to Iraq*. Santa Monica, CA.

Dobbins, James. (2007). *The Beginner's Guide to Nation-Building*. Santa Monica, CA.

Dobbins, James, *et al.* (2005). *The UN's Role in Nation-Building. From the Congo to Iraq.* Santa Monica, CA.

Doyle, Michael W. and Sambanis, Nicholas. (2000). International Peacebuilding. A Theoretical and Quantitative Analysis. *American Political Science Review*, 94 (4), 779–801.

Doyle, Michael W. and Sambanis, Nicholas. (2006). *Making War and Building Peace. United Nations Peace Operations.* Princeton: Princeton University Press.

Duffield, Mark. (2007). *Development, Security and Unending War.* London: Pluto.

Fearon, James D. (1998). Bargaining, Enforcement, and International Cooperation. *International Organization*, 52 (02), 269–305.

Fearon, James D. and Laitin, David D. (2004). Neotrusteeship and the Problem of Weak States. *International Security*, 28 (4), 5–43.

Fortna, Page Virginia. (2008). Peacekeeping and Democratization. In: Jarstadt, A. K. and Sisk, T. D. (eds), *From War to Democracy. Dilemmas of Peacebuilding.* New York: Cambridge University Press, 39–79.

Fukuyama, Francis. (2004). *State-Building. Governance and World Order in the 21st Century.* Ithaca: Cornell University Press.

Fukuyama, Francis. (2005). "Stateness" First. *Journal of Democracy*, 16 (1), 84–88.

Gheciu, Alexandra. (2005). International Norms, Power and the Politics of International Administration. The Kosovo Case. *Geopolitics*, 10 (1), 121–146.

Gigerenzer, Gerd and Selten, Reinhard. (2002). *Bounded Rationality. The Adaptive Toolbox.* Cambridge MA: MIT Press.

Hohe, Tanja. (2002). The Clash of Paradigms. International Administration and Local Political Legitimacy in East Timor. *Contemporary Southeast Asia*, 24 (3), 569–589.

Jabri, Vivienne. (2007). *War and the Transformation of Global Politics.* Basingstoke: Palgrave.

Jarstad, Anna and Belloni, Roberto. (2012). Introducing Hybrid Peace Governance. Impact and Prospects of Liberal Peacebuilding. *Global Governance*, 18, 1–6.

Jarstad, Anna K. and Sisk, Timothy D. (eds). (2008a). *From War to Democracy. Dilemmas of Peacebuilding.* Cambridge: Cambridge University Press.

Jarstad, Anna and Sisk, Timothy D. (2008b). *From War to Democracy: Dilemmas of Peace-building.* Cambridge: Cambridge University Press.

Kahnemann, Daniel. (2011). *Thinking, Fast and Slow.* London: Penguin Books.

Kappler, Stefanie and Richmond, Oliver. (2011). Peacebuilding and Culture in Bosnia and Herzegovina. Resistance or Emancipation? *Security Dialogue*, 42 (3), 261–278.

Knaus, Gerhard and Martin, Felix. (2003). Travails of the European Raj. *Journal of Democracy*, 14 (3), 60–130.

Krasner, Stephen. (2004). Sharing Sovereignty. New Institutions for Collapsed and Failing States. *International Security*, 29 (2), 85–120.

Krasner, Steven. (2005). The Case for Shared Sovereignty. *Journal of Democracy*, 16 (1), 39–54.

Lavenex, Sandra and Schimmelfennig, Frank. (2011). EU Democracy Promotion in the Neighbourhood. From Leverage to Governance? *Democratization*, 18 (4), 885–909.

Lederach, John Paul. (1997). *Building Peace. Sustainable Reconciliation in Divided Societies.* Washington.

Leininger, Julia. (2010). 'Bringing the Outside In': Illustrations from Haiti and Mali for the Re-Conceptualization of Democracy Promotion. *Contemporary Politics*, 16 (1), 63–80.

Mac Ginty, Roger. (2010). Hybrid Peace. The Interaction Between Top-Down and Bottom-Up Peace. *Security Dialogue*, 41 (4), 391–412.

Mac Ginty, Roger. (2011). *International Peacebuilding and Local Resistance. Hybrid Forms of Peace*. Basingstoke: Palgrave Macmillan.

Marten, Kimberly Zisk. (2004). *Enforcing the Peace. Learning from the Imperial Past*. New York: Columbia University Press.

Menkhaus, Ken. (2006). Governance without Government in Somalia. Spoilers, State Building, and the Politics of Coping. *International Security*, 31 (3), 74–106.

Merkel, Wolfgang. (2010). Systemtransformation. Eine Einführung in die Theorie und Empirie der Transformationsforschung. Wiesbaden: VS Verlag für Sozialwissenschaften.

Millar, Gearoid, van der Lijn, Jaïr and Verkoren, Willemijn. (2013). Peacebuilding Plans and Local Reconfigurations. Frictions between Imported Processes and Indigenous Practices. *International Peacekeeping*, 20 (2), 137–143.

Paris, Roland. (2002). International Peacebuilding and the 'Mission Civilisatrice'. *Review of International Studies*, 2002 (28), 637–656.

Paris, Roland. (2004). *At War's End. Building Peace after Civil Conflict*. Cambridge: Cambridge University Press.

Paris, Roland. (2005). *At War's End. Building Peace after Civil Conflict*. Cambridge: Cambridge University Press.

Paris, Roland and Sisk, Timothy D. (2007a). *The Dilemmas of Statebuilding. Confronting the Contradiction of Postwar Peace Operations*. London: Routledge.

Paris, Roland and Sisk, Timothy D. (2007b). *Managing Contradictions. The Inherent Dilemmas of Postwar Statebuilding*. New York: Routledge.

Paris, Roland and Sisk, Timothy D. (eds). (2009). *Dilemmas of Postwar Statebuilding*. Oxon: Routledge.

Pickering, Jeffrey and Peceny, Mark. (2006). Forging Democracy at Gunpoint. *International Studies Quarterly*, 50 (3), 539–560.

Pouligny, Béatrice. (2005). Civil Society and Post-Conflict Peacebuilding. Ambiguities of International Programmes Aimed at Building 'New' Societies. *Security Dialogue*, 36 (4), 495–510.

Przeworski, Adam. (1991). *Democracy and the Market. Political and Economic Reforms in Eastern Europe and Latin America*. Cambridge: Cambridge University Press.

Richmond, Oliver. (2009). Becoming Liberal, Unbecoming Liberalism. Liberal-Local Hybridity via the Everyday as a Response to the Paradoxes of Liberal Peacebuilding. *Journal of Intervention and Statebuilding*, 3 (3), 324–344.

Richmond, Oliver. (2010). Resistance and the Post-Liberal Peace. *Millennium – Journal of International Studies*, 38 (3), 665–692.

Richmond, Oliver. (2011a). Becoming Liberal, Unbecoming Liberalism. The Everyday, Empathy, and Post-Liberal Peacebuilding. In: Tadjbaksh, S. (ed.) *Alternatives to the Liberal Peace*. New York: Palgrave.

Richmond, Oliver. (2011b). Critical Agency, Resistance and a Post-Colonial Civil Society. *Cooperation and Conflict*, 46 (4), 419–440.

Richmond, Oliver and Mitchell, Audra. (2011a). Peacebuilding and Critical Forms of Agency. From Resistance to Subsistence. *Alternatives*, 36 (4), 326–344.

Richmond, Oliver P. and Mitchell, Audra (eds). (2011b). *Hybrid Forms of Peace. From the 'Everyday' to Post-Liberalism*. Basingstoke: Palgrave.

Roberts, David. (2011). Post-Conflict Peacebuilding, Liberal Irrelevance and the Locus of Legitimacy. *International Peacekeeping*, 18 (4), 410–424.

Ruggeri, Andrea, Gizelis, Theodora-Ismene and Dorussen, Han. (2012). Managing Mistrust. An Analysis of Cooperation with UN Peacekeeping in Africa. *Journal of Conflict Resolution*, 57 (3), 387–409.

Schneckener, Ulrich. (2006). Fragile Staatlichkeit. "States at Risk" zwischen Stabilität und Scheitern. Baden-Baden: Nomos.

Simon, Herbert A. (1956). Rational Choice and the Structure of the Environment. *Psychological Review*, 63 (2), 129–138.

Stedman, Stephen J. (1997). Spoiler Problems in Peace Processes. *International Security*, 22 (2), 5–53.

Suhrke, Astri. (2006). *The Limits of Statebuilding. The Role of International Assistance in Afghanistan*. International Studies Association Annual Meeting. San Diego, CA.

Tansey, Oisín. (2009). *Regime-Building. Democratization and International Administration*. New York: Oxford University Press.

Walter, Barbara. (2002). *Committing to Peace. The Successful Settlement of Civil Wars*. Princeton: Princeton University Press.

Zaum, Dominik. (2007). *The Sovereignty Paradox. The Norms and Politics of International Statebuilding*. Oxford: Oxford University Press.

Zürcher, Christoph. (2006). *Is More Better? Evaluating External-Led State Building after 1989*. Stanford: Stanford University Press.

Zürcher, Christoph. (2007). *Evaluating International Influences on Democratic Development. Volume 2*. Post-Conflict Countries. Research and Writing Guide. Berlin.

Zürcher, Christoph. (2011). Building Democracy While Building Peace. *Journal of Democracy*, 22 (1), 81–95.

Zürcher, Christoph, Manning, Carrie, Evenson, Kristie D., Riese, Sarah and Roehner, Nora. (2013). *Costly Democracy. Peacebuilding and Democratization after War*. Stanford: Stanford University Press.

Zürcher, Christoph, Röhner, Nora and Riese, Sarah. (2009). External Democracy Promotion in Post-Conflict Zones. Evidence from Case Studies. *Taiwan Journal of Democracy*, 5 (1), 241–259.

3 The analytical framework of peacebuilding interactions

Being interested in the external–domestic interplay in post-war Kosovo, and knowing the literature on the need for powerful international capacities, the importance of local resistance, and the role of strategic thinking, I was struck by two observations made during my field research in the Kosovo municipalities of Bregore/Brdašce and Zabel/Šumarak. First, I was surprised by the manifold instances of non-compliance at the local level despite the powerful international capacities employed in Kosovo. None of the peacebuilding reforms I investigated had been implemented right after their legal adoption by UNMIK or by the Kosovo parliament. Implementation started only after international actors actively voiced demands for reform execution, sometimes years after legal adoption. External–domestic interaction thus seems to be a necessary condition for peacebuilding reforms to be implemented. This widespread non-compliance is a recurring challenge for peacebuilders, I learned, even in everyday legislation such as building permits, housing or taxation.[1] A former UNMIK employee described the situation in his municipality with the following words:

> We could write down one thing in law, but people would not care and do whatever they wanted. If UNMIK had really cared about Kosovars following the law, they would have had to fire them all.
> (Interview 81, UNMIK Legal Officer, 26/09/2013)

Owing to the fact that peacebuilding organisations engage in the complete re-writing of a state's legislation, often without consideration for previous legal codes and context,[2] domestic actors might choose non-compliance simply because of the "law of least effort" that assumes that individual routine behaviour changes only in cases of urgency (Kahnemann 2011). In any case, the domestic tendency for non-compliance is a defining feature of any interaction process as it makes interactions a necessary condition for reform implementation to occur.

Second, given the discussion about local resistance, I had expected to find highly conflictive interactions between peacebuilders and domestic elites in Kosovo's municipalities, with peacebuilders using ever more pressure to reach their goals and domestic actors fiercely resisting unwanted reforms. Yet the second thing that struck me in the field was that I could hardly detect open conflicts or standoffs between international organisations and municipal elites – even though most of the peacebuilding reforms were apparently not implemented in full compliance with Kosovo's legal framework, if at all. The multitude of actors involved – international organisations such as Kosovo Force (KFOR), the United Nations (UN), World Bank, International Monetary Fund (IMF), the OSCE and various UN agencies as well as bilateral donors and (international) non-governmental organisations – negotiated rather quietly with domestic actors in the government, legislature or the state bureaucracy. Both sides frequently emphasised in my interviews how cooperative their relations are with their counterparts.

When analysing the data gathered in the two municipalities, I tried to understand the logic upon which these non-complying yet un-conflictive interaction dynamics unfold, and how these interactions facilitate reform capture in the end. The result is a new analytical framework that allows for a better understanding of the logic underlying external–domestic interactions in post-war transitions to peace and democracy. The analytical framework of peacebuilding interactions builds primarily on the inductive analysis of several cases of external–domestic interactions at the local level in Kosovo, not the deductive reasoning from existing theory.

The analytical framework of peacebuilding interactions proposes a set of categories that seem relevant to describing and analysing external–domestic interactions. These key categories include: (1) international ad hoc interaction tactics, (2) a set of domestic responses to counter international demands, (3) the domestic environment of interaction and (4) a set of possible peacebuilding outcomes. The framework allows the tracing of interaction processes over time, permits the identification of interaction patterns, and enables a systematic comparison of several cases of external–domestic interactions. The approach is thus helpful in understanding how, and under what conditions, external–domestic interactions influence post-war transitions. Based on this analytical framework, I show that international capacity is less relevant for post-war transitions than assumed and that the level of local resistance has an important impact on the course of the reform, but does not necessarily lead to reform failure. The framework also allows for the conclusion that interactions are not purely driven by rational, strategic considerations, but are equally shaped by bounded rationality, where the ad hoc interaction tactics of selectivity, prioritisation and leverage serve as a repertoire of heuristics to simplify decision-making.

Before proceeding, I would like to make explicit the basic assumptions on which this analytical framework rests and discuss the role of scope conditions – diverging priorities, mutual dependencies and the complexity of the post-war environment – in the evolution of any external–domestic interaction in post-war settings.

Scope conditions for peacebuilding interactions

The analytical framework rests on the assumption that external–domestic interactions in any peacebuilding context are significantly shaped by the following three scope conditions: diverging priorities, mutual dependencies and the complexity of the post-war environment. These three scope conditions constrain peacebuilders' ability to promote peace and democracy in peacebuilding contexts, and shape the external–domestic interaction in a way that it is marked by domestic non-compliance, mutual conflict avoidance and non-strategic behaviour. Divergent priorities, for example, are an incentive for domestic non-compliance or reform capture and preclude a completely cooperative interaction process. Mutual dependencies make both sides prone to compromise in order to avoid conflicts. The complexity of the post-war environment constrains peacebuilders' ability to control post-war developments and process all information available, thus fostering bounded rationality in the interaction.

The following section summarizes how the three scope conditions shape the logic of external–domestic interaction and what they look like in Kosovo specifically.

Diverging priorities

> I have the feeling that internationals wanted just peace, not development. Now and before we didn't have a good economic situation, And still we don't have an economic plan.
> (Interview 66 with former Mayor, Zabel/Šumarak, 07/11/2012)

The priorities of peacebuilders and domestic elites are seldom aligned in post-war countries (Barnett and Zürcher 2008, Jarstad and Sisk 2008, Paris and Sisk 2007a). This is a fundamental challenge for peacebuilders, who wish to fulfil their peacebuilding agenda, because domestic actors will prefer non-compliance or reform capture in order to push their own set of priorities. Diverging priorities are also a defining feature of the external–domestic interaction in Kosovo: While peacebuilders in Kosovo prioritise stability, democracy and minority rights, domestic actors prioritise socio-economic development, political power and the Kosovo status question (whether Kosovo should be independent or remain part of Serbia).[3]

Peacebuilders' priorities: stability, democracy and minority rights

For peacebuilders, ensuring stability and promoting the international norms of democracy and minority rights are top priorities in the international intervention in Kosovo (Doyle and Sambanis 2000, Mac Ginty and Richmond 2009, Newman *et al.* 2009, Paris 2004).

Stability represents the first priority for peacebuilding organisations in post-war settings because the success or failure of international interventions is ultimately measured against their ability to keep the peace (Barnett and Zürcher 2008, Doyle and Sambanis 2000, Paris 2004). The mission mandates of KFOR and UNMIK in Kosovo establish stability as a primary goal. KFOR is mandated to "deter renewed hostilities" and to "establish a secure environment and ensure public safety and order" (NATO 2013), and UNMIK strives to "maintain civil law and order" and to ensure the "safe and unimpeded return of refugees" (UN 1999). This has consequences for peacebuilding practice: UNMIK, for example, often tended to ignore legal breaches by domestic actors with the exception of inter-ethnic incidents or the violation of Serbian property rights, because these were regarded as de-stabilising factors.[4]

Democracy – the strengthening of participation, transparency and accountability – and *minority rights* – special rights and special representation – figure equally high on the priority list of peacebuilders in Kosovo. The two international norms are of particular importance in Kosovo[5]: Mission mandates of UNMIK, the International Civilian Office (ICO), the OSCE and the EU all emphasise democracy and minority rights. UNMIK's mandate comprises the "development of provisional institutions for democratic and autonomous self-government" (UN 1999), and the ICO is in "clear support of a democratic and multi-ethnic state" (ISG 2012). The OSCE is dedicated to "democratisation and governance" and the "monitoring, protection and promotion of minority rights" (OSCE 1999). The EU facilitates the "creation of a democratic and multi-ethnic society" (CEC 2005), and EULEX promotes "sustainability, accountability, multi-ethnicity, freedom from political interference, compliance with internationally recognized standards" (EULEX 2010).

Domestic priorities: development, political power and the status question

> Communicating directly with you helps me to understand your priorities to begin a new mission for Kosovo. After gaining freedom and independence and state-building, my focus will be to accelerate economic development and Euro-Atlantic integration.
>
> (Hashim Thaçi, former Kosovo Prime Minister, on his Facebook page, 23/02/2014)

When I asked local politicians about the most pressing issues in municipal politics, none referred to stability, democracy or minority rights – as peacebuilders would have done. Instead, socio-economic development, political power and the status of Kosovo emerged as key issues. These priorities guide the domestic logic of action when negotiating peacebuilding reforms with international counterparts and have to be understood against the backdrop of the hardships of everyday life in Kosovo and the war, which will be discussed in Chapter 4. This divergence of international and domestic priorities complicates peacebuilders' attempts to reach their peacebuilding goals, as Kosovo political elites strive to capture peacebuilding reforms for their own political agenda.

Socio-Economic Development. For most Kosovo citizens, the struggle for survival is the most pressing concern in everyday life. Development of the economy and infrastructure is therefore a top priority for Kosovo's political elites and more important than liberal democratic reforms.[6] Numerous studies in the past years have revealed that Kosovars are more concerned about economic and social development than about politics: When asked about the most pressing problems in their municipalities, unemployment was the answer of 57.7 per cent of Kosovo respondents, followed by poor supply of electricity (7 per cent), water (6.4 per cent) and poor standard of living (5.4 per cent) (UNDP 2012). Additionally, street pavements, uninterrupted electricity, water and waste disposal and individual pleas to help out with food or firewood emerged as the most common demands from citizens to politicians.[7] With 34 to 48 per cent of the population living below the poverty line, this might come as no surprise. Yet the mission mandates of peacebuilding organisations do not reflect the domestic preoccupation with survival and development. The liberal peacebuilders' abstract ideals of democracy and minority rights and their ensuing failure to address local needs for economic survival has dire consequences for the peacebuilders' great project of social transformation – all issues that have not yet been sufficiently analysed by scholars.

Political power is a further priority of Kosovo's elites. The structure of the Kosovar political system fosters the quest for political power via clientelist networks and the maintenance of patronage relations with citizens. Increasing the personal political power base through (internationally funded) infrastructure projects, the distribution of posts, and state resources is imperative for numerous politicians in many parts of the world, as well as in Kosovo (Englebert and Tull 2008).[8] In an environment of widespread poverty and under conditions of clientelism and patronage, the quest for political power might be in direct contradiction to peacebuilders' promotion of democracy: Accountability via institutional checks and balances or transparency in the form of citizen participation appear to be potential threats to one's personal clientelist network.

The Status Question – Independence, Integration or Boycott. Gaining ground on the status question of whether Kosovo should seek independence or remain part of Serbia is an equally important issue for Kosovo's political elites, although Kosovo Albanians and Kosovo Serbs have different visions of the ideal outcome. Kosovo Albanians' priority is the independence of Kosovo. Most Albanian municipal politicians I interviewed mentioned freedom from Serbian repression and independence as one major motivation to engage in politics.[9] Kosovo independence figures as the main goal in all Kosovo Albanian party programmes (Stojarova 2007). Kosovo Serbs, to the contrary, generally favour remaining part of Serbia. Moderate Serbs are inclined to accept Kosovo institutions, while Serbian hardliners demand their boycott. As both priorities (independence or remaining part of Serbia) still figure high on the domestic political agenda, they complicate peacebuilders' attempts to institutionalise minority rights.

Mutual dependencies

Mutual dependencies influence the logic of interaction in that they foster a tendency to avoid conflict and increase the willingness to compromise on one's own priorities. Mutual dependencies thus instil strategic elements in the interaction: For example, peacebuilders might be tempted to back down from their demands, while domestic actors might become inclined to give in. But what do these dependencies consist of?

Peacebuilders' dependencies: in need of cooperation

Peacebuilders are dependent on the cooperation of domestic actors to advance the peacebuilding agenda. To that end, peacebuilders are often willing to compromise on their goals and back down from their initial demands. The fact that peacebuilders need the cooperation of domestic elites to maintain stability and implement liberalising reforms has already been raised by Barnett and Zürcher (2007). In the case of Kosovo, the dependency of peacebuilders is based on the capacity of high-ranking former UÇK commanders to control the security situation and on the important role of domestic elites in implementing peacebuilding reforms. The latter is especially relevant for external–domestic interactions at the municipal level: Peacebuilders need domestic municipal elites' cooperation because these elites are either directly responsible for implementation or are in a position to order the implementation at the administrative level. Maintaining good relations with the municipal political power holders is, therefore, of utmost importance for peacebuilders' success, as the following quotes show:

> We try to acknowledge that because we also have a relationship to maintain with our interlocutors. We cannot go for every issue that we are aware of. We have to chose a little bit.
> (Interview 53, OSCE Community Team, 18/10/2012)

As a consequence, peacebuilders often back down from their demands in order to maintain domestic cooperation in other areas:

> But, you know, sometimes it is difficult – when you go there once, and you go there twice, and things don't change. You just feel bad. Sometimes they say, "You know, we have quite a lot of priorities", which means to say, "You know, this is not [a priority]".
> (Interview 54, OSCE field office, 19/10/2012)

Maintaining good relations with domestic counterparts is thus important for the success of peacebuilders' work. Sometimes peacebuilders might even fear that increasing pressure on domestic elites to enforce compliance might endanger their own position. One municipal politician commented on a situation in which an international employee witnessed legal breaches but refrained from increasing pressure on the Mayor, with the following words:

> No, me personally, I don't have bad feelings. I respect this man – but he only cares about not losing his job, keeping his salary, thoughts of that kind...
>
> (Interview 40, municipal politician, 02/10/2012)

In cases of corruption and organised crime, fear of political pressure might be a further reason for backing down:

> INTERVIEWER: Ok, so even if you observe it [corruption], nothing happens?
> INTERVIEWEE: We don't have the capacity. It's too big for us to take on. You know, we try to monitor that the procedures are adhered to [in budget development], but in terms of where money is allocated and where it is spent, it's simply, it's outside of our.... We can't do that.
>
> (Interview 14, OSCE headquarters, Prishtina, 08/05/2012)

Peacebuilders, then, tend to back down in an interaction in order to maintain good relations, to keep from losing their job or out of fear of political pressure.

Domestic dependencies: in need of resources

Domestic actors are primarily dependent on peacebuilders' financial resources. Faced with poverty and tight municipal budgets, the financial assistance offered by peacebuilders represents a powerful incentive for domestic actors to give in to peacebuilders' reform demands. Domestic elites are interested in financial resources for several reasons: First, political elites in clientelist systems typically use financial assistance to broaden their political power base (Englebert and Tull 2008). Second, financial assistance allows political actors to advance their priority of socio-economic development. Many times when I asked Kosovo politicians about their relations with the internationals, the first reaction was a praise of internationals' development activities and investment of financial resources.[10] The quote below exemplifies this:

> What I want to say is that we have very good relations with internationals, or if we don't, we always try to have better relations. USAID helps us a lot to rebuild: They gave us a projector, microphones, laptops,

cameras, and all the cars have GPS. We also have a big project for street-lights. As you can see, the municipality looks great and different because of the really nice contact with USAID.

(Interview 37, Municipal Director, Bregore/Brdašce, 01/10/2012)

Conversely, international actors without great financial resources are in a worse position to push their demands through in front of domestic actors:

The OSCE is many times interested only in some issues with the non-majority [population]. They do not have money to help us. They do not have work, they do not give out money – only for small projects up to €250, which are not so necessary. However, they help us on different issues.

(Interview 18, Municipal Official, 11/05/2012)

Financial resources are also an important incentive for prompting individuals to participate in municipal politics and, consequently, influence reform success. If citizens are not offered financial compensation, participation in committees or assembly meetings remains scarce because they prefer to work on their land instead of engaging in politics:

To tell the truth the law [on public budget hearings] already exists and citizens have the right to participate, but a very small number participates and only in rare cases. I want to get into details: People here are very busy; it is an agriculture territory and it is also in a big crisis, and they hardly survive the winter, and they always are running to provide food and they do not have time.

(Interview 44, former Mayor, 03/10/2010)

Domestic actors in poverty-stricken post-war countries, whether political actors or individual citizens, thus have a financial interest in conceding to peacebuilders' demands for liberal reforms.

Complexity of the post-war environment

Post-war states represent complex, ambiguous and unclear environments (Ljin 2013). This limits peacebuilders' capacity to fully control post-war politics and to act strategically, making way for non-strategic elements in the external–domestic interaction. Post-war environments are complex in several regards: First, the high volatility of the security situation makes organised planning difficult (Paris and Sisk 2007b). Second, peacebuilders' poor understanding of political dynamics restricts their ability to create targeted interventions in politics (Caplan 2005). And third, the simultaneity of peacebuilding tasks is difficult to process and simply overwhelming Caplan (2002). In post-war settings, international actors often have to act under pressure in combination with an information overload that is difficult to process (Ljin 2013). This makes it difficult to think about future interaction strategies in a purely rational manner (Ljin 2013). Simon (1956), who coined the term 'bounded rationality', states that "a great deal can be learned about rational decision-making ... by taking account of the fact that the environments to which it must adapt possess properties that permit further simplification of its choice mechanisms". Peacebuilders, unable to interact in a purely strategic way to enforce an optimum outcome, therefore resort to ad hoc tactics as heuristics in order to deal with overly complex environments. These ad hoc tactics then offer domestic actors leeway to pursue their own priorities.

It seems therefore important to take into account the overwhelmingly complex post-war environment in order to understand what drives interactions in peacebuilding contexts. Caplan (2002), one of the few conflict researchers taking on the issue of complexity, considers the simultaneity of peacebuilding tasks to be particularly challenging:

> The more fundamental challenge of international administration, however, is the sheer number of functions it must perform, many of them simultaneously and with great urgency, and the difficulty of identifying the priority tasks as the situation on the ground evolves.
>
> (Caplan 2002)

The complexity of the post-war environment severely limits peacebuilders' capacity to control post-conflict political developments, although control seems to be necessary to ensure success in a situation of widespread domestic non-compliance and mutual conflict avoidance. Complexity is particularly high at the local level, where peacebuilders are expected to ensure the practical implementation of a high number of reforms simultaneously. International staff at a local level describe the challenge as follows:

> UNMIK did not have the time to deal with every problem. It would have taken too long to respond and taken up too much energy. Because for every illegal rule the Kosovars would pass at the local level, six people in UNMIK would have to be discussing what to do.
>
> (Interview 81, UNMIK Officer, 26/09/2013)

> Let's say it is challenging to keep track of it. There is so much happening in the region that you need to be flexible to respond.
>
> (Interview 75, OSCE regional office, 23/11/2012)

The ability to keep track of political developments is furthermore diminished by the fact that peacebuilders' limited human resources force them to delegate political decisions to domestic actors.[11] Interactions are thus marked by deliberate acts of omission on the peacebuilders' side. In Kosovo, UNMIK soon delegated political decisions to domestic political elites at the municipal level.

As early as a few days after his arrival, the UNMIK Municipal Administrator of one of the investigated municipalities wrote the following:

> Given the sudden influx of visitors, the MA [Municipal Administrator] met with Mr. X, the Vice President of the Zabel municipality. The purpose of the meeting was to inform them that in the future, the MA expected all individuals – to as great an extent as possible – to meet first with the appropriate municipal official as the MA could not possible [*sic*] deal with the municipal population on an individual basis.
>
> (UNMIK Municipal Administrator, Zabel/Šumarak, Daily Report, 27/08/1999)

To cope with such complexity, peacebuilders structure and simplify their environment by selecting and prioritising issues (Kahnemann 2011) or by increasing leverage. At the local level, this does not take place due to long-term strategic considerations, but rather out of ad hoc considerations for how to best cope with unexpected and challenging situations, relying on ad hoc interaction tactics as heuristics to structure decision-making. These observations complement Barnett and Zürcher's national-level argument on strategic interaction, as my empirical investigation shows that bounded rationality does indeed matter at the local level.

The analytical framework of peacebuilding interactions: key categories

The analytical framework of peacebuilding interactions serves to analyse external–domestic interactions that take place on the backdrop of the scope conditions described above. The framework suggests a set of key categories relevant for describing external–domestic interactions, including (1) international ad hoc interaction tactics, (2) a set of domestic responses to counter international demands, (3) the domestic environment of interaction and (4) a set of possible peacebuilding outcomes. The framework has been inductively developed from the empirical material gathered in Kosovo as a tool to trace interaction processes over time, identify interaction patterns, and systematically compare external–domestic interactions across cases. The approach is thus helpful in understanding how, and under what conditions, external–domestic interactions influence post-war transitions and how these are shaped by bounded rationality. The central categories are as follows:

1   *Ad hoc interaction tactics of selectivity, prioritisation and leverage* have a significant influence on how a peacebuilding reform unfolds on the ground and offer domestic actors various points of leeway to capture peacebuilding for their own agenda. Selectivity, prioritisation and leverage can be seen as expressions of bounded rationality in interactions, as they are not of a strategic nature but rather represent coping strategies that peacebuilders use to deal

with fast-changing or unexpected developments. *Selectivity* refers to the peacebuilders' selection of a sub-set of rules from a reform initiative, which peacebuilders push to advance a reform. In this case, domestic actors gain leeway to ignore the non-selected rules at no cost. Yet if peacebuilders manage to cover the total set of rules over time, an outcome of full implementation is possible. *Prioritisation* refers to raising a reform to the top of the international agenda, which makes peacebuilders less inclined to tolerate non-compliance. Prioritisation makes an outcome of no implementation less likely. If, however, a reform is not prioritised, domestic actors gain leeway for non-compliance or reform capture at a low cost because on that reform peacebuilders tend to tolerate domestic resistance, modification or foot-dragging. *Leverage* describes the ability of peacebuilders to alter domestic actors' calculation of (non-)adoption costs through the use of higher leverage instruments such as coercion, conditionality or financial assistance. Higher leverage makes an outcome of no implementation less likely. If peacebuilders do not use higher leverage, domestic actors receive increased leeway for non-compliance or reform capture, as they can ignore, modify or delay the implementation of demanded rules at low cost. Peacebuilding outcomes are thus influenced by whether prioritisation occurs, which set of rules peacebuilders select and to what extent they apply leverage.

2   *Domestic responses* to international demands at rule implementation can take the form of cooperation, foot-dragging, modification or resistance. *Cooperation* means that domestic actors fully follow international demands. *Foot-dragging* implies that domestic actors show low commitment to international demands and invest insufficient time, financial resources or human resources. *Modification* means that domestic actors substantially depart from peacebuilders' intentions in their implementation. *Resistance* refers to outright refusal to follow international demands.

3   The *environment of interaction* influences adoption costs for domestic elites when implementing a peacebuilding reform. An environment can be enabling or constraining for peacebuilders' reform goals. In an enabling environment of interaction, domestic elites are willing to cooperate with the reform demands of peacebuilders, as domestic adoption costs are low. In a constraining environment of interaction, domestic elites might prefer to respond with strategies of foot-dragging, modification or even resistance, as domestic adoption costs are considerably higher.

4   Peacebuilding reforms can have several *outcomes*: full implementation, captured implementation or no implementation. Reforms can be captured for the domestic priority of political power or socio-economic development, or to push the Kosovo status question.

The above categories are explained in more detail below by drawing on the empirical material gathered in Kosovo.

Ad hoc interaction tactics: selectivity, prioritisation, leverage

Peacebuilders' ad hoc interaction tactics of selectivity, prioritisation and leverage have significant influence on how a peacebuilding reform unfolds on the ground. In the following pages, I intend to show that selectivity, prioritisation and leverage are primarily non-strategic coping mechanisms for dealing with the complexity of the post-war environment and as such are expressions of bounded rationality. At the same time, I do not deny that external–domestic interactions contain strategic elements inasmuch as actors intend to act rationally. However, since peacebuilders have to simplify and structure their environment in order to deal with information overload, they use selectivity, prioritisation or leverage as heuristics to make faster decisions. Kahnemann (2011) considers strategies such as prioritisation and selectivity to be typical responses for individuals in these situations. Also the use of leverage is seldom strategically tailored to the specific interaction situation at the local level, but instead follows standard peacebuilding pro-gramme prescriptions from the national level. These ad hoc interaction tactics offer domestic actors various points of leeway to capture peacebuild-ing for their own agenda. The occurrence of one tactic does not determine the peacebuilding outcome, but it does decrease the likelihood of one of the three possible outcomes.

It should also be noted that international ad hoc tactics are tools that peacebuilders resort to *during* an interaction process. They are thus subjected to changes over time: A reform that is at the lower end of peacebuilders' pri-ority list can become a top priority at another point in time, the set of selected rules that peacebuilders want to see implemented can change as the reform implementation evolves, and the international leverage deployed to push for rule implementation is equally in flux.

Using selected quotes from Kosovo, the section below exemplifies how prioritisation, selectivity and leverage influenced interaction dynamics and peacebuilding outcomes in the two municipalities.

Selectivity

Peacebuilders rarely address the entire catalogue of rules pertaining to a reform when interacting with their domestic counterparts. Instead, they con-centrate on a few rules for improvement; selecting only a sub-set of rules at one point in time. This selectivity enables peacebuilders to focus on limited aspects of a peacebuilding reform at a given moment, leaving aside rules con-sidered too demanding, too time-consuming, or simply just forgotten. Such selectivity provides domestic actors leeway to ignore those rules left out by peacebuilders and to capture reform at literally no cost. Over time, I have carefully traced which rules peacebuilders demanded to be implemented and which rules they left out of the interaction with domestic elites. In every reform, I have identified selectivity shifts in which peacebuilders widened and/or shifted the sub-set of rules expected to be implemented at a certain time. This means that while peacebuilders might emphasise one set of a reform's rules initially, they might change their focus to a completely different set of rules during the course of the reform. Such selectivity shifts are reflected in donor programmes, projects and activities and the triggers for selectivity shifts can be international routine evaluations, broader changes in the international agenda or local security incidents.

Selectivity is a widespread coping strategy among peacebuilders for managing the enormity of the social engineering programme entailed in peacebuilding. It allows individuals to deal ad hoc with complex environments through the reduction of the information to be processed (Kahnemann 2011): It's not ten rules that have to be negotiated, but only two or three. As a heuristic tool for navigating unclear situations, selectivity is not a strategic exercise, but rather an expression of the bounded rationality inherent in the interaction. The selective allocation of attention to a sub-set of rules enables international actors to be "orienting and responding quickly" (Kahnemann 2011), even in situations of potential danger. This simplifying and structuring also helps in the formulation of "concrete and attainable goals" (Ljin 2013).

In various interviews, international actors have described selectivity as a tactic for negotiating with their counterpart:

> But it is also an important issue that we are choosing where to intervene, because we cannot intervene in all situations.... We cannot go for every issue that we are aware of. We have to chose a little bit.
> (Interview 53, OSCE regional office, 18/10/2012)

The practice of evaluating peacebuilding initiatives to prove their effectiveness to donor agencies or headquarters enforces this selectivity because it motivates peacebuilders to concentrate on achieving 'success' only for concrete indicators:

> Third, performance indicators should be selective. There must be a limited number of focused targets, and they must be prioritized to offer sequenced strategic direction.
> (Dobbins 2007)

Due to the fact that domestic actors pursue different priorities than peacebuilders, the interaction pattern emerging from selectivity is one in which domestic actors implement only those rules that have been part of the selected sub-set of rules, if they implement any at all. Non-selected rules are most likely not to be implemented, as there is only low intrinsic motivation on the domestic side to make the reform happen. This means that *if selectivity is high, a full implementation outcome of a peacebuilding reform is less likely*. Selectivity thus might influence external–domestic interactions in such a way that a peace-building outcome of full implementation becomes less likely, while captured implementation and no implementation are both possible outcomes. Given the above-described tendency for non-compliance on the domestic side, full implementation is only possible if peacebuilders manage to tackle the total set of rules during the interaction process.

Prioritisation

Prioritisation means that peacebuilders raise a reform initiative to the top of the international agenda, which leads to increased attention, expectations and resources for the reform. The use of prioritisation is limited to special occasions and bound to the occurrence of certain exogenous triggers endangering the core interests of peacebuilders. For example, if non-compliance threatens Kosovo's stability or if a reform is mentioned as a benchmark in international reports (like the UN Security Council reports or EU reports), this non-compliance would then also threaten the peacebuilders' ability to proclaim 'success' in front of the wider international community. In the case of prioritisation, peacebuilders are less inclined to tolerate domestic non-compliance and insist on the implementation of a minimum sub-set of rules that guarantees success in the short-term and is easy to measure. Ljin (2013) makes similar observations: "To satisfy their need for order, people prioritise quick, easy and attainable solutions". Peacebuilders also increase the frequency of interactions with their local counterparts and the resources for the reform. If a particular reform is not a priority on the international agenda, peacebuilders tolerate domestic resistance, modification or foot-dragging. Such non-prioritisation of a peacebuilding reform provides domestic actors with the leeway to ignore or capture those reforms, because they only incur low costs.

Just like selectivity, prioritisation is a coping strategy to help peacebuilders navigate a highly complex post-war environment. Prioritisation does not result from strategic considerations geared to reach the optimum outcome in a reform, as is expected by strategic interactionists, but from unexpected ad hoc developments on the ground such as security incidents or broader political developments. In such situations, random prioritisation allows peace-builders to cope with the challenge of complexity in post-war settings (Kahnemann 2011). Peacebuilders thus deal with ambiguous post-war environments by prioritizing certain reforms while leaving others aside, thereby reducing the volume of information with which they are confronted (Kahnemann 2011). Prioritised peacebuilding reforms are then perceived as more important than others and receive more attention and resources. At the same time, policy options that guarantee more success in the short-term are preferred over longer-lasting, more solid solutions (Ljin 2013). This is why peacebuilders often prioritise a reform but then limit their attention to a minimum sub-set of rules that is easy to measure.

Prioritisation is described as a coping strategy in numerous interviews I held with the staff of peacebuilding organisations in Kosovo, for example, the OSCE regional offices:

> Sometimes you have to make a trade off. You have to sacrifice some success in one component in order to have some more success in the other.
>
> (Interview 22, USAID, 14/05/2012)

Prioritisation is not necessarily the result of a well-planned strategy of the peacebuilding community. On the contrary, prioritisation is often an ad hoc strategy, as one former UNMIK employee admitted:

> On the one hand there is the mandate and international legislation, but on the other hand, there is the 'ground', and SRSG has to set 'priorities of the moment' depending on personality, events and a complex environment of factors.
>
> (Interview 82, former UNMIK Legal Officer, 03/10/2013)

The triggers for priority shifts can thus be random, ad hoc and dependent on personalities, as the same UNMIK employee explained:

> UNMIK did not have the time or resources to deal with every problem. There was little conscious priority setting on the side of UNMIK. Issues were assigned priority or not, more or less on a random basis, often depending on individuals charged with the case.
>
> (Interview 82, former UNMIK Legal Officer, 26/09/2013)[12]

The interaction pattern that follows from prioritisation is one in which domestic actors are likely to drop their resistance against peacebuilders' demands as peacebuilders have raised the costs of non-adoption. *If prioritisation is high, a no implementation outcome of a peacebuilding reform is less likely.* Prioritisation thus influences external–domestic interactions in such a way that a peacebuilding outcome of no implementation becomes unlikely, while captured implementation and full implementation remain both possible outcomes.

Leverage

Leverage refers to the ability of peacebuilders to alter domestic actors' calculations of (non-)adoption costs and must be seen in relation to the vulnerability of governments, to external pressure and to existing dependency relations (Levitsky and Way 2005). Zürcher *et al.* (2013) also hold that peacebuilding outcomes "are to a great extent shaped by the costs they incur in adopting democracy, as well as the leverage that peacebuilders can muster to increase the costs of nonadoption". Due to domestic dependencies on financial support – or on good relations to receive such support – peacebuilders have a certain influence over domestic elites through the higher leverage norm promotion instruments of supervision, coercion, conditionality or financial assistance. Leverage, then, is concerned with the power that peacebuilders are able to mobilise in order to induce changes in domestic contexts. Yet the amount of leverage applied at the local level seems seldom strategically tailored to the specific interaction situation but instead results from standard program prescriptions at the national level.

International leverage is grounded in the fact that domestic actors are interested in maintaining good relations with peacebuilders in order to have better access to financial resources. Peacebuilders can increase domestic actors' adoption costs by using higher leverage instruments such as supervision, coercion, conditionality or financial assistance. At the same time, peacebuilders can also use lower leverage norm promotion instruments, which mainly draw on the mechanisms of learning and persuasion, to attain their goals. Checkel (2001) describes these lower leverage strategies as "a social process of interaction that involves changing attitudes about cause and effect in the absence of overt coercion". I thus distinguish between situations of high leverage and low leverage.

Higher leverage instruments:

- *Supervision* formally permits international actors to take over executive, legislative, judicial and administrative tasks, as well as to veto laws or to oust politicians from office (Caplan 2005, Chesterman 2004, 2005, Grimm 2010, Tansey 2009). It increases international leverage due to the formal powers given to peacebuilders.
- *Coercion* relies on the exertion of pressure in the field of diplomacy through international advocacy coalitions, high level visits, official statements, or threats to cut diplomatic relations or financial assistance. It increases international leverage because it signals the potential worsening of good relations with peacebuilders (which are needed to access financial resources).
- *EU conditionality* is "a bargaining strategy of reinforcement by reward, under which the EU provides external incentives to comply with its conditions" (Schimmelfennig and Sedelmeier 2004).[13] It can take the form of EU membership accession conditionality, policy conditionality or pre-conditionality and is controlled by clear benchmarks and regular progress reports. It increases international leverage because it offers domestic actors attractive material rewards (access to EU funds) for compliance with international demands.
- *Financial assistance* through programs and projects usually form a part of a development cooperation and draw on financial incentives as a mechanism to change domestic behaviour. It increases peacebuilders' leverage because it satisfies domestic actors' interests in financial resources.

Lower leverage instruments:

- *Capacity building* through seminars or workshops is a mechanism based on learning through teaching (Riddell 2007).
- *Public outreach activities* also aim to induce learning processes on the domestic side through teaching (Riddell 2007).
- *Advice through expert consultants* refers to exclusively non-material and non-coercive means to tell individuals to adopt a new attitude or behaviour.
- *Monitoring* and *reporting* are equally non-coercive means to incentivise individuals to change behaviour.

Peacebuilders in Kosovo are aware of the increased influence they could exert through the use of higher leverage instruments. For example, they are aware that citizens expect financial compensation for participating in committees, and accordingly, newly established committees often grant financial compensation to their members in order to ensure citizen or minority participation:

> There are also, of course a lot of issues with payment. It's a voluntary position and people don't really like to do things like that without getting paid. That's always an obstacle when it comes to doing things like that here.
>
> (Interview 14, OSCE headquarters, Prishtina, 08/05/2013)

Yet if peacebuilders do not use such high leverage, domestic actors find that they have more leeway for non-compliance or reform capture, as they can ignore, modify or drag their feet on implementing rules at a low cost.

The interaction pattern emerging from leverage is one in which domestic actors are more likely to drop their resistance against peacebuilders' demands in case of high leverage because the cost of non-adoption is raised considerably. *If leverage is high, a no implementation outcome of a peacebuilding reform is less likely.* Leverage thus influences external–domestic interactions in such a way that a peacebuilding outcome of no implementation becomes less likely if higher leverage instruments are applied, while captured implementation and full implementation remain possible outcomes.

Domestic responses: cooperation, foot-dragging, modification, resistance

Domestic actors respond to international reform demands with cooperation, foot-dragging, modification and resistance. The category system of domestic responses was inductively developed based upon the empirical data gathered. It illustrates the actions used by domestic actors to react to external reform demands. Generally, these domestic responses can be ordered according to the degree of agreement with international demands.

Cooperation describes domestic actors' acceptance of international reform demands, whether it be demands for the adoption of legislation or the implementation of reform packages or single rules. Cooperation can be the result of their own commitment to the reform, persuasion or financial incentives and is thus neutral with regard to the domestic actors' motivation. Cooperation can, for example, be the result of learning:

> We have changed a lot during this decade. So it's a learning process and we are now pretty much aware of why we should do this and not that.
> (Interview 27, Ministry of Administration, 27/11/2011)

Foot-dragging refers to activities that decelerate the reform process and includes an issue being assigned low priority, the use of limited effort, the allocation of limited resources and other tactics of deceleration. Foot-dragging describes the effect of domestic actors' activities but does not draw conclusions about whether domestic actors are opposed to reform demands or whether they simply have different priorities on their agenda. An example of foot-dragging could be a reduction in the number of meetings, which leads to the inefficient implementation of reforms:

> We had, I think, two meetings, both in spring 2010, but after the summer break, we were not acting in any way.
> (Interview 15, Committee member, 12/11/2011)

Modification describes the domestic actors' substantial alteration of international demands, implying that they have added to, changed or left out international demands. An international actor describes an act of modification in the following words:

> The people in the workshop were happy with our draft, but when we presented the ministry with the results of the workshop, they changed it to something totally different.
> (Interview 05, British Council, 17/10/2011)

Resistance refers to the explicit rejection of international demands and can include resistance to reform adoption, resistance to reform implementation, resistance to the implementation of specific international demands or resistance to participation in a particular reform.

> The decision of the municipality foresaw that it is now up to the Communities Office to ensure nominations from the Serbian community. But nominations never came.
> (Interview 53, OSCE, Bregore/Brdašce, 18/10/2012)

Environment of interaction: enabling or constraining

The domestic *environment of interaction* is also important for the evolution of external–domestic interaction dynamics because it is related to the adoption costs of peacebuilding reforms for domestic elites and, in turn, impacts on the domestic responses. The environment of interaction can be enabling or constraining. In an *enabling environment*, domestic actors face lower adoption costs for the implementation of peacebuilding reforms and are therefore more willing to respond cooperatively to international demands. In a *constraining environment*, domestic actors are confronted with higher adoption costs when implementing peacebuilding reforms and are therefore more apt to respond to international demands with resistance. The domestic environment of interaction thus determines to a certain extent the kind of interaction dynamics that evolve between external and domestic actors as well as the possible outcomes. In the cases I have studied, full implementation of reforms was only possible in an enabling environment. In such situations, domestic actors were more likely to fully cooperate with peacebuilders in their reform agenda because they were faced with lower adoption costs. In a constraining environment, domestic elites were much more likely to respond to international demands with resistance, modification or foot-dragging, which in turn made full implementation less likely.

The environment of interaction is influenced by two factors in particular: the *domestic support* for a promoted international norm, which can be more or less favourable, and the *style of politics* between domestic political actors, which can be cooperative or competitive. In an enabling environment, there is both a supportive attitude towards the promoted norm *and* a cooperative style of politics among the political actors. In a constraining environment, there is low domestic support for the promoted norm and/or a competitive style of politics.

Domestic support of an international norm refers to the widespread agreement with an international norm amongst the post-war population. The level of domestic support for a promoted norm is important because it influences the domestic elites' calculation of adoption costs: If there is strong support for (and hence popular pressure to respect) an international norm, domestic elites might be more willing to change their behaviour and follow external demands (Checkel 1997). In the case of a weakly supported norm, however, they might be more reluctant to implement such unpopular reforms out of fear of losing support and diminishing the chances of an incumbent government being re-elected (Schimmelfennig and Sedelmeier 2005). Domestic elites in post-war states thus play a two-level game (Putnam 1988) and can use weak domestic support to strengthen their position to oppose reforms vis-à-vis their international counterpart. The particular reforms I investigated in Kosovo either promoted the norm of democracy or the norm of minority rights. While *democracy* enjoys strong domestic support in Kosovo because it was associated with positive ideas of justice, equality and well-being, *minority rights* find only weak domestic support as they touch upon the politically sensitive question of Kosovo's status.[14]

The observation that international norms in peacebuilding enjoy both strong and weak support from the population breaks with the commonly held assumption in the critical peacebuilding scholarship that domestic actors *automatically* oppose liberal international norms (Mac Ginty 2010, Richmond 2011) and "resist, ignore, subvert or adapt liberal peace interventions" (Mac Ginty 2011). Because of this, researchers who aim to understand postwar transitions to peace and democracy require a more careful analysis of the discourses in the local population about international norms and the degree of support generated for them. Chapter 4 discusses in greater detail the meaning of democracy and minority rights within the local population and seeks to explain the positive or negative associations.

The *style of politics* refers to the general openness of political actors to share power with potential competitors within their own party or a rival party. The two municipalities I investigated practice different styles of politics. While politics in Zabel/Šumarak are marked by a cooperative style of politics, politics in Bregore/Brdašce are marked by a competitive style of politics. The style of politics is closely linked to the level of mistrust and vulnerability amongst the political elite that is common to find in states recovering from war (Talentino 2009). Informal networks of friendship are important in such situations for creating trust among decision-makers and fostering cooperative politics, as these relationships decrease the perception that peacebuilding reforms would cost a loss of power for themselves. A cooperative style of politics is expressed through (a) the absence of power struggles (transparent appointment of political officials, no political coups), (b) information sharing (between the executive and legislative branches, between the executive branch and caucus leaders, and between assembly factions), and (c) inclusive politics through consultations with the legislature, factions or third parties on legislative drafts. As most peacebuilding reforms require politicians or institutions to share power through control, transparency and inclusion, a cooperative style of politics lowers domestic elite adoption costs to implement peacebuilding reforms. Rules that increase compromise, accountability, transparency and participation are, however, more risky for the political elite practicing a competitive style of politics, as these reforms limit political elites' prospects of 'winning over the rival'.

In sum, the domestic environment of interaction influences the domestic calculation of adoption costs as well as the domestic responses chosen to counter international demands.

Peacebuilding outcomes: full, captured or no implementation

Peacebuilding reforms can result in three types of outcomes: full implementation, captured implementation or no implementation. *Full implementation* means that the total set of rules of a reform is implemented the way peacebuilders intended. *Captured implementation* means that the total set or sub-set of rules of the reform is implemented in a way that accommodates domestic priorities while diverting from peacebuilders' original intents. *No implementation* means that none of the rules of the reform are implemented. The middle ground category, captured implementation, leans on Barnett, Fang and Zürcher's (2014) description of captured peacebuilding as a situation where local elites reduce peacebuilding to an instrument of their preferences. Assuming that the external–domestic interaction offers domestic actors leeway to exploit reforms for their own priorities in various ways, captured implementation is further classified according to whether it serves the priority of socio-economic development, political power or the Kosovo status question.

Figure 3.1 below provides an overview of the central elements of the proposed interactive model of peacebuilding.

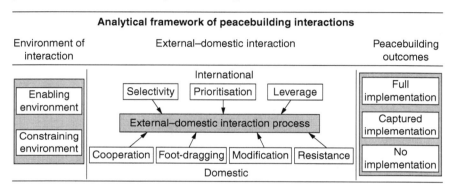

Analytical framework of peacebuilding interactions

Figure 3.1 The analytical framework of peacebuilding interactions.
Source: own compilation.

Notes

1 Please see the UNMIK Daily Reports, Zabel/Šumarak, 11/12/1999.
2 Interview 81 with former UNMIK Legal Officer, 26/09/2013.
3 The term 'priority' was chosen consciously instead of 'interests' or 'goals' because it points to the fact that peacebuilders' priorities do not have the same importance and urgency for domestic actors – and vice versa – but it does not imply domestic opposition to peacebuilders' priorities.
4 Interview 81 with former UNMIK Legal Advisor, 26/09/2013 and conversation with former high-ranking UNMIK employee, 30/01/2014.
5 Democracy and minority rights are, for example, prominent norms in the Comprehensive Proposal for a Status Settlement, which set out the Constitutional Provisions for an independent Kosovo (Muharremi 2010).
6 I base this claim on 16 interviews with municipal politicians. When asked about their motivation in politics, improving living conditions in Kosovo through economic and infrastructure development was the most frequent answer.
7 Interview 71 with USAID DEMI, Prishtina, 13/11/2012 and interviews 56 and 58 with members of the Communities Committee, Zabel/Šumarak, 29/10/2012.
8 There are many examples of clientelism in Kosovo: Interview partners talked about infrastructure projects accomplished a few weeks before elections or about

cousins being offered a job in the administration if able to assemble a certain number of votes.

9 For example in the interviews with municipal politician, Bregore/Brdašce, 22/09/2012, or municipal politician, Bregore/Brdašce, 03/10/2010.

10 For example in the interviews with municipal politician, Bregore/Brdašce, 22/09/2012, high-ranking municipal official, Bregore/Brdašce, 11/05/2012, municipal politician, Bregore/Brdašce, 03/10/2010, municipal official, Zabel/Šumarak, 31/10/2012, high-ranking municipal official, Zabel/Šumarak, 08/11/2012.

11 Even in highly staffed Kosovo, a team of five to six UNMIK municipal officers had to keep track of the political activities of 30 municipal politicians, 120 municipal officials and countless UÇK combatants (UNMIK, Daily Reports, Zabel/Šumarak, 21/08/1999).

12 The OSCE regional office in Prizren also told me they "decide on an ad hoc basis" about their annual priorities. Interview 15, OSCE regional office, Prizren, 09/05/2012.

13 I restrict my understanding to the specific form of EU conditionality, because it played a unique role in the peacebuilders' efforts to stabilise Western Balkan countries. Outside the EU, conditionality is also used in financial assistance, particularly by the International Monetary Fund and World Bank (Alexander 2008).

14 I draw this conclusion from focus group discussions I held with citizens in the two municipalities, where democracy was predominantly associated with positive connotations, while minority rights were predominantly associated with negative connotations.

References

Alexander, Marcus. (2008). Democratization and Hybrid Regimes. *East European Politics & Societies*, 22 (4), 928–954.

Barnett, Michael, Fang, Songying and Zürcher, Christoph. (2014). Compromised Peacebuilding. *International Studies Quarterly*, Online First, 1–13.

Barnett, Michael and Zürcher, Christoph. (2007). *The Peacebuilder's Contract: How External State-building Reinforces Weak Statehood*. Stanford: Stanford University Press.

Barnett, Michael and Zürcher, Christoph. (2008). The Peacebuilder's Contract. How External State-Building Reinforces Weak Statehood. In: Paris, R. and Sisk, T. D. (eds), *The Dilemmas of Statebuilding. Confronting the Contradictions of Postwar Peace Operations*. Abingdon: Routledge, 23–52.

Caplan, Richard. (2002). *A New Trusteeship? The International Administration of War-Torn Societies*. Oxford: Oxford University Press.

Caplan, Richard. (2005). *International Governance of War-Torn Societies. Rule and Reconstruction*. Oxford: Oxford University Press.

CEC. (2005). Communication from the Commission. A European Future for Kosovo. In: Communities, C. o. t. E. (ed.). Brussels: Commission of the European Communities.

Checkel, Jeffrey T. (1997). International Norms and Domestic Politics. Bridging the Rationalist-Constructivist Divide. *European Journal of International Relations*, 3 (4), 473–493.

Checkel, Jeffrey T. (2001). Why Comply? Social Learning and European Identity Change. *International Organization*, 55 (03), 553–588.

Chesterman, Simon. (2004). *You the People. The United Nations, Transitional Administration and State-Building*. Oxford: Oxford University Press.

Chesterman, Simon. (2005). Transitional Administration, State-Building and the United Nations. In: Chesterman, S., Ignatieff, M. and Thakur, R. (eds), *Making States Work. State Failure and the Crisis of Governance*. New York: United Nations University Press, 339–358.

Dobbins, James. (2007). *The Beginner's Guide to Nation-Building*. Santa Monica, CA.

Doyle, Michael W. and Sambanis, Nicholas. (2000). International Peacebuilding. A Theoretical and Quantitative Analysis. *American Political Science Review*, 94 (4), 779–801.

Englebert, Pierre and Tull, Denis M. (2008). Postconflict Reconstruction in Africa. Flawed Ideas about Failed States. *International Security*, 32 (4), 106–139.

EULEX. (2010). EULEX Program Report 2010. Prishtina.

Grimm, Sonja. (2010). Erzwungene Demokratie. Politische Neuordnung nach militärischer Intervention unter externer Aufsicht. Baden-Baden: Nomos.

ISG. (2012). Communiqué of 2nd of July. Vienna: International Steering Group.

Jarstad, Anna K. and Sisk, Timothy D. (eds). (2008). *From War to Democracy. Dilemmas of Peacebuilding*. Cambridge: Cambridge University Press.

Kahnemann, Daniel. (2011). *Thinking, Fast and Slow*. London: Penguin Books.

Levitsky, Steven and Way, Lucan A. (2005). International Linkage and Democratization. *Journal of Democracy*, 16 (3), 20–34.

Ljin, Jaïr van der. (2013). Imagi-Nation Building in Illusionstan. Afghanistan, Where Dilemmas Become Dogmas, and Models Are Perceived to Be Reality. *International Peacekeeping*, 20 (2), 173–188.

Mac Ginty, Roger. (2010). No War, No Peace. Why So Many Peace Processes Fail to Deliver Peace. *International Politics*, 47 (2), 145–162.

Mac Ginty, Roger. (2011). *International Peacebuilding and Local Resistance. Hybrid Forms of Peace*. Basingstoke: Palgrave Macmillan.

Mac Ginty, Roger and Richmond, Oliver P. (eds). (2009). *The Liberal Peace and Post-War Reconstruction*. Abingdon: Routledge.

Muharremi, Robert. (2010). The European Union Rule of Law Mission in Kosovo (EULEX) from the Perspective of Kosovo Constitutional Law. ZaöRV, 70, 357–379.

NATO. (2013). NATO's Role in Kosovo [Online]. Available at: www.nato.int/cps/en/natolive/topics_48818.htm [accessed 02/01/2014].

Newman, Edward, Paris, Roland and Richmond, Oliver (eds). (2009). *New Perspectives on Liberal Peacebuilding*. Tokyo: United Nations University Press.

OSCE. (1999). Decision No. 305. Vienna: OSCE Permanent Council.

Paris, Roland. (2004). *At War's End. Building Peace after Civil Conflict*. Cambridge: Cambridge University Press.

Paris, Roland and Sisk, Timothy D. (2007a). *The Dilemmas of Statebuilding. Confronting the Contradiction of Postwar Peace Operations*. London: Routledge.

Paris, Roland and Sisk, Timothy D. (2007b). *Managing Contradictions. The Inherent Dilemmas of Postwar Statebuilding*. New York.

Putnam, Robert D. (1988). Diplomacy and Domestic Politics. The Logic of Two-Level Games. *International Organization*, 42 (3), 427–460.

Richmond, Oliver. (2011). Critical Agency, Resistance and a Post-Colonial Civil Society. *Cooperation and Conflict*, 46 (4), 419–440.

Riddell, Roger C. (2007). *Does Foreign Aid Really Work?* Oxford: Oxford University Press.

Schimmelfennig, Frank and Sedelmeier, Ulrich. (2004). Governance by Conditionality. EU Rule Transfer to the Candidate Countries of Central and Eastern Europe. *Journal of European Public Policy*, 11 (4), 661–679.

Schimmelfennig, Frank and Sedelmeier, Ulrich (eds). (2005). *The Europeanization of Central and Eastern Europe*. Ithaca NY: Cornell University Press.

Simon, Herbert A. (1956). Rational Choice and the Structure of the Environment. *Psychological Review*, 63 (2), 129–138.

Stojarova, Vera. (2007). Nationalistic Features in the Programmes of the Serbian and Kosovo Albanian Political Parties. 10th Annual International Seminar "Democracy and Human Rights in Multiethnic Societies". Konjic, Bosnia and Herzegovina.

Talentino, Andrea Kathryn. (2009). Nation Building or Nation Splitting? Political Transition and the Dangers of Violence. *Terrorism and Political Violence*, 21 (3), 378–400.

Tansey, Oisín. (2009). *Regime-Building. Democratization and International Administration*. New York: Oxford University Press.

UN. (1999). Resolution 1244 (1999) adopted by the Security Council at its 4011th Meeting on 10 June 1999. In: *United Nations Documents* (ed.). New York.

UNDP. (2012). *The Kosovo Mosaic. Perceptions of Local Government and Public Services in Kosovo*. Prishtina.

Zürcher, Christoph, Manning, Carrie, Evenson, Kristie D., Riese, Sarah and Roehner, Nora. (2013). *Costly Democracy. Peacebuilding and Democratization after War*. Stanford: Stanford University Press.

4   Setting the stage

Everyday life and external–domestic interaction in Kosovo

To understand the external–domestic interaction as it unfolds in Kosovo, it is helpful to take a closer look at the everyday life of Kosovo citizens, the perception of international norms amongst Kosovo Albanians and Kosovo Serbs as well as the style of politics cultivated in the two municipalities of Zabel/Šumarak and Bregore/Brdašce. This is what this chapter is about. A better grasp on these aspects of Kosovo life provides valuable insights into the domestic logic of interaction – what drives domestic actors, why they choose certain priorities over others, and how this influences interactions with their international counterparts. The last part of the chapter then introduces the international and local actors who negotiate peacebuilding at the local level.

The tiny territorial stretch called Kosovo, situated between the Albanian Alps and the plains of southern Serbia, is probably the most notable laboratory for international norm promotion in the history of peacebuilding missions. The 1999 international intervention in Kosovo was a response to the violent conflict between Serbia and Kosovo Albanians over the question of whether Kosovo should become an independent state or remain part of Serbia.[1] On the eve of the conflict, Kosovo's multi-ethnic population was made up of 82 per cent Albanians and 10 per cent Serbs as well as Turks, Roma, Ashkali, Egyptians, Croats and Bosniaks.[2] While Kosovo Albanians sought to claim greater autonomy or outright independence, Serbs expected Kosovo to remain part of Serbia. The conflict took a violent turn in the mid-1990s, when Kosovo Albanian militants gained access to arms in an imploded Albania (Suhrke *et al.* 2000). On 24 March 1999, NATO started air strikes to pressure the Serbian government into accepting an internationally brokered peace deal. Soon afterwards, Serbian forces withdrew from Kosovo, and KFOR and the UNMIK were deployed. Nearly 11,000 people had died, 800,000 became refugees and 500,000 internally displaced persons had to be accommodated (AKUF 2007, UN 1999b). The ethnic distribution also changed: The Ibar River became the dividing line between a Serb-populated north and a predominantly Albanian south. Kosovo Serbs soon deserted formerly multi-ethnic cities like Prishtina, Prizren and Pejë/Peć. Mitrovicë/Mitrovica and Rahovec/Orahovac became divided along ethnic lines. Northern Kosovo – adjacent to Serbia itself – remained firmly under Serbian control and to this day continues to function to a considerable extent as part of Serbia (ICG 2009, OMIK and OSCE 2003, OSCE 2007a). At present, estimates project that the Kosovo Albanian population is at 92 per cent, the Kosovo Serbian population is at 4 per cent, and other minority groups equally constitute the remaining 4 per cent (Kosovo Agency of Statistics 2011).

To this day, the status of Kosovo remains contested between Kosovo Albanians and Kosovo Serbs, between Kosovo and the Serbian state and between members of the EU and the international community at large. Although the 1244 UN Security Council resolution that set up the UNMIK peacebuilding mission provided a mandate to facilitate a political dialogue on a 'final status' of Kosovo (UN 1999b), a final status settlement, including an official acceptance of Kosovo's independence by the Serbian state, has not been reached so far. There have been important attempts, however. UN Special Envoy Martti Ahtisaari facilitated status talks in 2006 between Serbia and the Kosovo Government, which resulted in the Comprehensive Proposal for the Kosovo Status Settlement (UN 2007b), also known as the Ahtisaari Plan. The Ahtisaari Plan envisioned Kosovo's independence under certain conditions and received backing from the Kosovo Albanian Government, the US and the EU. Yet it failed to be adopted in the UN Security Council due to objections from Russia and China, who were backing Belgrade (Kostovicova and Glasius 2008). As a consequence, Kosovo Albanian political leaders unilaterally declared Kosovo's independence on 17 February 2008, pledging to implement the provisions of the Ahtisaari Plan to gain international acceptance as an independent state (Kosovo 2008). The second important attempt at facilitating a status settlement was the Belgrade–Prishtina Dialogue, initiated under EU auspices in 2011. Its goal was the normalisation of relations between Belgrade, Kosovo Serbs and Kosovo Albanians, particularly through the dismantling of Serbian parallel structures in Kosovo territory. That said, the question of Kosovo's status remains contested.

Everyday life in post-war Kosovo: survival, politics and the dilemma of integration or boycott

Why, after all, do domestic actors pursue priorities different to those of peacebuilders? What is it that makes reform capture so attractive? To answer this question, it is important to take a closer look at the everyday life of citizens and investigate how widespread poverty, clientelist party politics and the status question shape domestic preferences and priorities. These factors are essential to understanding why domestic actors prioritise socio-economic development, political power and the status question instead of aligning with peacebuilders' priorities of stability, democracy and minority rights. Taking into account the widespread poverty in post-war Kosovo makes it easier to understand why socio-economic development is a priority for politicians and citizens. It also elucidates why clientelism and shifting alliances are such a common practice in the political party landscape. Looking at the structure of party politics is, in turn, helpful in understanding why political power is such a central priority for politicians and which strategies and practices help politicians to maintain it. The Kosovo Serbian dilemma about whether to choose integration or to boycott Kosovo institutions points to the political significance that the status question still possesses. If we are to understand reform capture, we need to understand these aspects of everyday life as they shape domestic motivations when negotiating peacebuilding reforms with internationals in post-war Kosovo.

Struggling for survival: what really moves Kosovo citizens

> I don't know what is difficult. It is necessary to have wood for the winter, to have electricity for the bathroom and to be able to provide for the family. Nothing special.
>
> (A municipal official's answer to my question about whether his job is difficult, Bregore/Brdašce, 05/10/2012)

For the majority of the rural population in Kosovo, life commonly means a struggle for survival. The peacebuilding literature seldom addresses the conditions of poverty dominating the lives of citizens in post-war states, although it is of fundamental relevance for peacebuilding.[3] Why should people care about democracy and minority rights if they don't know how they will stay warm during the winter? Taking into account the conditions of everyday poverty is necessary for understanding why domestic actors strive for socioeconomic development.

Life in Kosovo is a daily struggle. Even today, Kosovo is the poorest region in Europe: Kosovo's total GDP was $6.23 billion in 2012, while the annual per capita gross national income (GNI) was $3,640 in 2013 (World Bank 2013). These figures are low even compared to the Western Balkan region. The grim economic outlook is due to a mixture of historical legacies, a high rate of failed privatisation after the post-socialist transition, war-time destruction of factories and infrastructure and a standstill of the Kosovo economy in the 1990s with the rise of the informal sector (UNDP 2012). Poverty rate estimates indicate that between 34 per cent and 48 per cent of Kosovars live in absolute poverty, and between 12 per cent and 18 per cent live in extreme poverty.[4] Those falling under the poverty line have less than €1.42 to spend per day (UNDP 2012). Mainly children, female-headed households and members of Roma, Ashkali and Egyptian ethnicity groups are affected (UNDP 2006). Absolute poverty is rising sharply in rural areas.

Being poor means that citizens of Kosovo buy their groceries at the local market, not in stores. Clothes are worn through before new ones are bought, and cars are driven until they fall apart. It means that few families possess more than two to three books and that buying pencils and notebooks for school is considered an investment. Getting sick is one of the most serious worries of Kosovo citizens. Grave illnesses can lead to the financial ruin of families due to a lack of health insurance (UNDP 2012). To organise fire-wood for winter – the most widespread form of heating in Kosovo – many families engage in illegal woodcutting because they cannot afford the €350 needed to pay for it.[5] I saw men tearing down the roof of a burnt house to use the wooden beams for heating. Still, most households have a TV, washing machine, refrigerator and/or a mobile phone, but having a computer and an internet connection continues to be an exception (UNDP 2006).

Needless to say that the major preoccupation of most Kosovo families is how to earn money and be able to survive on it: Fifty per cent of Kosovars identify unemployment as the most pressing issue of all (UNDP 2006). The unemployment rate in Kosovo is the highest in Europe at 43 per cent, with youth unemployment rising to 73 per cent (Statistical Office of Kosovo 2009).[6] Even 30 per cent of the households with one employed member live below the poverty line, however, because of insecure, low-skill and low-wage jobs (UNDP 2012). The average monthly income is estimated at €170 per capita, with the average household expenditure being €352 (IMF 2011).[7] Fifty per cent of Kosovo's households spend between €201 and €400 per month, 19 per cent spend €200 or less (UNDP and USAID 2009).[8] This is not much considering that price levels are comparable to Western Europe (Narten 2009). Employment is evenly split between agriculture and industry although both are characterised by low productivity. In rural areas, monthly incomes usually figure below €400. Most farms are subsistence-oriented, with even large farms devoting more than 50 per cent of their crop production to meeting household needs (USAID 2008). The average peasant makes their living by working small acreages to obtain a minimal level of subsistence, earning roughly €150 (Duijzings 2000). The Kosovo state offers €300 to €400 to Municipal Directors and police station Commanders and €250 to other administrative positions in the municipality.[9] Teachers receive an average salary of €274, doctors receive €280 and nurses receive €180 (World Bank 2010). The private sector offers a monthly income of €300 (World Bank 2010). Social assistance is at €37 and pensions range from between €45 and €150 per month (RoK 2011).

Not only families suffer from a lack of resources, also the state infrastructure is in bad shape. In rural areas, there remain problems with even the most basic of public services: electricity, drinking water and sewage systems, roads and waste disposal. Ninety-seven per cent of Kosovars are connected to electricity, but only 84 per cent have a tap water supply at home, 67 per cent have access to a public sewage or sanitation system and only 9 per cent have central heating (UNDP 2006). Kosovo citizens wish for public service improvements most urgently in the areas of electricity, primary health care facilities and waste collection (UNDP and USAID 2009). Interruptions in the supply of water and electricity are frequent. In Bregore/Brdašce, I witnessed several electricity cuts during the five weeks I stayed there – diesel generators served as a bridge. In Zabel/Šumarak, drinking water is only available four hours a day, while one part of Bregore/Brdašce is provided with water only during the night. In summer and wintertime, water might even cease to run for several weeks and transports to private wells have to be organised. Improvements, however, are observable after the 1999 intervention, thanks to financial assistance for infrastructure projects.[10]

Under these conditions of poverty, Kosovo citizens have developed several survival strategies: family networks, clientelism and international support – the latter only since the arrival of UNMIK in 1999. The first survival strategy, family networks, provides support through remittances and nepotism. Remittances represent 15 per cent of Kosovo's GDP (UNDP 2012). Most families send some members abroad, mostly to EU countries, to work in order to survive economically (Duijzings 1999). Most people I met had a brother or sister in Europe. This, however, raises the social inequality between those who have someone abroad and those who don't. Nepotism – the preferential treatment of family members – is also a common practice (EC 2010). In the private sector, 45 per cent of employment decisions rest on recommendations and a further 36 per cent on family connections (UNDP 2012). Thirty-nine per cent of young Kosovars expect to be employed due to family connections, 18 per cent due to bribes and only 27 per cent based upon their educational or professional experiences (UNDP 2012). Nepotism thus amounts to a social expectation in a situation where jobs that provide much needed income are scarce.[11]

The second survival strategy, clientelism, draws on the attainment of jobs or financial advantages in exchange for party loyalty. One of the biggest providers of employment, the state, allows those in power to offer jobs in state-controlled institutions (EC 2010, UNDP 2012). Most Kosovars have an ambiguous relationship to clientelism: Theoretically, it is rejected; practically, few individuals would decline an offer as a teacher, municipal official or at the post office.

The third survival strategy is international support. Peacebuilders offer financial assistance and employment: Currently, foreign assistance makes up 9 per cent of Kosovo's GDP (UNDP 2012) and international organisations provide much wanted employment opportunities. The most skilled Kosovars obtain jobs with the peacebuilders, who offer between €850 and €1,100 a month, causing a post-conflict brain drain within the country.[12] A significant number of drivers, translators and security service providers have also found employment with internationals. Furthermore, international salaries have supported owners of small food stores, kiosks and restaurants, along with landlords in the urban centres. If peacebuilders leave, many Kosovars will be much worse off.

Against the backdrop of such widespread poverty, the domestic priority for socio-economic development and the ensuing incentive to capture peacebuilding reforms for these goals become more understandable.

Freedom and a better life: aspirations and realities of Kosovo politics

To have a better life for citizens in Kosovo. Here in Kosovo many things changed after the war. The population had a hope that it was only the Serbs' fault that we didn't have a good life, that we weren't free.... Now we have to fight with other things – not with weapons, with democratic means. As I said, it is the attempt to do good, so that the ordinary citizen has a better life and feels safe.[13]

(A Municipal Assembly member's answer to my question as to why he decided to go into politics, Bregore/Brdašce, 02/10/2012)

Freedom and a better life – if you ask a municipal politician in Kosovo why he or she started to engage in politics, this is the answer.[14] Politicians in Kosovo are deeply influenced by these motivations, though clientelist practices and shifting loyalties are an equally defining feature of Kosovo politics. Internationally promoted norms of democracy, minority rights and rule of law are of marginal importance in inner-Kosovo political discourses (Stojarova 2007). Kosovo Albanians want to make a change for their families, their fellow citizens and the piece of land called Kosovo, which has been too often neglected by, or succumbed to, big power politics. In everyday politics, the philosophically rich concepts of freedom and a better life translate into more manageable claims: independence and economic development. For many Kosovo Albanians, the quest for freedom signifies the absence of political repression from Belgrade that is to be attained through Kosovo's independence (Di Lellio and Schwandner-Sievers 2006). The idea of a better life is tightly connected to socio-economic development. The wish to overcome poverty and underdevelopment and to be able to provide for families was omnipresent in all the conversations I held with municipal politicians.[15] This is reflected in political life, which focuses to a great extent around the goals of independence and development.

There is, however, a second defining feature of the political system in Kosovo: Power politics, clientelist networks, and shifting political loyalties between and within parties characterize political actors' behaviour towards each other and in interactions with international actors. Kosovo's parties are characterised by clientelism, strong leaders and weak programmatic profiles (KAS 2012, OSCE 2007b). The major Kosovo Albanian parties dominating the political landscape are the LDK, the PDK and the AAK while new formations such as Lëvizja Vetëvendosje have recently entered the party landscape, and others, such as the AKR (Aleanca Kosova e Re/Alliance for New Kosovo) have disappeared. The LDK was formed in 1989 by a group of intellectuals under the Kosovo Albanian Ibrahim Rugova and is rooted in his peaceful resistance against Belgrade in the 1990s (ICG 1999).[16] The PDK and the AAK are rooted in the military resistance of the UÇK as both party leaders are influential former UÇK Commanders. The party strongholds are still concentrated in the regions formerly under their command and party loyalties overlap with family clan structures.[17] Leading party figures of the

PDK and the AAK are deeply entrenched in organised crime through a network dating back to wartime – from the smuggling of cigarettes, drugs and weapons to human trafficking (Bundesnachrichtendienst 2005). The youngest member of Kosovo's party system is Lëvizja Vetëvendosje, which emerged out of a social movement for independence, the fight against corruption and against international tutelage.

Personalist politics and the maintenance of clientelist networks through the distribution of state resources is a major source of power for Kosovo politicians. This leads to a vicious circle: Because political power is broadened by access to state resources, the fight for political positions that offer access to state resources is particularly fierce and merciless. Competition instead of cooperation is the rule. In a clientelist system – a common phenomenon in post-war environments and weak states (Englebert and Tull) – "[t]he patron needs the client's support to maintain their position and the client receives the benefits from supporting their patron" (Clapham 1982). It is a system in which a political elite gains political loyalty in exchange for the distribution of jobs or resources to its support base (Kitschelt and Wilkinson 2007). This mutual dependency also shapes clientelist relations in Kosovo:

> A Minister is expected to employ party members (without regard for competence) to show his loyalty to the party. If he does not employ party members, he will lose the support from his party and thus might not stay in power. Party leaders thus need patronage networks and proofs of their party loyalty to stay in power.
>
> (Interview 82, former UNMIK Legal Officer, 03/10/2013)

State resources are frequently used by political elites to ensure their power position (Englebert and Tull 2008). Kosovo politicians provide jobs in the administration, schools, health centres and remaining state-owned companies as rewards for political support, particularly to party members, family members or UÇK veteran families (Narten 2009).[18] Incumbents also offer small-scale financial rewards in the form of 'subsidies', phone cards or cash to supporters during election time.[19] Peacebuilder attempts to introduce merit-based principles in the civil service have been of limited success.

A consequence of these clientelist party structures is the shifting of loyalties from one party to another. Clapham explains this with the following words: "[C]lients are free agents and are rational, self-maximising individuals. If they believed they would benefit more greatly from a different patron, they could seek their patronage" (Clapham 1982). The possibility of shifting loyalties increases the pressure on politicians to practice clientelism and to succumb to the expectations of their party members, family members, or fellow ex-combatants to stay in power. Such shifting loyalties can also be observed at the municipal level in Kosovo.

Clientelist politics and shifting loyalties make the quest for political power even more important. The result is fierce political rivalries between and within parties in Kosovo because clientelist structures create enormous pressure to win over competitors and provide little incentive for cooperation.[20] The victor is able to broaden his or her support base even further through access to state resources. Political conflicts are, thus, often a consequence of clientelist structures. At the local level, fights over posts in committees, assemblies, directorships and civil servant positions have been the origin of the fiercest intra-party and inter-party fights. For example, the former Mayor of Bregore/Brdašce was pressured to resign because he refused to accept the person proposed by the central level for a director post. Similarly, the current Mayor of Bregore/Brdašce lost the support of his party faction in the Municipal Assembly because he refused to accept the candidates put forward by the central level and his local party. Both times, fights over posts had severe political consequences for the institutional stability of the municipality.

Against the backdrop of the party landscape's clientelist structure, politicians' priority of political power becomes comprehensible to the informed observer.

Integration or boycott: difficult choices for Kosovo's Serbs

> I don't care about Serbia, I don't care about Kosovo, I care about my family.
> (Conversation with a Kosovo Serb, Bregore/Brdašce, 14/10/2012)

Why do I call a Slovenian number if I want to speak to my Albanian translator, but a Serbian number if I want to contact my Serbian landlady? Why doesn't Amazon allow books to be shipped to Prizren in Kosovo, but instead offers to ship books to Prizren in Serbia? Living with an unsettled status question deeply permeates into everyday life. Indeed, what is considered to be Kosovo by some is Serbia to others. Kosovo Serbs face a dozen choices a day that raise the question of whether to integrate or to boycott Kosovo institutions. Taking into account the difficulties that Kosovo Serbs have in deciding this question is helpful in understanding why many minority rights promoting reforms are hampered by difficulties: Minority rights protection mechanisms require Kosovo Serbs' participation in Kosovo institutions and thus touch on the heart of the conflict of whether Kosovo should be its own state – and have its own institutions – or remain part of Serbia.

The remaining Serbs in North Kosovo and the 74,000 Serbs living in the enclaves south of the Ibar River are deeply divided over whether it is better to integrate or to boycott Kosovo's institutions (ICG 2012).[21] In general, Kosovo Serbs in North Kosovo take a more hardline stance, whereas Kosovo Serbs living south of the Ibar River are more moderate. At the time of writing, Serbia still maintains a dense network of so-called parallel institutions that run under the de-facto authority of Belgrade.[22] Kosovo Serbs can choose between two parallel worlds – Serbia or Kosovo: They can pay with dinar, have Serbian cell phone numbers and send packages and postcards from

Serbian post offices within Kosovo. The Serbian parallel structures provide services in the fields of administration, welfare, education and health care; they issue birth and death certificates, Serbian passports and license plates. Post offices disburse Serb salaries, pensions and welfare payments. In Serb-dominated territories, schools are run by the Serbian Ministry of Education, and healthcare centres function in line with the Serbian health system. In North Kosovo, Belgrade even maintained parallel courts and security institutions for many years (OSCE 2007a). The co-existence of parallel institutions and Kosovo institutions was tolerated in UNMIK times and even reinforced after the 2008 declaration of independence (ICG 2009). The EU-mediated Belgrade-Prishtina Dialogue envisages the slow dismantlement of parallel Serbian structures in Kosovo, but progress has been incremental. However, an increasing number of Serbs engage pragmatically with Kosovo institutions, using them for services, applying for Kosovo official documents and accepting Kosovo salaries (ICG 2009).

Whether to accept Kosovo's independence or to consider it part of Serbia is influenced to a great extent by the security situation, political ideology and pragmatic cost-benefit calculations. Many times, Serbian reluctance to engage with Kosovo institutions is due to a persistent feeling of insecurity, lack of freedom of movement, and experiences of discrimination and harassment (OSCE 2007a). After UNMIK's arrival, Kosovo Albanian violence against Kosovo Serbs and other non-Albanian minorities prompted 200,000 individuals to leave by 2000 (UN 2000).[23] The most serious outbreak of ethnic violence after 1999 was the March 2004 riots against Serbian, Roma and Ashkali communities – 19 people died and 954 people were injured (UN 2004): KFOR, UNMIK Police and Kosovo Police had completely lost control of the security situation (Bernabéu 2007). Although security has improved today, a feeling of insecurity still prevails due to frequent unreported cases of low-level, inter-ethnic violence and incidents (ICG 2012).

Political ideology also plays a role in the Kosovo Serbs' decision about whether to integrate into or boycott Kosovo institutions. Kosovo belonging to Serbia forms an integral part of the Serbian national narrative (Bieber 2002) and for this reason, many Kosovo Serbs refuse to cooperate with UNMIK structures or Kosovo institutions. Serbian participation, when it happens, is unstable and sensitive to the security and political situation: For example, following the March 2004 riots and following the 2008 declaration of independence, Serbian representatives withdrew from the UNMIK structures, and political forces opposed to participation gained momentum (ICG 2009). The only Serbian pro-integrationist force today is the SLS (Samostalna Liberalna Stranka/Independent Liberal Party) (SLS 2013), while there are various branches of Serbian non-integrationist parties active in the territory of Kosovo.[24]

Lastly, the clientelist structures, personalist politics and shifting loyalties of Kosovo Serbian parties enable rapid changes in Kosovo Serbs' stance towards integration or boycott. Local Serbian leaders tend to switch party affiliation regularly to expand their personal power, based on a hard-to-grasp mixture of strategic calculations of votes and intra-party rivalries – conforming to Clapham's observation that "…[C]lients, who in the system of clientelism are aspiring politicians, may have more than one patron and may switch mentors in order to increase their chances of climbing the political ladder" (Clapham 1982).Whether the chosen party favours integration or boycott will then decide on the Serb municipal politician's stance. For example, I met a political leader in Bregore/Brdašce who started his political career with the SPS and was then a candidate for the KP in 2002, the SNS in 2007 and the SLS in 2009.[25] He chose a strategy of switching party loyalties to remain politically influential at the municipal level because the central-level political parties either dissolved or decided to boycott municipal elections. Now, disappointed by the clientelist structures within the SLS, he is thinking of leaving for a new party project to start a career at the national level.[26] This is not an isolated incident but rather a common strategy for politically active Kosovo Serbs: Many political leaders nourish their personal power bases at the municipal level and take these votes to the party that makes the best offer.[27]

Due to shifting loyalties, the line between hardline and moderate Serbs is not clear-cut. Surrounded by Kosovo Government authority, Serbs in southern Kosovo are constantly balancing their political loyalties between Belgrade and Prishtina, also on the backdrop of their own cost-benefit calculations for economic survival:

> Well … I believe that two or three more years need to pass … so that people understand that they can't chose but that they live here and have to get around … I can sit at home and not recognise the municipality, but I cannot sit at home and not work and not obtain subsidies and [do] nothing … I can't live from air. I have to fight for myself and for my future.
>
> (Interview 59, Office for Communities, 30/10/2012)

It is thus common for Serbian individuals to switch between Belgrade and Prishtina-run institutions. For example, one Serb who acted as 'parallel Mayor' for the Serbian government in one of the investigated municipalities had previously worked for the Kosovo Municipal Office for Communities. The financial attractiveness of cooperating with parallel structures gives Serbia a certain amount of leverage to manipulate Kosovo Serbs and force them to take a hardline position, although Kosovo-run municipalities also start to boost financial benefits for the Serbian community.

The consequence of this pragmatic shift between Belgrade- and Prishtina-run institutions is that peacebuilding reforms that require Serbian participation in Kosovo institutions are highly contested and likely to be unstable.

The local view of international norms

Kosovo citizens make up their own mind about what the norms of democracy and minority rights mean to them and whether they welcome these norms or not. This local perception of international norms influences how strongly a norm is contested, whether it is resisted or not, and ultimately, how successful the peacebuilding reform attempt will be. The degree of resistance or support for an international norm is therefore an important factor in the environment of interaction. I held several focus group discussions with citizens of the two studied municipalities, in which I tried to find out what meaning Kosovo citizens attach to the international norms of democracy and minority rights and whether they were perceived positively or negatively. I found that democracy enjoys strong domestic support in Kosovo, while minority rights received only weak domestic support because democracy was predominantly associated with positive connotations, while minority rights were associated with negative connotations.[28] Yet the local interpretations of democracy or minority rights diverge from the interpretations given by peacebuilders in interesting ways (Groß 2015).

The observation that international norms in peacebuilding enjoy both strong and weak support from the population breaks with the commonly held assumption in the critical peacebuilding scholarship that domestic actors automatically oppose liberal international norms (Mac Ginty 2010, Richmond 2011). Thus, researchers who aim to understand post-war transitions to peace and democracy require a more careful analysis of the discourses in the local population about international norms and the degree of support generated for them. The following shows how the local population interprets democracy and minority rights and how this explains the positive or negative associations to these norms.

The positive view of democracy

People living in Kosovo have a very positive opinion of the norm of democracy and are likely to support its promotion by the international community. There are several reasons for this positive view: First, many Kosovo citizens have fairly liberal convictions about how politics should be organised and all agree that "elections are a key element of democracy".[29] Second, the very idea of democracy as 'rule by the people' can be used by Kosovo Albanians and Kosovo Serbs alike as legitimation for their respective claims to the status of Kosovo. Third, as people know the democracies of Western Europe, democracy represents people's wish for a 'better life' and is loaded with a range of positive attributes such as a life in security and without poverty. The local meaning given to democracy is thus slightly different from the purely liberal understanding of democracy, and there are also differences in the interpretations of democracy by Serbs and Albanians.

Kosovo Albanians' interpretation of democracy converges in many regards with liberal ideas of statehood. The Kosovo Albanian discourse on democracy includes free and fair elections,[30] respect for rules,[31] the transparency and accountability of institutions,[32] freedom of speech,[33] the participation of citizens[34] and politicians' respect for citizens' concerns.[35] One focus group participant explains:

> I think that my vote as a Kosovo citizen is important. Both prior to the elections and while voting I felt important, just because I knew that I was casting my vote for someone, and that my vote may bring into power that party or that person for whom I voted, though since the elections I have not been satisfied because all my expectations have not been met. I am not satisfied because they have failed to fulfil their promises.
>
> (Focus Group, 13/10/2012, par. 69)

The Kosovo Albanian discourse on democracy also emphasises respect for the will of the majority, independence and sovereign statehood as important values of democracy.[36] These values enhance the legitimacy of Kosovo Albanian independence claims based on an ethno-nationalist conception of statehood. Due to these positive associations with democracy, its promotion is strongly supported by most Albanian citizens.

Kosovo Serbs show an equally strong support for democracy. Instead of emphasising the will of the majority as a basic feature of democracy, Kosovo Serbs understand democracy as the 'rule of the people', referring to people in an ethnic sense.[37] In doing so, Serbs use the norm of democracy to enhance the legitimacy of their claim that Kosovo should remain part of Serbia because democracy means being ruled by 'the people', i.e. ethnic Serbs:[38]

> I have no use for them [Kosovo elections], and I don't consider Kosovo to be my state. My state is Serbia and it's normal that I support the party and the people that I think will do the best for me.
>
> (Focus Group, 17/10/2012, par. 85)

At the same time, democracy is also associated with positive experiences such as having a normal life, an end to poverty, living in security and respect for the principle of equality and for rights – things that many Serbs living in southern enclaves lack in their everyday life. Many Serbs, therefore, voice disappointment about the 'unfulfilled promises of democracy' in post-war Kosovo.[39]

In short, the norm of democracy enjoys support amongst Kosovo Albanians and Kosovo Serbs alike, although the meaning is coloured by their own differing interpretations.

The negative view of minority rights

Kosovo citizens possess a rather negative opinion of the norm of minority rights and therefore tend not to support externally induced reforms promoting minority rights. Minority rights are perceived as contradictory to Kosovo Serbian and Albanian political goals with regard to the Kosovo status.

Kosovo Albanians strongly reject the idea of minority rights. Minority rights are seen as a tool to weaken Kosovo statehood, particularly when it comes to the special autonomy rights granted to Serbian majority municipalities, which are considered to limit the control of Prishtina. Many Kosovo Albanians perceive minority rights as violating principles of equality and fairness[40] and as unjustified preferential treatment for a particular group:[41]

> If we as Kosovo citizens go in other countries, they treat you equally, as a common citizen, but here, Serbs, Montenegrins, Turks, Roma – they are all prioritised.
>
> (Focus Group, 27/11/2012, par. 145)

Ethnic quotas and special representation rules are particularly strongly criticised. Quotas are considered unfair because, "we as natives are deprived of ten per cent of our rights".[42] Also, quotas would impede equal competition for seats in the Assembly or the administration.[43] Some even consider quotas to be an obstacle to democratisation because they "automatically push them [Serbs] not to turn out for elections". Only a few Kosovo Albanians support quotas, as these would make the "whole community feel represented" and would be "a kind of bridge between them [Serbs] and the institutions".[44]

Similarly, minority rights enjoy only limited support amongst Kosovo Serbian citizens. For Kosovo Serbs, minority rights are seen as a strategy to legitimise the illegitimate Albanian rule over Kosovo territory, so they therefore regard it with suspicion. Of course, there are also Serbs who see minority rights positively, for example as the promise of a 'normal life' and as a means of keeping their linguistic, religious and national identity, but they are often disappointed by the actual implementation. Therefore, minority rights provisions are often regarded as "something that was made for political reasons; [they] only exist[] on paper".[45] There is a widespread feeling that there is a lack of mechanisms for enforcing their implementation:

> So, for example, if I complain about the work of the Office for Communities, I have to hand in my complaint directly to the Mayor. But the Mayor works with this Director every day. KFOR doesn't react because they say it's not their mandate. UN doesn't have a mandate anymore, but says we should come to them and they will talk to the Mayor. And then everybody knows that you were the one who complained, and you and your family and your friends will be punished.
>
> (Focus Group, 16/10/212, par. 256)

Kosovo Serbs had an especially negative opinion of quotas and special representative institutions. They were dismissed as ineffective and regarded as formal instrument of the international community to justify Kosovo independence:

All those [Serb] people that are in Kosovo institutions serve the Kosovo state so that it can say in front of the international community, "Here we integrate, we have people, they take care of those rights here".

(Focus Group, 17/10/2012, par. 205)

There is thus widespread reservation towards minority rights from Kosovo Albanians and Kosovo Serbs alike, which provokes resistance against minority rights promoting reforms on the ground.

Cooperative and competitive politics

The style of politics cultivated amongst the municipal elites influences political elites' openness to issues such as power-sharing, accountability rules, transparency or participation. It is therefore an important factor in the environment of interaction. Political elites in Kosovo foster either a cooperative or competitive style of politics. Yet the competitive style clearly dominates throughout all Kosovo due to the clientelist party structures, while a cooperative style of politics remains an exception. The two municipalities I investigated differed in that regard: While politicians in Zabel/Šumarak seemed to act cooperatively, politics in Bregore/Brdašce was marred by competition and conflict. The following briefly introduces the two municipalities and the politics prevailing in each place.

Zabel/Šumarak: the cooperative tomato-growers

But this mandate – even though we are opposition – we are constructive and a part of the credit belongs to the opposition. Destructive is when you want to accept only your opinions. But now that we are in the opposition, we approve when the majority is right and they also accept our proposals because it is for their own good. There are a lot of cases. When we criticise a proposal, they take notes and if it suits them, they implement it. This is a very good virtue.

(Interview 60 with Municipal Assembly member Zabel/Šumarak, 31/10/2012)

Zabel/Šumarak is situated in northeast Kosovo. Its 70,000 inhabitants base their survival mainly on agriculture and small trade businesses (Kosovo Agency of Statistics 2013, OSCE 2009). The municipality is the biggest producer of tomatoes in the country, and one of the biggest events in the municipality is the annual 'Tomato Day', a gathering of Zabel/Šumarak tomato producers (OSCE 2009). Of the 1,500 small businesses operating in Zabel/Šumarak, most are car repair shops, hairdressers or tailors, although there are also a few construction enterprises (OSCE 2013a). Yet the level of unemployment in the municipality is notably high, as many firms were destroyed during the war and large investments would be required for their rehabilitation (OSCE 2009). The infrastructure is also in bad shape: Water runs only a few hours a day in the entire municipality and frequent electricity cuts disturb daily routines.

Politics in Zabel/Šumarak are marked by a cooperative style of politics. At the time of research, the municipality was run by a Mayor from the PDK, who headed a government of nine Directors and oversaw a Municipal Administration staff of 170 (MLGA 2012). The municipal politicians have known each other for a long time and there exists a network of friendly relations between members of different parties.[46] Some were active together in the LDK during the 1990s and only after the war dispersed to different parties. Others were together in the LDK in the early 2000s but followed different leaders when the party split after Rugova's death in 2007. The particularity in this municipality is that these splits do not seem to have provoked personal conflicts, and relations between different party members entail a sufficient amount of mutual respect. The cooperative style of politics is shown in the following: There is currently no major competition between the executive and legislative branches.[47] The government regularly reports its activities and financial situation to the Municipal Assembly.[48] The opposition is included in decision-making. Caucus leaders consult with their factions. Because of its cooperative attitude, the municipality has received the 'Transparent Municipal Assembly' award from USAID twice already. The award means that the executive branch proved ready to share information with the Municipal Assembly, and the Municipal Assembly informed the public in turn.

Inter-ethnic relations in Zabel/Šumarak are stable. Several minority groups live here: 3,500 Kosovo Serbs live in the surrounding villages of Bralžja/Bralje, Trebulja/Trebulë, Sice/Sicë and Mojskë/Mojska (OSCE 2010). Of these, Bralžja/Braljë is the largest settlement. The Kosovo Serbian community in Zabel/Šumarak tends to be heavily affected by the dynamics in North Kosovo due to its geographic proximity and is vulnerable to boycott pressures from North Mitrovica and Belgrade. Most Kosovo Serbs are unemployed. If not, they work for either the Kosovo or Serbian municipality, school or health centre. The Ashkali population amounts to 170 people and predominantly lives in Zabel/Šumarak, Rikosh/Rikoš or Branovci i Epërm/Gore Branovce (OSCE 2010). The 1,000 members of the Turkish community are well integrated with the Albanians in the town of Zabel/Šumarak (OSCE 2013a).

Bregore/Brdašce: the competitive wine producers

> The law clearly says that the Policy and Finance Committee is responsible for developing municipal policies and drafting the budget request, but the problem is that the law here does not work and the Mayor bypasses the committee.
>
> (Interview 46 with Municipal Assembly member, Bregore/Brdašce, 03/10/2012)

The 50,000 inhabitants of Bregore/Brdašce have settled in a landscape that is well-suited for wine production (Kosovo Agency of Statistics 2013). Most families possess a vineyard and in Yugoslav times, wine production was organised by the state-owned enterprise in the area with an average annual production of 70,000 litres. Around 65 per cent of the population obtains their income from agricultural activities. Apart from wine, the region produces peppers, tomatoes, cucumbers, onion, garlic and watermelons (MA Bregore/Brdašce 2004). Small and medium sized enterprises such as car repair shops, pharmacies and bakeries spark further economic activity (OSCE 2013a). No formerly state-owned enterprises have taken up work again despite the internationally led privatisation process. Unemployment is, thus, remarkably high in Bregore/Brdašce. The municipality also has some infrastructure problems. The schools work in two shifts because there is not enough space for all of the students. In some parts of the town, water runs only at night and garbage collection is unsteady.

Bregore/Brdašce politicians maintain a competitive style of politics. The years since the 2009 municipal elections were particularly marked by increasing political struggles for power between the executive and legislative branches, within the Municipal Assembly and within the political parties.[49] At the time of research, the AAK-led Municipal Government and the PDK-dominated Municipal Assembly hardly cooperated. On some occasions, the government made municipal decisions without consulting the legislature.[50] More frequently, the government pressured the Policy and Finance Committee to pass 'emergency' municipal acts without consulting the Municipal Assembly.[51] 'Emergency' was also used as an argument to pressure the Assembly into adopting municipal acts without discussion (MA Bregore/Brdašce 2011b). All this behaviour points to a general unwillingness to cooperate and share power with other political actors.

Political stability in the municipality has also been shaken by severe personal or political conflicts over political posts. After the 2009 elections, a major conflict emerged between the re-elected PDK Mayor and the PDK national level party. As central-level political pressure to appoint a certain candidate increased, the Mayor resigned in June 2010.[52] These intra-party fights led to considerable institutional instability and made extraordinary elections necessary. Extraordinary mayoral elections surprisingly brought the AAK candidate – whose main power base was rooted in his past as a former UÇK Commander – into power in November 2010. This AAK Mayor did not manage to form a stable coalition and had to run a minority government, again due to disagreements over the appointments of director posts: First, he lost support from the PDK in the Municipal Assembly when he broke an informal coalition agreement that included appointing PDK members to director posts. Then he lost support from his own AAK Assembly delegates when he refused to follow their recommendations for the appointment of director posts. The Mayor preferred to select his own entourage of trusted confidantes, often friends from wartime, and decided to work with flexible coalitions in the Municipal Assembly.[53]

The Mayors' politics had negative effects on the quality of cooperation between the Assembly and Municipal Government (MLGA 2010). In addition, inter-party relations in the Municipal Assembly were strained: In 2010, the PDK-dominated Municipal Assembly elected a LDK member as Chairperson (MA Bregore/Brdašce 2011a), which led to a recurrent conflict within the Municipal Assembly because Assembly members from the PDK and the AAK tried to oust him.[54] There are also considerable intra-party conflicts within the municipal branches of the PDK, the AAK and the LDK. The LDK, for example, is plagued by intra-party competition, stemming from a rural-urban divide: In the 2013 mayoral run-off elections between the PDK and the AAK, the LDK officially announced a coalition with the AAK (the LDK President being from the same village as the AAK candidate), while a considerable portion of LDK members from town decided to informally support the PDK candidate.[55] The competitive style of politics in Bregore/Brdašce thus permeates all stages of municipal politics.

Inter-ethnic relations are considered stable in Bregore/Brdašce, and Kosovo Serbs are regarded as rather moderate. Fourteen hundred Kosovo Serbs currently live in the Bregore/Brdašce municipality in one part of the town and in the neighbouring village Dobro Selo (OSCE 2010). Seven hundred and fifty-six Roma and Ashkali also live in Bregore/Brdašce. The municipality is the only one with Serbian-run parallel structures in the region. Serbian parallel structures have a Mayor and a regularly convening Municipal Assembly, as well as health and education facilities. (OSCE 2010). The parallel structures employ 56 Kosovo Serbs, only 28 of whom actually work for the administration, while the rest receive minimal salaries of about €100 (Helsinki Committee 2012).

Negotiating peacebuilding beyond the capital

Who actually negotiates peacebuilding at municipal level? The massive influx of international peacebuilders into Kosovo after 1999 has led to a situation in which peacebuilders are involved in every step of the political decisions at national, regional and municipal level. The negotiation of peacebuilding reforms thus includes a multitude of actors from international organisations, national level institutions and municipal organs and stretches from policy formulation at national level to reform implementation at sub-national level. The following presents the international and domestic actors that interact in peacebuilding contexts in Kosovo's municipalities.

Peacebuilders in Kosovo's municipalities

Kosovo hosts a complex network of international actors at the municipal level including KFOR, UNMIK, the OSCE, the EU Rule of Law Mission (EULEX) and the ICO, as well as multi- and bilateral donor agencies. Each international organisation has a different mandate and organisational structure and pursues distinct activities. Before the unilateral declaration of independence in 2008, KFOR and UNMIK (and within UNMIK, the EU, the OSCE and UN High Commissioner for Refugees) were the main players. After 2008, international organisations handed most authority over to domestic institutions, while KFOR, EULEX, the OSCE, the ICO, multi- and bilateral donors and a nucleus of UNMIK remained on the ground.

Kosovo Force (KFOR)

KFOR was mandated to restore peace in Kosovo by UNSC Resolution 1244, following the NATO intervention in June 1999 (UN 1999b). At its peak, KFOR amounted to 46,000 persons. In 2013, about 5,000 members remained (NATO 2013). At the municipal level, KFOR Liaison and Monitoring Teams (LMTs) monitor the security situation and function as a security guarantee for all citizens. KFOR LMTs also gather intelligence on the security situation and closely follow political developments.[56] To this end, KFOR maintains daily contact with the Mayor, political representatives, ordinary municipal employees and the police.[57]

The United Nations Interim Administration Mission in Kosovo (UNMIK)

UNMIK officially administered Kosovo between 1999 and 2008. It was tasked with the interim administration of the territory, "while establishing and overseeing the development of provisional democratic self-governing institutions to ensure conditions for a peaceful and normal life for all inhabitants of Kosovo", to whom it would gradually transfer authority (UN 1999b). The mission enjoyed a power seldom witnessed in a post-conflict state: It was authorised to take over executive, legislative and judicative functions at the national as well as the regional and municipal levels (UN 1999b).[58] In every municipality, there was a UNMIK Municipal Administrator supervising municipal politics. The Municipal Administrator formally took over the role of Mayor and supervised a team of five to six UN municipal officials and the local Municipal Administration.[59] After the declaration of independence in 2008, a nucleus of UNMIK stayed on the ground, still on the basis of UN Security Council Resolution 1244, but without exercising its supervisory authority.

International Civilian Office (ICO)

The ICO was deployed after Kosovo's declaration of independence in February 2008 by an international steering group of states that recognised its independence (Koutrakos 2011). The ICO was mandated to supervise the implementation of the provisions set forth in the Ahtisaari Plan. It allowed the International Civilian Representative to 'remedy breaches' of the Ahtisaari Plan by annulling laws and decisions made by Kosovo institutions, and to sanction or dismiss officials if their actions breached the Ahtisaari provisions

(UN 2007a). The ICO maintained four small regional offices. While in theory communication took place with all 37 municipalities, ICO staff de facto focused on Serbian-majority areas.[60] ICO staff advised politically, occasionally provided technical support and lobbied for the specific rights and financial support of Serbian-majority municipalities. The ICO officially closed down in September 2012, declaring its mission to be fulfilled.

Organisation for Security and Co-operation in Europe (OSCE)

The OSCE's mandate is to promote human rights, democracy and good governance in Kosovo. The organisation holds the most encompassing field presence with five regional offices and 30 field offices in municipalities (OSCE 2012). Its mission statement pledges to monitor and advise Kosovo authorities, "with a view to bettering the quality of services and public participation in decision-making" as well as "community [minority] rights, including returns and reintegration of displaced persons, safety, freedom of movement, property rights, non-discrimination, participation in public life, language and culture preservation" (OSCE 2013b). At the local level, the OSCE monitors and advises municipal politicians, administrative staff, minority representatives and civil society but enjoys no supervisory powers. OSCE staff is closely involved in municipal policy-making and takes an active part in the day-to-day political life. It does so mainly behind the scenes, discussing issues of concern in one-on-one meetings with relevant local actors.[61] Their main local contact points include the Mayor, Chairperson of the Municipal Assembly, the Communities Office, the Human Rights Office, the Information Officer, specific directorates and some civil society groups.[62] In those informal meetings, the OSCE takes on an advisory role and provides recommendations for solving specific problems or raising issues of concern.[63] The OSCE's main instruments of power are the monitoring of Municipal Assembly sessions and the preparation of daily, weekly and monthly reports.[64] Field offices also provide capacity building and limited financial assistance for projects of between €250 and €5,000.[65]

European Union Rule of Law Mission (EULEX)

EULEX was formally deployed after Kosovo's unilateral declaration of independence in February 2008.[66] EULEX supports Kosovo's rule of law institutions in the judiciary and police fields. It is the flagship mission of the EU Common Security and Defence Policy and the first fully integrated mission comprising a police, justice and customs component. EULEX retains executive responsibility in some areas. EULEX's priorities in the field remain border management, the fight against corruption, organised crime and the trafficking of drugs and human beings, as well as public order and safety (EC 2009). EULEX functions as a 'status-neutral' organisation, providing assistance on rule-of-law issues to local authorities without endorsing or rejecting

Kosovo's independence. EULEX Rule of Law and EULEX Police are endowed with certain executive powers: EULEX Police are allowed to investigate and prosecute cases of serious crimes and to start investigations or conduct arrests, in exceptional cases, without Kosovo Police (UN 2007a). Additionally, EULEX provides so-called Mentoring, Monitoring and Advising (MMA) activities, in which one international policeman chaperones the work of a Kosovo policeman in order to give advice on routine tasks such as patrolling, reporting, investigations and arrests.[67] EULEX had permanent MMA staff in every municipal police station until mid-September 2011 and now maintains a regional presence. EULEX today concentrates MMA activities on mid- and senior management at the regional level (EULEX 2012) and monitors the municipalities with EULEX mobile teams:[68] Each municipality is visited two to three times a week to discuss criminality, traffic and other areas of concern.[69]

United States Agency for International Development Democratic Effective Municipalities Initiatives (USAID DEMI)

USAID DEMI (subsequently called USAID) is the most active bilateral donor agency promoting good governance at the local level. Through the Democratic Effective Municipalities Initiatives (DEMI), USAID engages to improve internal source revenues, service delivery and democratic governance in Kosovo's municipalities (USAID Kosovo 2009).[70] The programme's main reason for existing is to support de-centralisation and local governance reform for the Ahtisaari Plan. A great deal of attention, therefore, is focused on Serb-majority municipalities. In 2011, however, USAID agreed on individual partnerships with 21 municipalities – including Kosovo Albanian majority municipalities – in order to improve the Municipal Administration, Municipal Assemblies, public service provision, economic development and citizen participation (USAID DEMI 2011). These partnerships include a package of financial assistance, capacity building and expert advice, having Regional Governance Advisors meet with the Mayor and Directors on a weekly basis to discuss projects and politics.[71] The fact that USAID sponsors projects of up to €150,000[72] per municipality makes USAID an influential actor at the municipal level.

Domestic actors in Kosovo's municipalities

Local governance structures in Kosovo are in constant flux since the arrival of UNMIK. Numerous institutions have been created and subsequently abolished, re-named or endowed with different competences in the past years. This also means that peacebuilders have negotiated with different municipal institutions that had different degree of authority over the years. Yet the political protagonists have remained largely the same politically active individuals. The structure at the municipal level can be distinguished in four phases: Between 1999 and 2000, no participative structures existed. From 2000 to 2001, UNMIK introduced the Joint Interim Administrative Structure (JIAS) as a governance arrangement, which was, however, soon replaced by the UNMIK Provisional Institutions of Self-Government (PISG) between 2001 and 2008. In 2008, Supervised Independence was introduced and only slowly dismantled, starting in September 2012.

1999–2000: no participative structures

Between 1999 and 2000, UNMIK represented the only officially recognised authority in Kosovo. Serbian structures instantly collapsed in non-Serbian majority areas (Judah 2000). LDK-led institutions and the UÇK provisional government under Thaçi existed in parallel, but were formally dissolved by the end of 1999. UNMIK Municipal Administrators coordinated or supervised the work of municipal bodies and partly carried out management functions (UN 1999a).

2000–2001: UNMIK Joint Interim Administrative Structure (JIAS)

JIAS offered a temporary local government framework under UNMIK. It served to incorporate the local leadership in Kosovo's administration without providing them with decision-making power. Real policymaking and control remained with international representatives. At the municipal level, international UNMIK Municipal Administrators continued to be responsible for the municipalities and local services. Municipal Administrative Boards, composed of local actors, were responsible for the Municipal Administration, but were chaired and monitored by the International Administrator. Municipal councils represented the citizens of a municipality and acted as a consultative body to the UNMIK Municipal Administrator. Both were appointed and removed by the Municipal Administrator (please see UNMIK 2000a for more information).

2001–2008: UNMIK Provisional Institutions of Self-Government (PISG)

As the 2001 municipal elections provided more legitimacy to local municipal bodies, the Provisional Institutions of Self-Government were introduced, which transferred additional authority to local actors. Municipal bodies received the capacity to make decisions regarding municipality matters (UNMIK 2000a) and to implement central level regulations (UNMIK 2000a). UNMIK exercised administrative supervision over the municipalities to ensure compliance with the law, regulatory framework and established standards (UNMIK 2000b). Kosovo municipal bodies that were involved in negotiating reforms with peacebuilders included the Municipal Assembly (elected by citizens), President of the Municipality (elected by the Assembly), Chief Executive Officer (appointed by the President), Board of Directors (elected by the Assembly) and Assembly Committees. The Board of Directors, headed by the Chief Executive Officer, formed the Municipal Government. The Municipal Assembly was capable of adopting statutes, rules of procedure and regulations within their limit. The President chaired the Assembly and oversaw the financial administration (UNMIK 2000b). Since UNMIK/REG 2007/30, Mayors have been elected in direct elections.

2008–2012: supervised independence

Today, municipalities possess three kinds of competences: internal competences (decision-making), delegated competences (implementation of central-level regulation) and enhanced competences (autonomy rights for Serbian-majority municipalities in education, health and culture). The central bodies of Kosovo municipalities include the Mayor (elected by citizens), Board of Directors (appointed by the Mayor), Municipal Assembly (elected by citizens) and the Chairperson of the Municipal Assembly (appointed by the Municipal Assembly). The Municipal Government manages municipal affairs, whereas the Municipal Assembly controls the Municipal Government and makes decisions within its area of competence. It also forms the Committee of Policy and Finance and the Communities Committee, among others.

This chapter offered a better understanding of the everyday life of people living in post-war Kosovo, marked by a continuous struggle for survival, a clientelist political system, and a high level of political polarisation with regard to the status question of Kosovo. These features of Kosovo everyday life help to understand why domestic priorities centre on socio-economic development, political power, and the Kosovo status settlement and do not conform to the set of international priorities of stability, democracy and minority rights. Furthermore, in order to enhance the readers' understanding of the domestic environment of interaction in a given reform initiative, the chapter explained how the local population perceives international norms of democracy and minority rights and which style of politics prevails in the respective municipalities.

Notes

1 Malcolm (1998) provides in-depth knowledge of the conflict.
2 The Yugoslav Federal Statistical Office (FSO) estimated the composition of the Kosovo population in 1991 based on the 1981 census. Information from the Brunborg (2002) report for the ICTY.
3 Doyle and Sambanis (2000), for example, understand poverty as a 'lack of capacity' but do not discuss the fact that owing to their economic condition, domestic actors might set priorities that are different from the peacebuilders' liberal peace agenda.
4 The income is scattered so tightly around the poverty line that only a 10-cent shift can make a considerable difference percentage wise. UNDP refers to the World Bank Poverty Assessment of 2007 and the Statistical Office of Kosovo of 2009.

The World Bank estimates absolute poverty to be when an individual is living on €1.42 a day and extreme poverty is at €0.92 a day. The Statistical Office of Kosovo data is inflation adjusted and stands at €1.55 a day and €1.02 a day, respectively (UNDP 2012).

5　According to my landlady in Bregore/Brdašce, a metre of firewood costs €35 to €40 and eight to ten metres are needed to heat the house for the winter. Field Notes, 21/09/2012.

6　The percentage might be slightly lower if informal labour is included.

7　The apparent discrepancy between average income and household expenditure is explained by the fact that informal employment and remittances can also play a role in household economics.

8　Expenditure depends on household size. Sixty per cent of households have three to five members in their family, 23 per cent have six to nine members (UNDP and USAID 2009).

9　Interviews with police station Commanders, Municipal Directors and municipal officials.

10　For a comparison please see the UNDP Kosovo Mosaic reports from 2003 and 2012.

11　I remember a revealing discussion with a friend and taxi driver. He told me that UNMIK tried to recruit him for the Kosovo Police. He declined; I asked why. After all, I did not see why working as a taxi driver would be preferable to being a policeman. He told me that his family was too big: At every family reunion, people would be angry with him because he did not help them, stopped the car of a friend, or similar issues.

12　Information from conversations with the OSCE and EULEX, Field Notes, 21/09/2012.

13　Translated from German.

14　These claims are based on a content analysis of my interviews with municipal politicians.

15　Please see interviews with municipal politicians from 14/05/2012, 01/10/2012, 02/10/2012, 03/10/2012, 29/10/2012 and 08/11/2012.

16　After Rugova's death, internal succession struggles led to the split of the LDK in 2007. Some LDK members left and formed the Lidhja Demokratike e Dardanie (LDD), which, however, never developed into a relevant political force in Kosovo.

17　Interview 21 with KFOR, field office, 14/05/2012 and interview 81 with former UNMIK Legal Advisor (2005–2009), 26/09/2013.

18　In one of the investigated municipalities, a friend told me that he had organised 120 votes for one mayoral candidate because his brother had been promised a post in the administration. Field notes, 06/12/2013.

19　Conversations with citizens of Bregore/Brdašce. Field notes, 06/12/2013.

20　Interview 82 with former UNMIK Legal Officer, 03/10/2012.

21　The municipalities investigated in this work are located in southern Kosovo. Northern dynamics, where UNMIK, EULEX and the Kosovo state are barely present, will not form part of the discussion (ICG 2009).

22　'Parallel institutions' is the term used by the international community. It describes Belgrade-run institutions that remained operational after 10 June 1999 but were not mandated for under UNSC Resolution 1244 (OMIK and OSCE 2003). Many Kosovo Serbs would refer to these institutions as their legitimate government, while Kosovo Albanians tend to call them illegal institutions.

23　In 1999 Serbian departures were provoked by, "an increasing number of incidents committed by Kosovo Albanians against Kosovo Serbs, including high profile killings and abductions, as well as looting, arson and forced expropriation of apartments" (UN 1999a).

24 The non-integrationist Serbian parties with branches in Kosovo are Koštunića's DSS (Demokratska Stranka Srbije/Democratic Party of Serbia), the SNS (Sprska Narodna Stranka/Serb People's Party), the ND (Nova Demokratija/New Democracy) and the SKMS (Srpska Kosovsko-Metohijska Stranka/Serb Kosovo-Metohija Party).

25 Interview 47 with former Serbian Deputy Mayor for Communities, Bregore/Brdašce, 04/10/2012.

26 Ibid.

27 A similar observation can be made about Serbian leaders in Zabel/Šumarak. A member of the Community Committee, formerly active in the SLS, was running for a newly founded party called Zajednička Budućnost (Common Future) in the 2013 municipal elections.

28 Please see Appendix 3 for a list of positive and negative statements with regard to the norms of democracy and minority rights drawn from focus groups in the two municipalities. I decided to leave out the location when citing focus groups in order to better protect the participants.

29 Focus Group, 20/10/2012. The importance of elections was mentioned ten times in the Albanian groups, and 11 times in the Serbian groups.

30 Focus Group, 24/11/2012, par. 46. In total, there were 23 statements complaining about the widespread election fraud and eight statements referring to free and fair elections as a constitutive element of democracy.

31 Ibid. In total, four statements point to the importance of following the law, while 12 statements complain about the absence of the rule of law and corrupt practices in the government and political party system.

32 Focus Group, 27/11/2012, par. 34. Similar statements were made 11 times, and complaints issued five times.

33 Focus Group, 24/11/2012, par. 28. Similar statements were made nine times.

34 Focus Group, 13/10/2012, par. 155. Similar statements were made nine times.

35 Focus Groups on 13/10/2012, 20/10/2012, 24/10/2012 and 27/10/2012.

36 Seven statements refer to sovereign statehood as part of democracy, while three statements complain about the lack of such sovereignty. Two statements connect democracy to independence.

37 Kosovo Serbs use the word *narod*, which means *people* in an ethno-nationalist sense. Quotes like the following thus have a heavy ethno-nationalist connotation: "We can say that democracy is the will of the people [Serbs], in Kosovo as well as Serbia". Focus Group, 17/10/2012, par. 44.

38 The claim that Kosovo Serbs consider Serbia to be the legitimate state was voiced 11 times, whereas it was stated five times that Kosovo is not considered legitimate.

39 Disappointment with 'democracy' was voiced in 20 statements.

40 Similar statements were made seven times in all groups.

41 This statement was made five times, usually as the introductory statement to the question of what participants thought of minority rights in Kosovo.

42 This refers to a university quota of 10 per cent for minorities. Focus Group, 27/11/2012, par. 87.

43 Focus Group, 20/10/2012, par. 132. Similar statements were made three times.

44 Focus Group, 13/10/2012, par. 225.

45 Focus Group, 17/10/2012, par. 202. Similar statements were made five times. In one discussion, I even had to explain what the Communities Committee is.

46 Interview 60 with Municipal Assembly member, Zabel/Šumarak, 31/10/2012.

47 Surely part of the explanation is that both the Municipal Government and the Assembly are headed by the PDK (Partia Demokratike e Kosovës/Democratic Party of Kosovo) at the moment. Still, intra-party rivalries could be fierce and possibly affect executive-legislative relations.

48 During 2012, reports on the financial situation were handed over to the Assembly at least quarterly. Please see the Municipal Assembly Reports for Zabel/Šumarak for 2012.

49 Between 2000 and 2007 Bregore/Brdašce was led by the LDK. The balance of power changed in favour of the PDK in 2007.

50 Interview 40 with Municipal Assembly member, 02/10/2012.

51 Ibid.

52 The official reason for the Mayor's resignation was health problems. Yet it is an 'open secret' that the real reason was serious disagreements with the central level PDK. After the Mayor resigned, the central level PDK forced him to return to his office, as they feared losing the city to a rival party. Then-President Sejdiu (LDK) asked the Constitutional Court for its opinion, which declared it unconstitutional for him to return to his office after his formal resignation in September 2012. Extraordinary elections were ordered (Balkanweb 2011).

53 Interview 54 with OSCE, field office, 18/10/2012.

54 Municipal Assembly member attempts at dismissing the Chairperson from LDK were unsuccessful until March 2012, when the Chairperson resigned under pressure – a face saving step in order not to be dismissed. A former Chairperson from the PDK took over.

55 Informal conversations with several inhabitants of Bregore/Brdašce.

56 Interview 21 with KFOR, Bregore/Brdašce, 14/05/2012.

57 Ibid.

58 The International Administration was structured into four functional components: Pillar I (UNHCR) related to humanitarian affairs, Pillar II (UN) was concerned with civilian administration, Pillar III (OSCE) was tasked with democratisation and institution building and Pillar IV (EU) focused on economic development (UN 1999a).

59 For a thorough overview of Kosovo's governance structures under UNMIK see Brand (2003).

60 Interview 08 with Decentralization Unit, ICO, 04/05/2012.

61 Interview 18 with OSCE, field office, Bregore/Brdašce, 10/05/2012.

62 Ibid.

63 Interview 14 with OSCE, field office, Bregore/Brdašce, 08/05/2012.

64 Interviews 14, 15, 16, 23 with OSCE teams in Prizren, Mitrovica, Bregore/Brdašce and Skenderaj/Srbica.

65 Interviews 14 and 18 with OSCE, Prishtina and Bregore/Brdašce, 08/05/2012 and 10/05/2012.

66 EULEX deployment preceded a thorough planning and preparation phase led by a EU Planning Team as early as 2006 (Grevi 2009). Actual deployment of the mission was hampered by disagreements within the international community as Serbia, Russia and some EU states insisted on EULEX being a 'status neutral' mission based on Resolution 1244.

67 Interview 50 with EULEX, regional office, 10/10/2012.

68 EULEX reduced its staff from 1,950 international and 1,250 local workers in 2009 to 1,250 international and 1,000 local workers in 2012 (EULEX 2012).

69 Interview 19 and 28 with Kosovo Police, Bregore/Brdašce, 14/05/2012 and Skenderaj/Srbica, 18/05/2012.

70 USAID DEMI is a programme sponsored by USAID and implemented by the Urban Institute in Prishtina. It formerly operated under the name of Effective Municipalities Initiative (EMI).

71 Interview 11 with USAID DEMI, Prishtina, 07/05/2012.

72 Interview 07 with USAID DEMI, Prishtina, 03/05/2012.

References

AKUF. (2007). Jugoslawien (Kosovo). Kriegs-Archiv. 31 December 2007 ed. Hamburg: Arbeitsgemeinschaft Kriegsursachenforschung (AKUF).

Balkanweb. (2011). Constitutional Court Decision [Online]. Available at: www. balkanweb.com/ [accessed 05/05/2013].

Bernabéu, Irene. (2007). Laying the Foundations of Democracy? Reconsidering Security Sector Reform Under UN Auspices in Kosovo. *Security Dialogue*, 38 (1), 71–92.

Bieber, Florian. (2002). Nationalist Mobilization and Stories of Serb Suffering. The Kosovo Myth from the 600th Anniversary to the Present. *Rethinking History*, 6 (1), 95–110.

Brand, Marcus G. (2003). *The Development of Kosovo Institutions and the Transition of Authority from UNMIK to Local Self-Government*. Genf.

Brunborg, Helge (2002). *Report on the Size and Ethnic Composition of Kosovo*. ICTY. The Hague: International Criminal Tribunal for the Former Yugoslavia.

Bundesnachrichtendienst. (2005). BND-Analyse vom 22/02/2005.

Clapham, Christopher. (1982). *Private Patronage and Public Power. Political Clientelism in the Modern State*. Basingstoke: Palgrave Macmillan.

Di Lellio, Anna and Schwandner-Sievers, Stephanie. (2006). The Legendary Commander. The Construction of an Albanian Master-Narrative in Post-War Kosovo. *Nations and Nationalism*, 12 (3), 513–529.

Duijzings, Ger. (1999). Kosovo. The End of a Mixed Pilgrimage. Leiden, 9.

Duijzings, Ger. (2000). *Religion and the Politics of Identity in Kosovo*. London: C. Hurst & Co.

EC. (2009). Kosovo 2009 Progress Report. Brussels.

EC. (2010). Kosovo 2010 Progress Report. Brussels.

Englebert, Pierre and Tull, Denis M. (2008). Postconflict Reconstruction in Africa. Flawed Ideas about Failed States. *International Security*, 32 (4), 106–139.

EULEX. (2012). EULEX Program Report 2012. Prishtina.

Grevi, Giovanni. (2009). The EU Rule-of-Law Mission in Kosovo (EULEX Kosovo). In: Giovanni Grevi et al. (ed.) *European Security and Defence Policy. The First 10 Years*. European Union Institute for Security Studies.

Groß, Lisa. (2015). The Journey from Global to Local. Norm Promotion, Contestation and Localization in Post-War Kosovo. *Journal of International Relations and Development*, (18), 311–336.

Helsinki Committee. (2012). *Serb Community in Kosovo*. Belgrade.

ICG. (1999). *Who Is Who in Kosovo?* Prishtina.

ICG. (2009). *Serb Integration in Kosovo. Taking the Plunge*. Prishtina.

ICG. (2012). *Setting Kosovo Free. Remaining Challenges*. Prishtina.

IMF. (2011). *Republic of Kosovo: 2011 Article IV Consultation and the Initiation of a Staff-Monitored Program*. Washington D.C.

Judah, Tim. (2000). *Kosovo. War and Revenge*. New Haven: Yale University Press.

KAS. (2012). *Internal Party Democracy in Kosovo*. Prishtina.

Kitschelt, Herbert and Wilkinson, Steven I. (2007). *Patrons, Clients, and Policies. Patterns of Democratic Accountability and Political Competition*. Cambridge: Cambridge University Press.

Kosovo Agency of Statistics. (2011). Kosovo Census 2011 [Online]. Prishtina: Kosovo Agency of Statistics. Available at: http://esk.rks-gov.net/rekos2011/?cid=2,1 [accessed 01/11/2013].

Kosovo Agency of Statistics. (2013). *Estimation of Kosovo Population 2011.* Prishtina.

Kosovo, Republic of. (2008). *Constitution of the Republic of Kosovo.* Prishtina: Republic of Kosovo.

Kostovicova, Denisa and Glasius, Marlies. (2008). The European Union as a State-Builder. Policies towards Serbia and Sri Lanka. Südosteuropa. Zeitschrift für Politik und Gesellschaft, 01, 84–114.

Koutrakos, P. (2011). *European Foreign Policy. Legal and Political Perspectives.* Cheltenham, UK/Northampton, USA: Edward Elgar Publishing.

MA Bregore/Brdašce. (2004). Development Agenda.

MA Bregore/Brdašce. (2011a). Procesverbal. 15/03/2011. In: Assembly, M. (ed.). Bregore/Brdašce.

MA Bregore/Brdašce. (2011b). Procesverbal. 29/09/2011. In: Assembly, M. (ed.). Bregore/Brdašce.

Mac Ginty, Roger. (2010). No War, No Peace. Why So Many Peace Processes Fail to Deliver Peace. *International Politics,* 47 (2), 145–162.

Malcolm, Noel. (1998). *Kosovo – A Short History.* Oxford: Macmillan.

MLGA. (2010). *Monitoring Report of Municipalities of the Republic of Kosovo. January–June 2010.* Prishtina.

MLGA. (2012). *Annual Report of Monitoring of Municipalities of the Republic of Kosovo 2011.* Prishtina.

Narten, Jens. (2009). Assessing Kosovo's Postwar Democratization. Between External Imposition and Local Self-Government. *Taiwan Journal of Democracy,* 5 (1), 127–162.

NATO. (2013). NATO Troop Contributions [Online]. Available at: www.aco.nato. int/kfor/about-us/troop-numbers-contributions.aspx [accessed 15/05/2013].

OMIK and OSCE. (2003). *Parallel Structures in Kosovo.* Prishtina.

OSCE. (2007a). *Parallel Structures in Kosovo 2006–2007.* Prishtina.

OSCE. (2007b). *Remarks of Ambassador Wendt.* Prishtina.

OSCE. (2009). *Municipal Profile Zabel/Šumarak.* Prishtina.

OSCE. (2010). *Kosovo Communities Profile.* Prishtina.

OSCE. (2012). OSCE in Kosovo [Online]. Available at: www.osce.org/kosovo [accessed 21/06/2012].

OSCE. (2013a). *Municipal Profile Zabel/Šumarak.* Prishtina.

OSCE. (2013b). OSCE Mission Mandate [Online]. Available at: www.osce.org/ kosovo/43381 [accessed 23/08/2013].

Richmond, Oliver. (2011). Critical Agency, Resistance and a Post-Colonial Civil Society. *Cooperation and Conflict,* 46 (4), 419–440.

RoK. (2011). Law on Amending and Supplementing the Law No. 02/L-17 on Social and Family Services. In: *Assembly of Kosovo* (ed.). Prishtina.

SLS. (2013). Homepage Samostalna Liberalna Stranka [Online]. Available at: www. sls-ks.org/ [accessed 01/11/2013].

Statistical Office of Kosovo. (2009). *Labour Force Survey.* Prishtina.

Stojarova, Vera. (2007). Nationalistic Features in the Programmes of the Serbian and Kosovo Albanian Political Parties. 10th Annual International Seminar "Democracy and Human Rights in Multiethnic Societies". Konjic, Bosnia and Herzegovina.

Suhrke, Astri, Michael, Barutciski, Sandison, Peta and Garlock, Rick. (2000). *The Kosovo Refugee Crisis. An Independent Evaluation of UNHCR's Emergency Preparedness and Response.* Geneva, 159.

UN. (1999a). *Report of the Secretary-General on the United Nations Interim Administration Mission in Kosovo.* In: United Nations Documents (ed.). New York.

UN. (1999b). Resolution 1244 adopted by the Security Council at its 4011th Meeting on 10 June 1999. In: United Nations Documents (ed.). New York.

UN. (2000). Report of the Secretary-General on the United Nations Interim Administration Mission in Kosovo. In: United Nations Documents (ed.).

UN. (2004). Report of the Secretary-General on the United Nations Interim Administration Mission in Kosovo. In: United Nations Documents (ed.).

UN. (2007a). Addendum. Comprehensive Proposal for the Kosovo Status Settlement. In: UN Security Council (ed.). New York: United Nations.

UN. (2007b). Comprehensive Proposal for the Kosovo Status Settlement. UN Security Council.

UNDP. (2006). The Kosovo Mosaic. Perceptions of Local Government and Public Services in Kosovo. Prishtina.

UNDP. (2012). Kosovo Human Development Report. Private Sector and Employment. Prishtina.

UNDP and USAID. (2009). The Kosovo Mosaic. Perceptions of Local Government and Public Services in Kosovo. Prishtina.

UNMIK. (2000a). On Municipal Self-Government in Kosovo. In: UNMIK (ed.) UNMIK Regulation 2000/45.

UNMIK. (2000b). UNMIK/REG/2000/45 On Self-Government of Municipalities in Kosovo. In: UNMIK (ed.).

USAID. (2008). Kosovo Economic Performance.

USAID DEMI. (2011). USAID Democratic Effective Municipalities Initiative [Online]. Available at: www.demi-ks.org/?cid=2,1 [accessed 03/11/2013].

USAID Kosovo. (2009). Kosovo Effective Municipality Initiative. Mid-Term Evaluation. Final Report. Prishtina.

World Bank. (2010). *Kosovo. Public Expenditure Review.* Washington.

World Bank. (2013). World Bank Dataset [Online]. Available at: http://data.worldbank.org [accessed 20/12/2012].

5 Negotiating local governance reform

Local governance is a policy field in which peacebuilders invested only low international capacity. The reform was initiated by international actors in 1999 and introduced international principles of democracy, minority rights and rule of law into governance structures at the municipal level (Ebel and Péteri 2007). This required a complete overhaul of existing municipal structures,[1] and peacebuilders were engaged in constant negotiations with their domestic counterparts to ensure implementation. In the following chapter, I trace the external–domestic interaction process of two local governance reform initiatives: Participatory Budget Planning (low capacity/weak resistance) and the Communities Committee (low capacity/strong resistance). Participatory Budget Planning is a case of weak resistance because it promotes the widely accepted international norm of democracy by introducing rules that ensure accountability, transparency and citizen participation. The Communities Committee, in contrast, is a case of strong resistance because it promotes the highly contested international norm of minority rights by setting up special representation organs for minority groups in each municipality.

Compared to other policy fields in Kosovo, peacebuilders invest only a low level of international capacity in local governance reform: Peacebuilders do not possess a far-reaching mandate, the civilian personnel are limited and the amount of financial resources invested is low compared to other policy fields. Until 2008, UNMIK's mandate formally gave UNMIK Municipal Administrators supervisory powers, which allowed them to act as 'international Mayors' (KFOS 2010) and to perform their duties jointly with domestic representatives in the administrative councils and boards (Ebel and Péteri 2007). Yet as early as 2005, UNMIK handed complete executive, legislative and administrative responsibility over to the municipal authorities while retaining the right to intervene in extra-legal decisions. Since 2008, the position of UNMIK Municipal Administrator has been abolished and the international mandate for local governance reduced to monitoring. The civilian personnel employed for local governance reform are also limited: UNMIK, ICO, the OSCE and USAID support local governance activities Kosovo-wide. Of these, only the OSCE and USAID are present in

Albanian-majority municipalities, while the rest either focus on Serbian-majority municipalities or the national level (USAID Kosovo 2009).[2]

Given the low level of international capacity invested in local governance, advocates of the international capacity explanation would expect limited success with peacebuilders' reform attempts. No implementation would be the most likely outcome according to this line of argument. A closer look at the outcomes of the two cases shows, however, that the international capacity explanation was not able to correctly predict the peacebuilding outcomes: In the case of Participatory Budget Planning, the peacebuilding outcome was full implementation in Zabel/Šumarak and captured implementation in Bregore/Brdašce. In the case of the Communities Committee, the peacebuilding outcome was captured implementation in both municipalities. If the standard explanation cannot justify the results, maybe an interaction-based argument can.

So what was the role of the external–domestic interaction in producing the peacebuilding outcomes in these two cases? Analysing the reform negotiations according to the analytical framework of peacebuilding interactions, I was able to identify how the international ad hoc tactics of prioritisation, selectivity and leverage were particularly relevant in shaping peacebuilding outcomes during external–domestic interactions. In the case of the Communities Committees, prioritisation made no implementation less likely, but the high selectivity increased domestic elites' opportunities for reform capture and made captured implementation more likely. The high international leverage in addition made no implementation less likely. In the democracy-promoting reform of Participatory Budget Planning, full implementation became possible because of the lack of selectivity and the high leverage that made no implementation less likely. Yet the final outcome was also influenced by the environment of interaction.

The two case studies have the following structure: First, I start with a brief overview of the reform initiative, including which domestic and international actors are involved and which concrete rules are negotiated. Second, the operationalisation of the reform outcome is presented. Third, the role of prioritisation, selectivity and leverage is discussed. Fourth, the external–domestic interaction process is analysed in three phases, each of which relates to the different sub-set of rules negotiated at that given point in time. Lastly, I discuss peacebuilding outcomes for each municipality.

Promoting democracy in a low capacity policy field: the participatory budget planning reform

Participatory Budget Planning is a relatively young reform, having been introduced in February 2008. Peacebuilders aimed at strengthening democracy by promoting transparency, accountability and citizen participation in budget decisions. For peacebuilders, municipal budget planning symbolises a key exercise for democratic decision-making in local governance:

Public budgets determine public resource allocation, and as such serve as a reflection of a society's priorities. For this reason, involvement of the public in budget development is necessary to ensure that public priorities are taken into account, especially when public coffers are limited. Public participation in local budgeting can also build trust between the public and elected officials, legitimatize government decisions, and increase oversight and therefore efficiency and effectiveness of public spending.

(OSCE 2012)

As such, the reform requires the Municipal Executive to be more transparent in budget planning with the Municipal Assembly and with their citizens; strengthens the accountability of the Municipal Executive to the Municipal Assembly; and introduces citizen participation in municipal budget decisions, particularly in the case of 'capital projects',[3] where municipalities decide on investments in the construction of roads, school buildings, sewage systems, theatre renovations or support for civil society organizations.

Participatory Budget Planning is a case of low international capacity and weak resistance against the promoted norm of democracy. Yet the case studies lead to different outcomes in the two municipalities, pointing to the fact that neither standard explanation had correctly predicted the outcome: In Zabel/Šumarak, Participatory Budget Planning resulted in full implementation and in Bregore/Brdašce it resulted in captured implementation. How can the external–domestic interaction explain these outcomes? First of all, the negotiations for Participatory Budget Planning took place in a complex environment, and peacebuilders resorted to the ad hoc tactics of prioritisation, selectivity and leverage to cope with multiple exigencies at once. For example, peacebuilders' selectivity provided domestic actors in Bregore/Brdašce with the leeway to drop learned rules (rules that had been promoted by peacebuilders in a previous period and adhered to by domestic actors) and thus facilitated captured implementation. External leverage, which had been increased in the last interaction period, made no implementation less likely in both municpalities. Second, the environment of interaction influenced the reform outcome. The enabling environment in Zabel/Šumarak facilitated municipal elites' cooperation and made learned rules sustainable over time. The fact that peacebuilders covered the total set of rules over time then made full implementation a possible outcome. In contrast, external–domestic interactions in Bregore/Brdašce took place in a rather constraining environment. Here, municipal elites often responded with foot-dragging and the modification of international demands, and learned rules proved less sustainable once peacebuilders had shifted to a different sub-set of rules. Full implementation became a less likely outcome.

If one is interested in following the external–domestic interaction in Participatory Budget Planning, it is useful to get acquainted with the multiple actors involved in negotiating this particular peacebuilding reform. In Participatory Budget Planning, the international side of the interaction is represented by the OSCE headquarters, regional offices and field offices as well as USAID headquarters staff and regional advisors.[4] The OSCE supports the reform through monitoring, advising, outreach activities, capacity building opportunities and minor financial support. USAID provides advice, capacity building and financial assistance to the municipalities. On the side of domestic actors, the Municipal Government, especially the Mayor and the Director of Budget and Finance, the Municipal Assembly and its Policy and Finance Committee, plus civil society representatives and ordinary citizens are involved. At the central level, the Ministry of Local Government Administration (MLGA) is involved by supervising the legality of decision-making and the Ministry of Finance (MoF) by supervising the legality of the budget.

Participatory Budget Planning requires domestic actors to implement a particular set of rules. For example, the reform envisions that the Ministry of Finance allocates a fixed amount of money for budget planning to each municipality by 30 April every year. By 30 September the Municipal Assembly has to approve the budget (rule 1) (RoK 2008b).[5] In the meantime, at least two public budget hearings have to be organised (rule 2) (OSCE 2012, RoK 2008b). By 1 September at the latest, the Mayor will propose a first budget draft to the Municipal Assembly (rule 3) (RoK 2008c). The Policy and Finance Committee (PFC) will then review the budget draft, submit its recommendations to the Municipal Assembly for further discussion and then give its recommendations to the Municipal Government (RoK 2008b). Public budget hearings have to be held by both Municipal Government and the Municipal Assembly, either separately or jointly (rule 4)(OSCE 2012, RoK 2008b).[6] Public hearings have to be announced according to a set of specific rules (RoK 2008b): Notification has to be made 14 days in advance – in all official languages – and must include information on the date, time and

Table 5.1 Outcome operationalisation – participatory budget planning

Rules	Selected rules			Source
	1	2	3	
Formal dimension				
1 MA approves budget within deadline	1	2	3	LLSG Art. 40
2 2 Budget hearings held	–	2	3	LLSG Art. 68
Practice dimension				
3 MA and/or PFC consulted on 1. draft	1	–	–	LLSG Art. 52
4 Budget hearing by Government & PFC			3	LLSG Art. 68
5 Outreach on budget hearing	–	2	3	LLSG Art. 68.1
6 Publication of budget	–	–	3	LLSG Art. 68.4
Content dimension				
7 MA & PFC alter budget proposal	1	–	–	LLSG Art. 40, 52
8 Citizen requests included	–	–	3	Recommendation

Source: Law on Local Self-Government 2008.

location, the agenda and any related materials. Public notifications must be placed in the most frequented places of the municipality, posted on the municipal website and dispersed via written and electronic local media (rule 5) (RoK 2008a). The budget has to be published and accessible to citizens (rule 6). Municipal Assembly and its Policy and Finance Committee have to have the opportunity to make changes to the budget proposal (rule 7) (OSCE 2012, RoK 2008b) and also citizens should get the chance to have requests included (rule 8). Based on these rules, I propose following the operationalisation to judge the peacebuilding outcome of Participatory Budget Planning:

Prioritisation, selectivity and leverage in participatory budget planning

In the case of Participatory Budget Planning, the environment of interaction was particularly challenging and complex in that the reform started directly after Kosovo's declaration of independence, at a time when a multitude of other changes were simultaneously being introduced into the municipal governance structure. The negotiations for Participatory Budget Planning thus took place in a quickly changing environment that often required peacebuilders to use the ad hoc tactics of prioritisation, selectivity and leverage to simplify decision-making in the negotiation process. The following provides a brief overview of the role of prioritisation, selectivity and leverage in the external–domestic interplay for this case.

Prioritisation

There were no instances of prioritisation in the case of Participatory Budget Planning. The usual triggers leading to prioritisation such as security threat due to non-compliance with the reform or the reform being part of the EU conditionality catalogue were simply absent in this interaction process.

Selectivity

Selectivity was a relevant ad hoc tactic for helping peacebuilders deal with the many simultaneous reform requirements on the ground. By following the interaction process closely, one can discern three interaction periods in which peacebuilders selected a different sub-set of rules for negotiation, while leaving out other rules. Such selectivity offered domestic actors ample leeway to capture reforms for their own ends. Selectivity periods can be broken down into the following time brackets: Between 2007 and 2008, peacebuilding initially focused on legislative oversight (rules 1, 3 and 7). Then, between 2009 and 2010, international attention centred on facilitating citizen participation in municipalities in general (rules 2 and 5). Lastly, peacebuilders concentrated on fostering public budget hearings (rules 2, 4, 5, 6 and 8) between 2001 and 2012. Selectivity shifts were triggered ad hoc by changes in the international agenda (Kosovo independence 2008) or by routine programme evaluations. By 2012, peacebuilders had covered the total set of rules belonging to the reform at least once. This made full implementation possible.

Period I (2007–08): legislative oversight (rules 1, 3 and 7)

In the first period, peacebuilders focused on rules to ensure legislative oversight of the budget planning process. External–domestic interactions were limited to this aspect of the reform. Peacebuilders emphasised the need for the Municipal Assembly to approve the budget within the deadline (1) as well as the need for the Municipal Government to consult the PFC and Municipal Assembly on a first draft of the budget (3) and to enable the legislative branch to alter the draft (7). Yet during this time, peacebuilders ignored the citizen participation rules.[7]

Period II (2009–10): citizen participation (rules 2 and 5)

After Kosovo independence, peacebuilders selected a sub-set of rules fostering citizen participation in municipal politics in general. They emphasised the need to hold public hearings (2) and to organise outreach for public hearings (5). Peacebuilders paid less attention to rules on legislative oversight. The selectivity shift to this sub-set of rules was related to the fact that citizen participation became more important as a 'watchdog' strategy for controlling municipal politicians, whom UNMIK was not able to control after Kosovo independence.[8]

Period III (2011–12): public budget hearings (rules 2, 4, 5, 6 and 8)

In the third period, peacebuilders focused on a sub-set of rules related to public budget hearings. They emphasised the need to hold public budget hearings (2), for public budget hearings to be organised by the executive and legislative branches (either jointly or separately) (4), to organise outreach for public hearings according to the rules (5), to provide the draft budget and other information to the citizens (6) and to try to include citizens' requests (8). Rules on legislative oversight were largely left out. This selectivity shift was triggered by programme evaluations that concluded that citizen participation was not effective and needed to be connected to 'concrete content'.[9]

Leverage

The leverage that peacebuilders applied in order to promote reforms also changed during the different interaction periods. Most activities were planned by headquarters but were to be implemented at the local level. They were thus not necessarily strategically tailored to the specific situations in the municipalities.

Period I (2007–08): lower leverage

In the first period, peacebuilders used lower leverage instruments in the form of capacity building or monitoring and advice. The OSCE pushed legislative oversight through monitoring and advice;[10] USAID organised capacity building for the Mayors and Directors on new technical budget requirements (USAID Kosovo 2009).[11]

Period II (2009–10): lower leverage

Peacebuilders continued to apply lower leverage with capacity building, outreach, monitoring and advice. The OSCE initiated a Kosovo-wide outreach campaign to promote citizen participation in radio and TV,[12] printed leaflets for public hearings[13] and monitored and advised municipal authorities.[14] USAID organised a capacity building workshop called 'Municipal Transparency and Citizen Participation'.

Period III (2011–12): higher leverage

In the third period, peacebuilders increased their leverage over domestic elites, providing considerable financial assistance in addition to increasing activities for outreach, monitoring, reporting and advice. The OSCE put a major focus on Public Budget Hearings: The OSCE Headquarters created a new funding line to finance projects in the area of 'participation in decision making',[15] and field offices made municipal budget planning a monitoring priority.[16] The 2012 OSCE monitoring report 'Budget Development Process in Kosovo Municipalities' (OSCE 2012) allowed for more targeted advice to municipalities. The outreach campaign for citizen participation continued.[17] The OSCE's field offices provided limited financial assistance for leaflets and catering at budget hearings.[18] USAID started a major programme in April 2011 to support 21 Kosovo municipalities based on 'municipal partnerships'. This included financial assistance for development projects[19] as well as capacity building and advice for, amongst other things, participation in municipal budgeting. USAID organized several workshops and conferences: the 'Municipal Budget Process' workshop with Municipal Government and Municipal Assembly representatives,[20] the 'Enhance Municipal Transparency' workshop with Press Officers[21] and several budget related conferences.[22] USAID also implemented weekly monitoring and advising activities in the municipalities.[23]

Participatory budget planning in Zabel/Šumarak

> You probably know that we review a regulation after the board prepares it, they deliver it to our Committee and we give our suggestions. Then, at sessions every member has the right to give his comments or suggestions,

the regulation goes to public hearings, and then it is returned for approval. We also give citizens the right to express their opinion.

(Interview 60 with a member of the Policy and Finance Committee Zabel/Šumarak, 31/10/2012)

If one questions that peacebuilding reforms can ever be successful, the budget planning reform in Zabel/Šumarak is an excellent example to show that peacebuilding initiatives can lead to success: The budget planning reform resulted in full implementation. Such a result might be surprising for advocates of the international capacity explanation because the budget planning reform actually took place in a low capacity policy field. By taking the external–domestic interaction into account, however, the outcome can be better understood: Although the interaction process was shaped by the ad hoc tactic of selectivity, peacebuilders had covered the full set of rules at least once by 2012. This made a peacebuilding outcome of full implementation possible. Given the enabling environment of interaction in this case, characterised by both domestic support for the promoted international norm and a cooperative style of politics, domestic actors were more inclined to cooperate with peacebuilders' demands and kept up learned rules from previous periods of interaction. Furthermore, the increase of leverage in the last period through the offer of financial assistance in exchange for proper budget hearings also influenced the outcome: As the municipality was interested in receiving financial resources for urban development, it was additionally motivated to implement budget hearings.

The negotiations for the budget planning reform in Zabel/Šumarak involved the Mayor, the Director for Budget and Finance, the Chairperson of the Municipal Assembly, and the Policy and Finance Committee, as well as civil society organisations and citizens (although they did not directly interact with peacebuilders). On the international side, the OSCE Local Governance Section and Municipal Teams as well as representatives from USAID's headquarters and regional advisors were involved.

The following section traces the external–domestic interaction process, discussing the rules negotiated in each period, the leverage international actors used to push these rules and the responses of domestic actors.

Period I (2007–08): legislative oversight (rules 1, 3 and 7)

In this first phase, international actors in Zabel/Šumarak selected rules to ensure executive-legislative cooperation in the budget, using the low leverage instruments of capacity building, monitoring and advice. Capacity building activities, for example, invitations to expensive hotels, were often combined with 'individual incentives'.

USAID was the first to promote participatory budget planning and organised a Kosovo-wide capacity building workshop on the new budget legislation and technical budget procedures, to which the Zabel/Šumarak Mayor and Directors were invited (USAID Kosovo 2009).[24] The OSCE regularly monitored and advised the Mayor, Directors and Municipal Assembly Chairperson concerning new requirements on legislative budget oversight.[25]

The Mayor, Directors and Municipal Assembly members of Zabel/ Šumarak cooperated and followed international recommendations. International activities were evaluated positively.[26] The Mayor consulted the Policy and Finance Committee and the Municipal Assembly on the municipal budget proposal,[27] and the budget was approved before the deadline on 30 September (MLGA 2009). The cooperative style of politics practiced in the municipality between the Municipal Government, the Municipal Assembly and the opposition, as well as the absence of inter-party and intra-party competition, increased municipal elites' inclination to consult potential rivals. Yet peacebuilders' selectivity with the rules of legislative oversight and simultaneous neglect of rules promoting budget hearings led to selective implementation by domestic actors: The legally required public budget hearings did not take place (MLGA 2009). This supports the conclusion that implementation depends on peacebuilders' attention to specific reform aspects.

Period II (2009–10): citizen participation (rules 2 and 5)

In 2009, international actors shifted their attention to rules promoting citizen participation while not explicitly demanding public budget hearings. International actors used the lower leverage instruments of capacity building, outreach, monitoring and advice to promote these rules.

USAID invited Zabel/Šumarak Assembly members to a Kosovo-wide capacity building workshop on transparency, citizen participation and public hearings (USAID Kosovo 2009), and OSCE Headquarters started a Kosovo-wide outreach campaign to promote citizen participation in municipal decision-making on radio and TV.[28] On the ground, the OSCE field team regularly monitored and advised Zabel/Šumarak's officials on the legally required public hearings.[29]

Municipal actors sustained learned rules related to legislative oversight from the previous phase: The Municipal Government and Municipal Assembly collaborated on the budget so that legislative oversight was ensured,[30] and the budget was approved within the deadline (MA Zabel/Šumarak 2010d, MLGA 2009). Local actors, however, responded with a mixture of cooperation and foot-dragging to the international demand for citizen participation through public hearings. This does not mean that the municipality was opposed to citizen participation per se. In fact, Municipal Assembly members were frustrated by the meagre turnout of citizens at public hearings (MA Zabel/Šumarak 2010c). Yet unless peacebuilders insisted, the municipality refrained from committing financial, human and time resources to public hearings because other items on the municipal agenda such as drinking water and sewage were seen as priority. There was thus only one budget hearing organised in 2010 by the Mayor and Municipal Assembly, instead of the two required per year.[31] Other public hearings, however, took place.[32] There was further foot-dragging demonstrated in the limited effort the municipality invested in outreach activities to win citizen participation: The date and time was advertised only on the municipal webpage and municipal billboard (Municipality Zabel/Šumarak 2010c). As a result, only a few citizens attended – sometimes not more than ten (ibid.).

Period III (2011–12): public budget hearings (rules 2, 4, 5, 6 and 8)

In the third period, peacebuilders in Zabel/Šumarak focused on a sub-set of rules related to the organisation of public budget hearings and citizen participation. At that point, peacebuilders, over time, had tackled every rule of the reform at least once. Peacebuilders used not only high leverage instruments such as financial assistance but also the lower leverage instruments of capacity building, outreach, monitoring, reporting and advice. The change in selectivity and leverage had been triggered by routine evaluations of the OSCE and USAID's donor programmes, which found citizen participation to be insufficient.

Since citizen participation in budget development had become an OSCE monitoring priority,[33] the OSCE field team provided more focused advice to their local counterparts on the legal requirements of public budget hearings and the OSCE headquarters issued a report on citizen participation in budget planning in 2012. The OSCE particularly targeted the requirement to post announcements 14 days in advance, hold public hearings in villages and use alternative media (OSCE 2012), and it provided Zabel/Šumarak with financial support for outreach activities in TV and radio.[34] USAID became extremely involved in supporting the organisation of budget hearings with financial assistance, capacity building and weekly advising activities.[35] They also offered Zabel/Šumarak $120,000 for development projects[36] on the condition that the municipality successfully cooperate with USAID's 'good governance' activities (including Participatory Budget Planning). In addition to that sum, Zabel/Šumarak's Municipal Assembly received $25,000 from USAID for being the most transparent Municipal Assembly in 2011 and 2012 (USAID DEMI 2012d). Furthermore, USAID offered the Zabel/Šumarak Press Information Office cameras, microphones and a computer[37] and organised several capacity building workshops to improve citizen participation in budget hearings with Municipal Directors, Policy and Finance Committee members and the Public Information Officer.[38] USAID also helped Zabel/Šumarak to develop a leaflet on the budget process and provided financial assistance for printing (Municipality Zabel/Šumarak 2011c).[39] USAID regional advisors followed up on activities with municipal officials on a weekly basis.

The Mayor, Municipal Directors and Municipal Assembly members responded cooperatively, possibly because they saw the various forms of financial assistance as an incentive to increase efforts. For sure, the increased leverage in this period – particularly the financial assistance offered by USAID for implementing 'participatory budget planning' – presented an important motivation for domestic actors to strive for full implementation of the reform and stop foot-dragging. In all my interviews, municipal politicians spoke very highly of USAID, mentioning the various financial benefits received from such cooperation.[40] The Mayor publicly thanked USAID on several occasions for its support.[41] The Press Department regarded USAID financial assistance as crucial to the municipality's success in increasing citizen participation:

> To speak realistically, [citizen relations are good] because of [USAID's] DEMI project. They also help us with technical equipment. The other organizations, they only support the process, but what we need is only technical support.
>
> (Interview, Municipal Official, 31/10/2012)

But there was also a genuine interest in increasing citizen participation in the budget process[42] and it is possible that the enabling environment of interaction facilitated a certain openness towards inclusionary and participatory approaches. For example, USAID's advice to improve outreach to citizens was immediately taken up: A few days after the 2011 workshop, the municipal website invited citizens to get involved in budgeting (Municipality Zabel/Šumarak 2011b, 2011d), and four public budget hearings were organised by the Mayor, Directors and Municipal Assembly for the year[43] and were advertised on the municipal website and with USAID supported leaflets.[44] However, citizen attendance was below municipal politicians' expectations and Assembly members complained about the "merely symbolic" number of participants (MA Zabel/Šumarak 2011c). In 2012, the Mayor and the Municipal Assembly stepped up efforts to organise joint public hearings. Following OSCE and USAID advice, 11 public hearings were organised in the city and surrounding villages, 300 citizens participated and 116 priorities for capital projects were identified for the budget (USAID DEMI 2012b). Yet Municipal Assembly members criticised the government for indiscriminate inclusion of citizen's requests at the expense of strategic priority setting (MA Zabel/Šumarak 2012b). With elections coming up in 2013, some might also have feared that the incumbent government would profit more from citizen participation than the opposition.

Peacebuilding outcome: full implementation

The external–domestic interaction resulted in full implementation in the case of Participatory Budget Planning in Zabel/Šumarak.[45] Peacebuilders' ad hoc tactics of selectivity and leverage significantly influenced the outcome. The municipality would not have fully complied with all the legal requirements of Participatory Budget Planning if peacebuilders had not managed to tackle every single rule at least once and thus reduced selectivity. Leverage was also influential. The peacebuilders' use of significant amounts of financial assistance to support compliance with budget hearing regulations certainly increased domestic actors' cooperation in the last period. Furthermore, the enabling environment of interaction facilitated domestic cooperation as adoption costs for the reform were low: The absence of significant intra-party and inter-party competition increased the Municipal Government's readiness to share information and consult the Assembly and the opposition, and facilitated the joint organisation of public budget hearings.

FORMAL DIMENSION

Rule 1. MA approves budget within deadline: The Municipal Assembly approved the annual budget within the deadline (MA Zabel/Šumarak 2011a).[46]
Rule 2. Two public budget hearings held: The municipality even held 11 public hearings between July and August 2012 – two in the town of Zabel/Šumarak town and nine in neighbouring villages, including the largest Serbian village of the municipality. Two hundred and ninety-three citizens participated (USAID DEMI 2012b).

PRACTICE DIMENSION

Rule 3. Municipal Assembly and/or PFC consulted on 1st draft budget: The Government consulted the Municipal Assembly on a first draft proposal on 26 July 2012. Prior to that, they had discussed the draft with the Policy and Finance Committee (MA Zabel/Šumarak 2012a).
Rule 4. Public public hearings by Government and Municipal Assembly: All public hearings were organised jointly between the Municipal Government and the Municipal Assembly. At all meetings, representatives from both the executive and legislative branches were present. Sometimes, civil society groups were also invited to the organizational team for public hearings (USAID DEMI 2012b).
Rule 5. Outreach for public hearings: The citizens were informed about each meeting on municipal billboards, the municipal website and posters, at least 14 days in advance.
Rule 6. Publication of budget for citizens: The municipality put together an information brochure and uploaded the budget proposal to its website. In this way, citizens were able to inform themselves about the municipal budget in an exemplary manner (Municipality Zabel/Šumarak 2012, USAID DEMI 2012b).

CONTENT DIMENSION

Rule 7. Municipal Assembly requests included: The Mayor promised to include the recommendations of the Assembly members (MA Zabel/Šumarak 2012a).[47]
Rule 8. Citizen requests included: Zabel/Šumarak included 23 citizen requests from the public budget hearings into the list of capital projects amounting to €2.7 million (USAID DEMI 2012b).

Participatory budget planning in Bregore/Brdašce

> I: You voted for Mr. [the Mayor]?
> YOUNG MALE: Yes, and I will vote again. He works more than the others. He changed Bregore. Now we have electricity on the street. So many things.
> (Conversation with a young Kosovo Albanian from Bregore/Brdašce after the municipal elections 2013, 04/11/2013)

Bregore/Brdašce was a place with a less cooperative external–domestic interaction process when it came to the reform of Participatory Budget Planning, and the interactions resulted in captured implementation. The Municipal Government, especially the Mayor, used the leeway inherent in the interaction process to capture the reform in order to centralise and broaden his political power base. The peacebuilders' selectivity of only a sub-set of rules provided the Mayor with leeway to ignore 'constraining' rules on legislative oversight at no cost in the third period. The variance in leverage also changed domestic elites' (non-)adoption costs over time. For example, municipal elites had a greater incentive to comply with international demands in the third period due to USAID's financial assistance with infrastructure projects. The rather constraining environment of interaction, characterised by a competitive style of politics, made it seem more advantageous for municipal actors to capture reform for their own ends: Peacebuilders' demands were met with a mixture of cooperation, foot-dragging and modification, and learned rules did not prove sustainable over time. At the same time, peacebuilders tolerated domestic foot-dragging, modification and ignorance – probably because 'correct' implementation of Participatory Budget Planning was not one of the top international priorities. The low capacity vested in this policy field may have had a negative effect on the outcome, as peacebuilders lacked the supervisory powers required to interfere, but it remains questionable whether they would have interfered and to what effect.

Similar to Zabel/Šumarak, the budget planning reform was negotiated between the Mayor, the Director for Budget and Finance, the Chairperson of the Municipal Assembly and the Policy and Finance Committee members on the domestic side; and on the international side, USAID and its regional advisor as well as the OSCE Local Governance Section and Municipal Teams.

The following paragraphs present the external–domestic interactions in Bregore/Brdašce over three interaction periods in which different sub-sets of rules were negotiated.

Period I (2007–08): legislative oversight (rules 1, 3 and 7)

At first, peacebuilders selected only a small sub-set of rules from the reform because international attention was bound up in the broader process of Kosovo independence. Institutional cooperation between the Municipal

Government and Municipal Assembly was central; public budget hearings were left out. The OSCE and USAID used the lower leverage instruments of capacity building, dialogue facilitation, monitoring and advice to support rule implementation. Furthermore, capacity building activities were made attractive to municipal politicians through dinner or hotel stays.

International actors organised several capacity building training sessions on the budget reform. For instance, USAID invited the Mayor and department heads of Bregore/Brdašce municipality to the Kosovo-wide budget management training in April 2008 (USAID Kosovo 2009). The OSCE field office also organised a budget-planning capacity building weekend for the Mayor, Directors and Policy and Finance Committee members with the goal of facilitating an executive-legislative budget collaboration and offering continued monitoring and advising on legislative oversight in budget planning.[48] Although domestic actors generally responded with cooperation to international requests, the selectivity of peacebuilders' demands led, in turn, to selective rule implementation on the domestic side: The Municipal Government and Municipal Assembly members did follow rules for legislative oversight[49] but ignored all rules connected to public budget hearings.[50] According to the Mayor at the time, the municipality was "not so well organised" in the first year after Kosovo's independence, and international advice was welcome.[51] The OSCE-facilitated budget-planning workshop, in particular, was remembered positively.[52] Still, only those rules asked for by peacebuilders were also implemented by the municipal bodies.

Period II (2009–10): citizen participation (rules 1, 2, 3 and 5)

In the second period, peacebuilders selected a sub-set of rules about citizen participation, while maintaining its activities in the field of legislative oversight. Peacebuilders did not ask, however, for the legally required budget hearings.[53] International actors used the lower leverage instruments of capacity building, dialogue facilitation, monitoring and advice to promote the selected sub-set of rules.

The OSCE and USAID both organised capacity building activities for Bregore/Brdašce: USAID invited Municipal Assembly members to a Kosovo-wide workshop on transparency and citizen participation in Assembly work (USAID Kosovo 2009),[54] and the OSCE field office continued to organise joint budget planning weekends in 2009 and 2010 with the Mayor, Directors and Policy and Finance Committee members.[55] The OSCE also regularly monitored and advised the municipality on how to organise legislative oversight, public hearings or outreach for citizens.[56] The OSCE's national outreach campaign for citizen participation also reached Bregore/Brdašce.

The domestic response to peacebuilders' norm promotion activities was marked by both cooperation and foot-dragging. The Mayor and Municipal Assembly were generally willing to follow peacebuilder recommendations for the selected rules although the Municipal Government was plagued by severe inter- and intra-party competition.[57] Thanks to the customary OSCE-sponsored budget planning weekend, the Municipal Assembly was able to provide its input to the budget proposal for the executive branch[58] and to pass the budget (almost) on time (MA Bregore/Brdašce 2011b).[59] Peacebuilders' selectivity, however, led to a situation in which municipal actors simply ignored non-selected rules: Because the OSCE and USAID had not explicitly pushed public budget hearings, no public budget consultations were organised.[60] The Municipal Assembly Chairperson and Mayor organised two public hearings in 2010 that were not related to the budget (MLGA 2009), but invested only limited effort in reaching out to citizens, putting up announcements only on the municipal billboard (MLGA 2009).[61] Only a handful of people attended.[62] While the Mayor was satisfied with having organised public hearings according to the legal requirements[63] and did not mind the low attendance rate – which he explained as citizens' lack of interest and frustration with politics[64] – peacebuilders expected the municipality to work more proactively on increasing citizen participation through outreach activities.[65]

Period III (2011–12): public budget hearings (rules 2, 4, 5, 6 and 8)

In the third phase, peacebuilders concentrated on a sub-set of rules related to public budget hearings that were designed to boost citizen participation. The OSCE and USAID sent out similar messages: Respect budget approval deadlines (2), organise a minimum of two public budget hearings (4), respect announcement rules (5), enhance outreach activities (6) and integrate citizens' proposals (8) (OSCE 2012). Rules on legislative oversight were not mentioned at all. At the same time, peacebuilders increased their leverage in order to push the selected rules, using financial assistance in addition to capacity building, dialogue facilitation, monitoring and advice. This made it more costly for domestic actors to possibly resist or drag their feet on rule implementation.

USAID tied their offer of $150,000 in financial assistance for infrastructure projects[66] to the demand to improve public participation in budget planning. It also supported press offices with video cameras and other equipment,[67] and organised several capacity building training sessions such as the Municipal Directors' training on good governance, the Policy and Finance Committee members' workshop called 'Municipal Budget Planning and Encouragement of Citizen Participation', or the Press Officers' workshop called 'Enhance Municipal Transparency'.[68] The USAID regional advisor conducted weekly visits to Bregore/Brdašce to discuss public budget hearings.[69] The OSCE equally increased its engagement: The OSCE Municipal Team closely monitored the budget-process in Bregore/Brdašce, provided regular advice on how to improve citizen participation and offered small-scale financial assistance for the printing of budget hearing leaflets.[70] The OSCE field office again sponsored a budget-planning weekend in 2011, but lacked the financial means to do so in 2012. As the Municipal Government was not willing to commit its own resources to such a meeting, the OSCE, as a compromise, hosted a 'budget dinner' in mid-August 2012 to facilitate informal consultations between the Mayor, the Director of Budget and Finance, and five Policy and Finance Committee members in a rather hostile atmosphere.[71]

The domestic response to peacebuilders' requests remained cooperative on the surface, but hidden conflicts of interests led to domestic foot-dragging and modification, even though peacebuilders had applied higher leverage to promote the selected sub-set of rules. The reasons behind domestic foot-dragging and modification were rooted in the constraining environment of interaction, marked by a competitive style of politics with fierce inter- and intra party rivalries and fights for political power between the Mayor, who headed a minority government, and the Municipal Assembly members. Additionally, peacebuilders tolerated domestic foot-dragging and modification and did not intensify the pressure to ensure full compliance with their demands.[72] The reason was that correct implementation of these rules was not a priority for international actors because it was neither needed for security nor for fulfilling EU benchmarks. Furthermore, peacebuilders were in dire need of the municipality's cooperation with regard to two highly contested laws from the Ahtisaari Plan, and they used all the leverage they had to pressure the municipality into compliance there.[73] Therefore, peacebuilders did not have the capacity or interest to pay attention to the implementation of 'less important' reforms such as participatory budget planning.

The implementation of Participatory Budget Planning in this period exemplifies once more how selectivity influences reform outcomes: While the 2011 budget capacity building workshops with the executive and legislative branches held by the OSCE managed to ensure executive-legislative budget cooperation, the lack of such external facilitation in 2012 led to a breakdown of executive-legislative cooperation: The Mayor excluded Municipal Assembly members from the public hearings and provided the Policy and Finance Committee with the budget plan only after the official submission deadline and two weeks before the deadline for approval.[74] The Municipal Assembly passed the budget by the deadline of 30 September,[75] but the adoption of the budget turned into a farce: The Municipal Assembly's budget session had been scheduled exactly on the deadline of 30 September. As the Municipal Assembly could be declared dysfunctional and be dissolved if it did not adopt the budget by the deadline, Municipal Assembly members were pressured to accept the Municipal Government's budget proposal.[76] Bregore/Brdašce thus witnessed a breakdown of institutional cooperation in budget matters, which international actors were powerless, or not interested enough, to prevent.

At the same time, the Mayor of Bregore/Brdašce strongly embraced the international push for citizen participation in budget planning. For the Mayor, the public hearings presented an opportunity to broaden his power base and win votes: He could show the citizens that he cared and that he was working hard to improve their lives. The Mayor's power-driven interest in holding public hearings, in combination with massive support from peacebuilders, led to an abundance of public hearings in 2011 and 2012: Twenty hearings were organised in 2011 (USAID DEMI 2012b), and 23 were organised in 2012 in almost all of the villages of Bregore/Brdašce, even the Serbian village. Seven hundred people attended these hearings (USAID DEMI 2012b). However, the Municipal Government used foot-dragging and modification when it came to *how* to organise public budget hearings: The Municipal Assembly was excluded; not all meetings were publicly announced on time and via municipal billboards, media, posters or leaflets;[77] and most public hearings were based on the Mayor's last-minute phone calls to village leaders, meaning that it would be mostly the Mayor's power base that would join.[78] The OSCE financed posters and leaflets were put up only in a few villages.[79] USAID and the OSCE were aware of these shortcomings but nevertheless were satisfied by the high number of budget hearings conducted.[80]

The Mayor's high commitment to public hearings was furthermore supported by the fact that USAID had conditioned financial assistance for infrastructure projects upon the organisation of budget hearings:

> They say to us, ok, you have to do this in order to reform your administration if you want to receive fifty thousand dollars for this and this project. So it's a very, very good and simple cooperation that we have with this DEMI program...
> (Interview 18, Municipal Director, Bregore/Brdašce, 11/05/2012)

This financial assistance from USAID further helped the Mayor in his quest to broaden his political power: He was well informed about the priorities of his citizens – a new sewage system, new lighting, new roads and socio-economic and infrastructure development – and spent the $150,000 from USAID on new street lighting (the project named in the quote at the beginning of the section), the renovation of the Municipal Assembly hall and a citizen service centre.[81] These were the things that the citizens cared about and that would get him re-elected. The Participatory Budget Planning reform thus turned into a power-support machine for the Mayor through the domestic strategies of selective implementation, modification and foot-dragging.

Peacebuilding outcome: captured implementation

The outcome of Participatory Budget Planning in Bregore/Brdašce shows the clear traits of a captured implementation that primarily served the Mayor's interest in broadening his political power base and excluding political competitors. Heading a minority government and confronted with fierce intra-party and inter-party competition, the Mayor had a strong interest in expanding his political power while neglecting democratic procedures of transparency and accountability in such a constraining environment of interaction. The Municipal Government, thus, used the budget planning reform – which the peacebuilders had envisaged as promoting democratic norms – to generate power for its own political survival by ignoring, modifying or dragging their feet on rule implementation. The Mayor sidelined the Municipal Assembly using several strategies: No effective formal consultation on the budget proposal by the Policy and Finance Committee or Municipal Assembly took place. No willingness to integrate the Assembly's proposals was shown. The Municipal Assembly was pressured into budget adoption as the possibility of its dissolution loomed should they reject it. In fact, the Municipal Assembly was excluded from the budget hearings to prevent rival parties or rival colleagues from gaining sympathy from the citizens. The Mayor used budget hearings first of all to expand his power base to win votes in the next election. The Mayor's heavy reliance on village leaders and personal networks, as well as the use of Assembly rooms that were closed to women, point to a practice of nurturing personal power bases while giving less importance to aspects of equal access for all citizens. The implementation of each rule of the reform is discussed below.

FORMAL DIMENSION

Rule 1. MA approves budget within deadline: The municipal budget was approved within the deadline,[82] but legal compliance in this matter can be partly attributed to the Municipal Assembly's fear of their own dissolution.

Rule 2. Two public budget hearings held: The Mayor held 23 public hearings with a total of 700 participants (USAID DEMI 2012b), but the Municipal Assembly held none.

PRACTICE DIMENSION

Rule 3. Municipal Assembly and/or PFC consulted on 1st draft budget: Consultation on the budget proposal with the legislative did not take place. The budget proposal was officially submitted to the PFC after the deadline, but the PFC was not expected to comment on the budget.[83]

Rule 4. Public budget hearings by Government and Municipal Assembly: The Mayor organised public budget hearings without the Assembly. The Assembly members – although interested in participating – were neither invited nor did they feel they should organise their own meetings.[84]

Rule 5. Outreach for public hearings: Outreach for budget hearings was partly organised through announcements on the municipal billboard and website and through the media.[85] However, not all meetings were publicly advertised. Sometimes the Mayor simply called the village leader and relied on their personal networks to bring people to the hearing. Sometimes these meetings took place in the *oda*, a traditional Albanian room in which only men are permitted.[86] This means that the general public – women and individuals outside the village leader's network – were excluded from some budget hearings.

Rule 6. Publication of budget for citizens: No information about the budget plans was provided to the citizens.[87]

CONTENT DIMENSION

Rule 7. Municipal Assembly requests included: The Municipal Assembly's recommendations were not included.[88]

Rule 8. Citizen requests included: Three citizen requests were included in the municipal budget, which amounted to €90,000 (USAID DEMI 2012b). Assembly members criticised this as an indiscriminate inclusion of citizens' requests at the expense of strategic priority setting.[89]

Summary: external–domestic interactions in participatory budget planning

The following summarizes the findings on the role of external–domestic interactions in the Participatory Budget Planning reform based on the key categories of the analytical framework: peacebuilding outcomes; the ad hoc tactics of prioritisation, selectivity and leverage; and the environment of interaction. As a reform with low international capacity invested but with weak local resistance against the norm of democracy, both standard explanations failed to predict the ultimate outcomes of Participatory Budget Planning. I therefore argue that the results of the Participatory Budget Planning reform can be better understood through the analytical framework of peacebuilding interactions. If one follows the interaction process closely, one can see that the reform implementation only started in summer 2008 after peacebuilders got engaged in the reform with capacity building and dialogue and not right after the new law was adopted in February 2008. Interaction thus seems a necessary condition for reform implementation to start. Still, peacebuilders were not always capable of fully reaching their reform goals through negotiation, particularly in Bregore/Brdašce: Different sets of priorities made full compliance unlikely; the complexities of the post-war environment made it difficult for peacebuilders to keep track of reform progress; and mutual dependencies let both sides agree to compromises otherwise rejected.

Peacebuilding outcomes

In Zabel/Šumarak, external–domestic interactions resulted in full implementation, while external–domestic interactions in Bregore/Brdašce resulted in captured implementation that served the Mayor's priority to enhance his political power. The fact that the reform was fully implemented in one of the municipalities is evidence that the lack of major international capacity seems to be less relevant for the success of peacebuilding than assumed by scholars emphasizing the importance of mission mandates and material investment. The high level of cooperation in Zabel/Šumarak also defies the expectations of critical peacebuilding scholarship that international interventions necessarily provoke domestic resistance. In Bregore/Brdašce, peacebuilders were also able to strengthen the norm of democracy during the reform process, but municipal elites used the leeway inherent in the external–domestic interaction

Table 5.2 Peacebuilding outcomes of participatory budget planning

Budget planning outcomes

Dimension	Zabel/Šumarak	Bregore/Brdašce
Formal dimension		
1 MA approves budget	Yes	Yes
2 2 Budget hearings held	Yes	Yes
Practice dimension		
3 MA and/or PFC consulted on 1. draft	Yes	No
4 Budget hearing by Gov & PFC	Yes	No
5 Outreach budget hearing	Yes	In-Between
6 Publication of budget		No
Content dimension		
7 MA & PFC alter budget proposal	Yes	No
8 Citizen requests included	Yes	Yes
Outcome	Full implementation	Captured implementation

to push their own domestic priorities: The Mayor exploited the reform initiative to enhance his political power, sidelining the Assembly and using the obligatory public budget hearings to broaden its political support base for the next round of elections. Participatory Budget Planning also served to advance the domestic priority of development in both municipalities: The provision of financial assistance for infrastructure projects in exchange for organising public budget hearings presented a powerful incentive for domestic actors to cooperate with international actors.

Prioritisation, selectivity, leverage

The ad hoc tactics of selectivity and leverage significantly shaped the evolution of the external–domestic interplay and influenced the reform outcome.

Selectivity offered domestic actors leeway to capture the reform for their own ends by ignoring those rules of the reform initiative that peacebuilders were not capable of paying attention to in a specific interaction period. The process tracing shows clearly that domestic actors respond with selective implementation to the peacebuilders' ad hoc tactic of selectivity: Rules selected by international actors were implemented (correctly or not), while those rules left out by international actors were ignored by the municipality. Unless interactions took place in an enabling environment, previously learned rules did not prove sustainable in the next interaction period. This, of course, had an effect on the reform outcome. I identified three interaction periods in which different sets of rules were selected: First, peacebuilders paid attention to a sub-set of rules on legislative oversight (rules 1, 3, 7), then to citizen participation (rules 2, 4, 5) and lastly to public budget hearings (rules 2, 4, 5,

6, 8). These selectivity shifts were triggered ad hoc by changes to the international agenda due to (a) Kosovo's independence and (b) routine programme evaluations. Over time, international actors managed to cover the total set of rules from 1 to 8. This was an important pre-condition for full implementation given the observed pattern that only those rules selected by peacebuilders are taken up for implementation by domestic actors. Yet, the learned rules only proved sustainable in the case of Zabel/Šumarak thanks to its enabling environment of interaction, while in Bregore/Brdašce, rules on legislative oversight were ignored without incurring any costs once peacebuilders had shifted their attention to public hearings.

Leverage changed from low to high during the different interaction periods because peacebuilders used different kinds of norm promotion instruments to push the selected sub-set of rules. In the first interaction period, peacebuilders used lower leverage instruments such as capacity building, dialogue facilitation, monitoring and advice. In the second period, the lower leverage instruments used were capacity building, outreach, dialogue facilitation, monitoring and advice. As the lower leverage instruments did not cause significant costs of non-adoption, domestic actors used this leeway for modification or foot-dragging. In the third period, peacebuilders increased their leverage and added financial assistance and financial rewards to the usual instruments of capacity building, outreach, monitoring, reporting and advice. The offer of financial assistance for public budget hearings sparked high levels of activism in both municipalities: The prospect of financial support increased domestic actors' willingness to cooperate as they saw the chance to push their priority of socio-economic development. Foot-dragging strategies became less prevalent. Yet even higher leverage cannot guarantee full domestic cooperation: In Bregore/Brdašce, domestic actors formally complied with international demands but substantially modified budget hearing rules to match up with the Mayor's priority to increase political power.

In general, peacebuilders were inclined to tolerate ignorance, modification and foot-dragging by domestic actors: For example, in Bregore/Brdašce, peacebuilders backed down from demanding more substantive rule implementation instead of increasing pressure through the withdrawal of financial assistance or by making reports to headquarters in order to enforce compliance. Backing down might have been the result of peacebuilders' dependency on domestic cooperation in other reform areas[90] or the need to preserve their reputation (by calling a failure a success) in front of their own agency or donor.[91] This international reluctance to punish obvious legal violations increased the leeway for domestic actors to capture reforms at a low cost.

Environment of interaction

The environment of interaction also had an influence on the evolution of the interaction process and the reform outcome. External–domestic interactions in Zabel/Šumarak took place in an enabling environment of interaction, marked by domestic support for the norm of democracy and a cooperative style of politics. In such an environment, municipal elites are more likely to respond with full cooperation to international demands, as transparency, accountability and participation are not perceived as a threat to local power holders. On the other side, external–domestic interaction in Bregore/Brdašce took place in a rather constraining environment with strong domestic support but a competitive style of politics. Municipal elites in Bregore/Brdašce perceived municipal politics as a zero-sum game, and were inclined to use extra-legal means to gain power and exploit the budget reform in order to dominate over their political rivals. Here, municipal elites responded with foot-dragging and modification of international demands. They tested the tolerance of international actors, but refrained from using outright resistance, as they were still interested in maintaining good relations with their international counterpart.

Promoting minority rights in a low capacity policy field: the Communities Committees

In Kosovo, Communities Committees are the most important minority rights protection mechanism at the municipal level (OSCE 2009b).[92] The Committees had already been introduced in 2000 as part of UNMIK Regulation 2000/45, "On the Self-Government of Municipalities in Kosovo" (UNMIK 2000). Communities Committees strengthen minority rights because they provide minorities with a special representative organ and, thus, offer space for institutionalised inter-ethnic dialogue between the municipality, the majority population and the minority populations. The Committees' mandates serve to ensure the municipalities' respect for minority rights and interests: that every local community regardless of its size, language, religion, ethnic origin or any other characteristic should receive equal treatment by the municipality, and that minorities have equal protection, opportunities and access to services (RoK 2008b).

The Communities Committee reform is a case of low international capacity and strong local resistance against the international norm of minority rights. In both Zabel/Šumarak and in Bregore/Brdašce, the Communities Committee reform results in captured implementation. Communities Committees were set up, but members re-interpreted its mandate, concentrating on socio-economic development while leaving aside politically contested issues. Neither the international capacity nor the local resistance approach can easily explain such a result. Based on the analytical framework of peacebuilding interactions, I show that analysing the external–domestic interaction helps to explain the peacebuilding outcomes in the case of the Communities Committees. Ad hoc tactics of prioritisation, selectivity and leverage, for example, influenced peacebuilding outcomes in different ways: Prioritisation, which international actors resorted to after the March 2004 riots, made no implementation less likely as peacebuilders were less inclined to tolerate domestic non-compliance. Selectivity offered domestic actors opportunities to ignore rules not taken up by international actors at no cost. The fact that peacebuilders did not manage to tackle the total set of rules over time made captured implementation more likely. Leverage was also important for the outcome of captured implementation: In the second interaction period, peacebuilders successfully used the higher leverage instruments of financial assistance and coercion to overcome domestic resistance but tolerated domestic foot-dragging and modification. In both cases, interactions took place in a constraining environment of interaction. Above all, the weak domestic support for minority rights increased the prospect of domestic resistance against international demands for reform implementation.

Implementation of the Communities Committee reform was negotiated between multiple actors. On the international side, KFOR, UNMIK and the OSCE were the main interlocutors. The KFOR field offices frequently monitored Communities Committee meetings. UNMIK Municipal Administrators played a crucial role until 2008, using supervisory powers for the Committee's formal establishment, the appointment of members and their subsequent invitation to meetings, and, more importantly, the facilitation of informal meetings between Albanian and Serbian leaders and provision of advice to both sides. Today, the OSCE remains the only peacebuilding organisation actively engaged in the implementation of Communities Committees. OSCE regional offices and Municipal Teams are involved in capacity building, outreach, monitoring and advising, and minor financial assistance, while OSCE Headquarters are involved in the legal drafting of new laws or regulations.[93] On the domestic side, the Mayor, the Municipal Assembly, the Municipal Office of Communities and Returns and minority leaders are the most important actors. The role of the Serbian community is particularly crucial, as the functioning of this minority rights mechanism depends to a great extent on the Serbian communities being willing to cooperate with Kosovo institutions.

The Communities Committee requires domestic actors to follow a particular set of rules.[94] First and foremost, the Committee has to be formally established (rule 1). The committee is composed of members of the Municipal Assembly (which should reflect party composition) and minority community representatives of each ethnic group in the municipality (rule 2) (RoK 2008b). The latter constitute the majority of the Committee. Usually, Committee members are appointed by the Mayor in coordination with the Officer for Communities and approved by the Municipal Assembly. However, there are no concrete rules regulating the selection of Committee members, which makes the selection procedure prone to political appointments and nepotistic practices (UNMIK 2004). Communities Committees are to meet ten times per year and should report their work at least once to the Municipal Assembly (rule 3) (RoK 2008b). Representatives of all ethnic groups should be present at these meetings (rule 4) (RoK 2008b). The Committee is required to provide an annual report about its work to the Municipal Assembly (rule 5) (RoK 2008b). The Committee's mandate is to ensure respect for minority rights (rule 6) and minority interests (rule 7) in the municipalities by reviewing municipal legislation, policies and practices (RoK 2008b). This includes the Committee's participation in municipal drafting of regulations and/or the making of decisions, or the review of existing regulations and decisions with regard to community rights and interests (UNMIK 2003). The committee also reviews the implementation of policies by the municipality to ensure that respect for minority rights and interests are included (UNMIK 2003). It is allowed to formulate recommendations for the Municipal Assembly to "promote, express, preserve and develop their ethnic, cultural, religious and linguistic identities" (rule 8) (RoK 2008b). Since 2004, Committee members have received the same amount of financial compensation as the Policy and Finance Committee (RoK 2008b). Compensation varies from municipality to municipality. In Bregore/Brdašce, members receive €100 per meeting, while Zabel/Šumarak members receive €50.[95] Such financial compensation can be an important incentive for individuals to participate in the Committees as €100 equals the monthly income of some families in the rural areas of Kosovo.

Based on these rules, I propose the following operationalisation for judging the peacebuilding outcome of the Communities Committees:

Table 5.3 Outcome operationalisation – communities committee

Rules	Selected rules			Source
	1	2	3	
Formal dimension				
1 Community Committee established	1	2	3	LLSG Art. 53
2 Members of each ethnic group appointed	1	2	3	LLSG Art. 53.1
Practice dimension				
3 Regular meetings (10)	–	2	3	Municpal Statute Art. 39
4 Each ethnic group participates	–	2	3	LLSG Art. 53
5 Annual report	–	–	–	LLSG Art. 53
Content dimension				
6 Review municipal regulations/decisions to ensure respect of minority rights/interests	–	–	3	LLSG Art. 53.2 UNMIK AD 2003/02
7 Review municipal policies, practices, activities to respect minority rights/interests	–	–	3	LLSG Art. 53.2
8 Recommend measures to promote, preserve, develop ethnic, cultural, religious, linguistic identities	–	–	–	LLSG Art. 53.2 UNMIK AD 2003/02

Source: Law on Local Self Government 2008, LLSG = Law on Local Self-Government, UNMIK AD = UNMIK Administrative Instruction.

Prioritisation, selectivity and leverage in the Communities Committee

The use of the ad hoc tactics of prioritisation, selectivity and leverage tactics not only helped international actors to simplify decision-making in the volatile post-war environment of Kosovo but also shaped interaction processes and outcomes as will be explained below.

Prioritisation

Prioritisation was used by international actors after the March 2004 riots, where (mostly) Kosovo Serbs in many multi-ethnic areas of Kosovo were violently attacked by Kosovo Albanians. This violent event, which came as a surprise to many in the international community, was the trigger for the Communities Committees becoming a priority on the international agenda. After March 2004, the international community perceived non-compliance with the reform as a direct security threat. Therefore, peacebuilders showed less tolerance for non-compliance with the reform, insisted on the implementation of a minimum sub-set of rules and engaged in more frequent interactions. This made non-compliance more costly for domestic actors and no implementation less likely.

Selectivity

Selectivity was an important factor in the Communities Committee reform. Peacebuilders were so busy keeping track of several reforms at once that they never demanded the implementation of the full set of rules, nor did they manage to tackle the full set of rules over time. In fact, rule 5 and 8 were never really taken up by peacebuilders. Selectivity thus made full implementation less likely because it provided domestic actors with leeway to capture reforms for their own ends, as they could ignore the rules not selected by peacebuilders without cost. I observed three interaction periods in the case of the Communities Committee reform. First (2000–03), peacebuilders selected a sub-set of rules related to the formal establishment of Communities Committees (rules 1 and 2). Then (2004–08), the selected sub-set of rules was expanded to an inter-ethnic dialogue between ethnic groups (rules 1, 2, 3, and 4). Lastly (2008–12), selectivity shifted to a sub-set of rules promoting the oversight of minority rights at the municipal level (rules 1, 2, 3, 4, 6 and 7). The shifts to new interaction periods were triggered ad hoc by security incidents and changes in the international agenda.

Period I (2000–03): formal establishment (rules 1 and 2)

At first, the selected sub-set of rules centred on the formal establishment of the Communities Committees. Peacebuilders emphasised the need to formally establish the Committees (1) and to appoint representatives of each ethnic group in the municipality to the Committees (2). Shortly after the war, establishing a Committee with both Albanians and Serbs was in and of itself a daunting task. Kosovo Albanians, on the one hand, had little interest in empowering those viewed as responsible for years of oppression. Kosovo Serbs, on the other hand, had little interest in cooperating with Kosovo/UNMIK institutions as they regarded Belgrade as their government and mistrusted Albanian politicians. It was only in 2003 that UNMIK issued more concrete guidelines for the functioning of Committees once they were established.

Period II (2004–08): inter-ethnic dialogue (rules 1, 2, 3 and 4)

In the second period, international actors selected a sub-set of rules fostering inter-ethnic dialogue. Peacebuilders not only emphasised the need to formally establish the Committees (1) and to appoint representatives of each ethnic group in the municipality to the Committees (2) but also emphasized the need to hold regular meetings (3) with the participation of all ethnic groups (4) and to implement common activities or projects for minority communities. This selectivity shift towards inter-ethnic dialogue was triggered by the March 2004 riots, after which UNMIK commissioned a comprehensive 'Assessment of Municipal Communities Committees' (UNMIK 2004).

Period III (2008–12): oversight of minority rights (rules 1, 2, 3, 4, 6 and 7)

In the third period, peacebuilders concentrated on a sub-set of rules to strengthen the oversight mechanism for minority rights at the municipal level. Correspondingly, the international focus shifted to the content dimension of the reform. Aside from emphasizing the need for formal establishment (1), the appointment of representatives of each ethnic group (2) and regular meetings (3) with the participation of all ethnic groups (4), peacebuilders demanded that committees review municipal regulations (6) as well as municipal policies and practices (7) to ensure that they respected minority rights and interests in order to strengthen the role of the Committee as an oversight mechanism for minority rights compliance. The selectivity shift was triggered by changes in the international agenda after Kosovo's independence and by routine programme evaluations. With UNMIK's withdrawal, international actors considered domestic control of municipal politics to be more relevant. Furthermore, two OSCE reports that were rather critical of the Committee's functioning, the 'Communities Rights Assessment Report' (OSCE 2009b) and 'Protection and Promotion of the Rights of Communities in Kosovo' (OSCE 2009b), proposed to focus more on the substantive content of the Committee's work.[96]

Leverage

Period I (2000–03): higher leverage

In the first period, peacebuilders only occasionally used the higher leverage instruments of supervision, preferring instead to rely on lower leverage instruments such as dialogue facilitation, monitoring and advice. UNMIK Municipal Administrators were in a position to use executive power to appoint representatives, formally establish Communities Committees or schedule meetings. However, UNMIK also depended on domestic cooperation, meaning that international actors had to find individuals ready to be appointed and ready to attend meetings. UNMIK, therefore, mainly used lower leverage means, such as the facilitation of informal meetings between Albanian and Serbian local leaders in an attempt to (re-)build trust, or the providing of advice to municipal authorities and Serbian leaders to establish such Committees.

Period II (2004–08): higher leverage

In the second period, peacebuilders resorted to the high leverage instruments of supervision and financial assistance, but also made use of capacity building, outreach, monitoring, reporting and advice. UNMIK Municipal Administrators remained in a position to use executive power to appoint representatives, formally establish Communities Committees and schedule meetings, but handed over the responsibility of leading Communities Committees to local municipal actors. A variety of donors started to provide small amounts of financial assistance for projects developed by Communities Committees. Furthermore, UNMIK asked municipalities to provide financial compensation to committee members as a further financial incentive. UNMIK's post-March 2004 monitoring report on Communities Committees recommended an increase in round tables, outreach activities to minority communities, capacity building for Communities Committee members and more advice to municipal authorities to provide an 'encouraging environment' for the Committees (UNMIK 2004). In 2005, the OSCE invited all Communities Committee Chairpersons to a capacity building workshop called 'Discriminatory Practices and Mediation Techniques' and developed a capacity training package to be delivered to all Committee members (Wyart and Simpson 2005). The OSCE also started an outreach campaign in 2005 and printed 20,000 leaflets to inform citizens about the existence of these Committees (Wyart and Simpson 2005). Kosovo-wide coordination of such activities, however, decreased after 2006.

Period III (2008–12): lower leverage

In the third period, peacebuilders decreased the intensity of their activities and applied only lower leverage instruments of capacity building: monitoring, reporting and advice. The OSCE was the only organisation left to continuously support the reform. Field offices provided capacity-building workshops based on individual needs assessments and offered advice to municipal authorities and Committee members. They required municipalities to continue to provide Committee members with financial compensation as an incentive to attend and participate in meetings.

Communities Committee reform in Zabel/Šumarak

At the Committee? We discuss there, for example, the Ashkalis' requests: they ask to clean the road, to do something, or they have request for food for poor peoples. Serbs want – as Serbs are ... (laughing) They always make trouble for us. On the one hand, they accept Kosovo's structures, and on the other, they keep their relations with Serbia's structures. They must acknowledge that Kosovo is now a state for all citizens, not only for Albanians, but also for all people who live in Kosovo – Turkish, Ashkalis. Serbs shall change their opinion.

(Albanian member of the Communities Committee in Zabel/Šumarak, 29/10/2012)

External–domestic negotiations over how to implement the Communities Committee reform in Zabel/Šumarak were not as cooperative as in the previous case of Participatory Budget Planning. The reform resulted in captured implementation, as it was used by domestic actors to advance their priority of socio-economic development. Both the international capacity and local resistance theories would instead have predicted no implementation as an outcome due to the fact that Communities Committee reform took place in a low capacity policy field and because the norm of minority rights was met with resistance in the population. Peacebuilders' ad hoc tactics help to explain why the reform did not result in a no implementation outcome. For example, prioritisation made no implementation less likely after the 2004 March riots: The growing international insistence on implementing a minimum sub-set of rules made it more costly for Kosovo Albanians and Kosovo Serbs to continue with outright resistance, and domestic actors gave in to international demands. Selectivity, however, enabled domestic actors to drop those rules that had never been raised by international actors, and made full implementation less likely. The fact that increased leverage in the form of coercion or financial compensation was limited to a minimum sub-set of rules offered domestic actors leeway to exploit the Communities Committee for their own development concerns at a low cost. The constraining environment of interaction, characterised by weak support for minority rights, proved conducive to a peacebuilding outcome of captured implementation because international demands were often met with resistance or modification and less often cooperation.

The most important actors in the external–domestic interactions over the Communities Committee reform were the Mayor, his Municipal Officer for

Community and Returns, and members of the local Serbian community on the domestic side; and, on the peacebuilders' side, the UNMIK Municipal Administrator and the OSCE Community Team and Municipal Team.

The following section presents the external–domestic interaction process according to the three interaction periods with their particular sub-set of rules.

Period I (2000–03): formal establishment (rules 1 and 2)

The first years after the intervention, establishing a Communities Committee in Zabel/Šumarak seemed almost impossible. The Serb population in the surrounding villages declined any cooperation with UNMIK and Kosovo Albanian dominated institutions. Mistrust prevailed on both sides, and the feeling of insecurity among Kosovo Serbs remained strong, as did the pressure from Belgrade and North Mitrovica not to engage (OMIK and OSCE 2003).[97] The UNMIK Municipal Administrator decided to use a persuasion-based strategy to start an inter-ethnic dialogue between Kosovo Serbs and Albanians in Zabel/Šumarak. Especially members of the Kosovo Serbian community reacted with resistance to international advances to establish the Committee at first. It took until February 2001 to organise a first formal meeting between Serbian and Albanian representatives (Lane and Brown 2006). The UNMIK Administrator then regularly held meetings with individuals from both sides to convince them of the benefits of cooperation (Lane and Brown 2006), and facilitated informal meetings between representatives from both sides, which took the form of dinners at his private home.[98] Further UNMIK-facilitated meetings were needed to gain acceptance for the Communities Committee among Serbian party members and village leaders (Lane and Brown 2006). For the first time in 2003, some Serbian village leaders agreed to join the Communities Committee. The UNMIK Municipal Administrator used his supervisory powers to appoint Communities Committee members only after having received consent from both sides to establish a Communities Committee (OSCE 2003).[99]

A first inaugural meeting took place in 2003 (UNMIK 2004), but domestic actors reacted with foot-dragging strategies to further international attempts at making the Committee work: Serbian Committee members in particular regularly cancelled their participation in scheduled meetings (UNMIK 2004). This was due to a variety of reasons: Inter-ethnic incidents or political conflicts at the local or national level served as a catalyst for Serbian abstention, but pressure to abstain also emanated from within Kosovo Serbian political structures, most notably from North Mitrovica.[100] UNMIK only occasionally worked on re-activating the Committee through dialogue, but mainly backed down when confronted with resistance.[101] There were several reasons for UNMIK's capitulation: First, the priority requirement of formal establishment was met; second, the UNMIK Administrator was aware that the Committee was highly dependent on the general attitude of the Serbian community and that UNMIK's influence on these general dynamics was limited (Lane and Brown 2006); and third, UNMIK had only a limited capacity to take care of the reform. Amidst the fragile security situation, minority returns and regular water and electricity cuts, making the Communities Committees work did not figure as a priority on UNMIK's local agenda.[102] The non-functioning of the Committee was, thus, the result of domestic resistance and peacebuilders' subsequent capitulation in the face of a huge array of simultaneous tasks.

Period II (2004–08): inter-ethnic dialogue (rules 1, 2, 3 and 4)

Kosovo Serb resistance to participation in Kosovo institutions hardened in Zabel/Šumarak after the March 2004 riots, even in relation to the Communities Committee. The fact that Zabel/Šumarak was so close to North Kosovo, with its Serbian majority municipalities, encouraged an even more hard-line stance. Yet the March 2004 riots against Kosovo Serbs also put minority protection at the top of the peacebuilding agenda and made functional Communities Committee a top priority for peacebuilders. Peacebuilders therefore intensified diplomatic persuasion and the facilitation of informal meetings after the March riots. Both the UNMIK Municipal Administration and the OSCE field offices tried to gain support by lobbying for the Communities Committee within Municipal Government bodies and among Serbian leaders.[103] The UNMIK Administrator invited members to informal meetings as well as to official Communities Committee meetings.[104] The OSCE Headquarters invited the Mayor and involved Directors of Zabel/Šumarak to a capacity building training on Communities Committees, and the OSCE field office organised a capacity building workshop for the Committee members (Wyart and Simpson 2005).[105] The OSCE also distributed leaflets on the work of the Communities Committee in Zabel/Šumarak (Wyart and Simpson 2005). An international humanitarian NGO simultaneously started to work on facilitating inter-ethnic dialogue in one of Zabel/Šumarak's villages, Samodrezhë/Samodreža. The NGO rewarded domestic cooperation with financial assistance for infrastructure projects for the water supply, electricity and sewage, which already points to the fact that Committees were used to address development concerns of the minority community, but not to address minority rights related issues. International activities, however, declined over the course of 2006.

These international efforts yielded limited impact on Kosovo Albanians and Serbs, who mainly responded with resistance or foot-dragging. Although the Communities Committee had been formally established, it remained largely non-functional as Kosovo Serbs regularly refused to accept invitations to Committee meetings (UNMIK 2004). Kosovo Albanians were more open to cooperating with Serbs and Roma but were not willing to invest time and resources or to compromise in order to overcome Serbian resistance. For example, the municipality of Zabel/Šumarak refused to provide financial compensation for attending meetings. In general, if domestic actors conceded to peacebuilders' demands to meet, both sides did so reluctantly and without investing time or financial resources.

Reform implementation in that period was therefore sluggish. The Municipal Assembly approved no new members between 2003 and 2009 – despite municipal elections in 2002 and 2007 that would have required a re-election of the Committee members – because finding members from the Serbian minority who were willing to participate was difficult. The composition of the Communities Committee thus remained the same. Meetings took place on a highly irregular basis and only on the initiative of the UNMIK Administrator. Whether or not meetings actually took place depended to a large extent on the larger political climate. The few meetings that took place provided space for discussions regarding the concerns of minority groups, such as humanitarian bus transportation, firewood for schools or waste collection in minority quarters and villages.[106] The Committee, however, did not plan projects to solve the problems or provide recommendations for measures to the Municipal Administration or Assembly, nor did it tackle minority rights.[107]

The main forum for addressing and solving the concerns of the minority population remained informal meetings facilitated by international actors. This was the alternative strategy peacebuilders had developed to address the issue of minority protection in the municipality – the organisation of informal meetings between municipal representatives and Serbian leaders to support a dialogue on the concerns of minority citizens (Lane and Brown 2006).

Period III (2008–12): oversight of minority rights (rules 1, 2, 3, 4, 6 and 7)

Kosovo's 2008 unilateral declaration of independence led to further increases in international attention to minority protection at the local level (CSSP 2007). Peacebuilders were not only determined to ensure a minimum sub-set of rules (ruels 1, 2, 3 and 4), but also aimed at transforming the Committee into an effective institution that engaged in protecting minority rights and interests (rules 6, 7). The OSCE made Communities Committees a monitoring priority for 2008 and the following years.[108] The OSCE Municipal Teams and Community Teams thus closely followed the development of the Communities Committee and, if deemed necessary, intervened with advice based on their monitoring data. For example, OSCE used advice to ensure that meetings took place or to motivate disappointed members to stay engaged. In November 2011, the OSCE Community Team invited the Communities Committee members to two capacity building workshops in a nearby hotel to discuss the oversight functions of the Committee (Communities Committee Zabel/Šumarak 2011).

During this third phase, domestic actors responded more with cooperation and modification and less with resistance. As a result, there was considerable improvement in the functioning of the Communities Committee. This was not, however, a mere result of peacebuilders' activities, but of changing local political dynamics, especially within the Serbian community. Indeed, the Serbian attitude towards cooperation with Kosovo institutions had shifted within Zabel/Šumarak's Serbian villages after Kosovo's independence. Younger Serbs from Zabel/Šumarak had started to become active in the SLS, the only Serbian party participating in Kosovo's institutions. Their reasoning was that if they wanted to stay in Kosovo (and be employed), they had no alternative than to cooperate with Kosovo institutions.[109] This meant that for the first time since the war, there was a politically organised group of local Serbian citizens that promoted integration into Kosovo and that actively sought institutional cooperation with municipal authorities in Zabel/Šumarak (OSCE 2009a).

Feeling that support in the Serbian community had increased, the long-standing Serbian Chairperson of the Communities Committee started regularly sending out invitations for meetings in 2009 (OSCE 2009b).[110] The OSCE advice to elect new members to the Communities Committee was taken up after the municipal elections in November 2009 (OSCE 2009b). The Assembly approved a list of new Communities Committee members in January 2010,[111] the constituting session was held in April 2010 (MA Zabel/Šumarak 2010a, Municipality Zabel/Šumarak 2010a), and regular meetings convened thereafter (MLGA 2011). The offer of €50 financial compensation for attendance at each session certainly sparked further motivation to cooperate in some.[112] The Mayor was critical of the Committee's work because, in his opinion, members always discussed the same problems but did not develop solutions (MA Zabel/Šumarak 2010b).[113] The Mayor then issued a decision in January 2011 to limit the number of Committee meetings to four per year (meaning that the municipality would have to pay less in meeting allowances),[114] which triggered an internal discussion in the Committee about the quality of its work.[115] This resulted in the appointment of a new Chairperson and in the election of two additional Serbian representatives (MA Zabel/Šumarak 2011c) so that the Mayor restored the previous rule of ten meetings per year.

The Committee dedicated its discussions to the development and welfare concerns of the communities.[116] The Committee did not systematically review municipality policies for the protection of minority rights or interests, nor did it recommend measures to promote minority identities. It also refrained from regularly overseeing Municipal Assembly legislative activities. Sensitive political topics were thus circumvented. Instead, the Committee concentrated on advancing the domestic priority of socio-economic development and discussed intensively problems of social housing, waste collection and water provision in Serbian and Ashkali areas.

Peacebuilding outcome: captured implementation

The outcome of the budget planning reform in Zabel/Šumarak shows clear traits of captured implementation that helped minority communities to advance their priority of socio-economic development. Issues with a higher potential of politicisation – use of all official languages, property related issues or education – were less likely to be discussed. Instead, the Committee engaged with the most pressing issues of the day-to-day life of the Serbs and the Roma: the development of infrastructure and basic public services.[117] One Communities Committee member described the work as follows:

> In every meeting, we try to discuss and solve every one of their [the minorities] problems to treat them as a part of our citizens and make them feel equal to us.
>
> (Interview 58, Communities Committee member, Zabel/Šumarak,
> 29/10/2012)

The work of the Committee is thus devoted to the improvement of the economic and social situation of minority communities and connected to socioeconomic development: sewage systems, garbage collection, social housing and food. The reform was thus exploited to push forward development issues, which was what minority communities – just like the Albanian majority – cared about most.

The findings are discussed according to the indicators in the formal, practice and content dimensions of the outcome.

FORMAL DIMENSION

Rule 1. Community Committee established: The Committee was first formally established in 2003 (OSCE 2003).

Rule 2. Members of each ethnic group appointed: Representatives of all ethnic groups were appointed – three Albanians, one Turk, one Serb and two Roma (MA Zabel/Šumarak 2011b) and two additional Serbian seats were established in 2011.

PRACTICE DIMENSION

Rule 3. Regular meetings: Nine meetings were held in 2012, which is one meeting less than projected (MLGA 2013).

Rule 4. Each ethnic group participates: Representatives of all ethnic groups participated in the meetings[118] as well as the Municipal Assembly Chairperson and the Officer for Communities.

Rule 5. Annual reports: An annual report for 2012 was submitted to the Municipal Assembly in January 2013. Albanian Assembly members complained that the report did not contain enough information about the impact of the Committee's work, particularly whether the Committee had an impact on 'increasing Serbian willingness to integrate into Kosovo' (MA Zabel/Šumarak 2013). This shows how each side re-adapts the institution for its own goals.

CONTENT DIMENSION

Rule 6. Review municipal regulations to ensure respect for minority rights/interests:
The Communities Committee did not review municipal acts drafted or
approved by the Municipal Assembly to ensure they respected community
rights.[119]

Rule 7. Review municipal policies/practices with regard to minority rights/interests:
The Committee did not review policies related to political rights, but rather
those related to social welfare and the quality of services provided in minority
areas. Most discussion in the Committee centred on problems of social
housing, waste collection and water provision in Serbian and Ashkali areas.[120]
The committee filed a few recommendations with the Mayor and the
responsible Directorates for how to improve the situation with regard to these
social and developmental issues.[121]

*Rule 8. Recommend measures to the Municipal Assembly to promote their ethnic iden-
tity, culture and language:* There were no recommendations to protect or
promote the ethnic, cultural or linguistic identity of the minority groups.

Communities Committee reform in Bregore/Brdašce

> INTERVIEWEE: The cooperation with the OSCE is positive. However,
> sometimes they are also boring. For example, we have put signs at
> the entrance of the town, and "Welcome to" is written in three lan-
> guages – in Albanian, Serbian, and English, and then Bregore was
> written only in Albanian. So they came to us, "Yeah, you should
> also write this in Serbian, which is a legal obligation". They're small
> things, very boring things.
>
> I: So, you don't really agree with their focus on minority rights.
>
> INTERVIEWEE: We say, "Oh, good idea, now we are going to do this".
> But we are not doing anything.
>
> (Interview 18 with municipal official, Bregore/Brdašce,
> 10/05/2012)

The Communities Committee reform in Bregore/Brdašce resulted in
captured implementation – just like in Zabel/Šumarak. Domestic actors also
used it to exploit the reform for their own development concerns. Again, the
international capacity and local resistance arguments would have expected no
implementation as an outcome due to the fact that the Communities Committee reform took place in a low capacity policy field and only enjoyed
weak support from the population. The analytical framework of peacebuilding interactions helps explain why the reform did not end up as no implementation: First of all, prioritisation after the March 2004 riots led to growing
international insistence on implementing a minimum sub-set of rules, which
made outright resistance more costly for Kosovo Albanians and Kosovo Serbs.
No implementation thus became less likely, although the functioning of the
Committee proved unstable over time. The selectivity of international actors

allowed domestic actors to ignore rules not paid attention to by peacebuilders. Full implementation thus became less likely. Increased leverage in the form of coercion or financial compensation to advance the implementation of a minimum sub-set of rules again made no implementation less likely. Furthermore, the constraining environment of interaction, characterised by weak support for minority rights and a competitive style of politics, led to a situation in which international demands were often met with resistance, modification, foot-dragging, and, less often, cooperation.

The negotiation of the Communities Committees reform in Bregore/Brdašce was shaped by three groups: The domestic side was represented by the municipality leaders (including the Mayor and the Serbian Officer for Communities) and the political leaders or representatives of the minority communities, and the peacebuilding side was represented by UNMIK, the OSCE Community Team and Municipal Team.

The following section analyses external–domestic interactions in three interaction periods with a particular sub-set of rules for each.

Period I (2000–03): formal establishment (rules 1 and 2)

In the first phase, peacebuilders in Bregore/Brdašce focused on formally establishing the Communities Committee. As in Zabel/Šumarak, setting up institutions fostering cooperation between Kosovo Serbs and Kosovo Albanians proved to be difficult: The majority of the Serbian community in Bregore/Brdašce clearly favoured boycotting Kosovo institutions, and Kosovo Albanians, although not openly opposed, proved reluctant to support the Committee. To initiate the reform process, peacebuilders first used dialogue and advice to re-establish trust between the two groups: UNMIK facilitated informal meetings between the Kosovo Serbs and Albanians and provided advice to individual actors from both sides.[122] UNMIK also met regularly with village leaders and those considered to be moderate Serbs in order to gain their cooperation to participate in Kosovo institutions.[123] The Kosovo Serbian community reacted first with resistance and later with foot-dragging. Pressure from Belgrade and the Bregore/Brdašce Kosovo Serbian community kept most individuals from agreeing to join the Committee.[124] Albanian municipal actors were also reluctant to support the reform, as the Committee was perceived as a source of potential inter-ethnic conflict. Most Albanians were not ready to give power to those who, as they saw it, had dominated their lives for so long.[125]

By March 2003, after several years of advice and facilitation, UNMIK had managed to compile a list of moderate individuals from the Serbian and Roma, Ashkali and Egyptian (RAE) minorities to formally join the Committee. UNMIK used its supervisory powers to propose this list of Committee members to the Municipal Assembly and the Committee was formally established in March 2003 (OSCE 2006).[126] Yet the Committee proved dysfunctional due to the resistance and foot-dragging strategies on the domestic side:

Most sessions were boycotted due to political conflicts between the different Kosovo Albanian parties or, more frequently, due to Serbian representatives' abstention (UNMIK 2004). In general, Serbian representatives enjoyed limited backing within their community for cooperating with Kosovo institutions and were vulnerable to pressure from the wider Serbian community (UNMIK 2004).[127] In the volatile, post-war situation, pressure to abstain from meetings increased when inter-ethnic incidents of local or national importance occurred (UNMIK 2004). Confronted with domestic resistance, UNMIK backed down on their demands for regular meetings. If peacebuilders were in need of inter-ethnic cooperation, they resorted to the facilitation of informal meetings, a strategy I would call substitution.[128]

Period II (2004–08): inter-ethnic dialogue (rules 1, 2, 3 and 4)

After the March 2004 riots, prioritisation of the Communities Committee reform made peacebuilders in Bregore/Brdašce insist more emphatically on the implementation of a minimum sub-set of rules. Formal establishment (rule 1, 2) did not suffice; peacebuilders insisted on regular meetings (rule 3) and the participation of all ethnic groups (rule 4) to improve inter-ethnic dialogue. This posed a challenge because most Kosovo Serbs had withdrawn from the Communities Committee right after the March 2004 violence.

As the Communities Committee now represented a top priority on the international agenda, the UNMIK Municipal Administrator was less willing to tolerate domestic non-compliance. He used the higher leverage instruments of financial assistance and financial rewards alongside facilitation and advice and furthermore increased the frequency of meetings with domestic counterparts. UNMIK made sure that Committee members were provided with financial compensation from the municipal budget to provide additional incentive for participation.[129] The OSCE Municipal Team increased monitoring and advice activities, provided capacity building workshops for all Communities Committee members and offered small-scale financial assistance for local inter-ethnic projects (Wyart and Simpson 2005).[130] In addition, a German NGO, in cooperation with the OSCE field office, started a capacity building project in 2007 to improve inter-ethnic dialogue and cooperation between the Communities Committee and the Municipal Assembly (CSSP 2007).[131] During three workshops, municipal officials and Committee members worked on improving cooperation (CSSP 2007).

Domestic actors responded to the international activities with a mixture of cooperation, foot-dragging and resistance. At first, Kosovo Serbs resisted international demands to participate again in the Community Committee. By autumn 2004, they had consented, however, to participate once more in Committee meetings (Wyart and Simpson 2005) – most probably because UNMIK had ensured that financial compensation would be provided and because of a planned NGO project. Meetings took place on a more regular basis (Wyart and Simpson 2005). The problems facing minority communities

– freedom of movement, garbage, water and electricity – were discussed (Wyart and Simpson 2005). This two-year boost of activity was not made to last, and at the end of 2006, Serbian boycott of meetings increased. International advice to resume meetings failed (OSCE 2006). A UN report describes the problems of the Committee in Bregore/Brdašce with the following words:

> Specifically, the non-attendance of Kosovo Serbian representatives has been a particular issue in many municipalities [referring to Bregore/ Brdašce], where it had quite often obstructed and negatively impacted on the work of the Committees for several months. Root causes of these challenges range from an inadequate selection of members representing the communities (generating a deficit of legitimacy at the grassroots level with a consequent misrepresentation of communities' needs and interests) to the internal power struggles among and between community representatives in the established Committees.
>
> (UN and CCPR 2006)

The de-motivation of Committee members might have been caused by the lack of concrete projects after 2006 but was also caused by the lack of a financial incentive, resulting from irregular payments from the municipality. A politically active Serb told me that Committee members complained: "I don't have time to go to the municipality for free".[132] With the start of the German capacity building project in spring 2007, the regularity of Communities Committee meetings and Serbian participation increased again (CSSP). The impact of the project was short-lived, however: The Committee came to a new standstill in 2007 when a Mayor from the PDK – whom Serbs mistrusted because of PDK's strong connections to the UÇK – resumed office.[133] Reform implementation thus alternated between phases of activity and phases of boycott. The work of the Committee was far from consolidated and mainly kept alive by financial incentives.

Period III (2008–12): oversight of minority rights (rules 1, 2, 3, 4, 6 and 7)

After the unilateral declaration of independence in February 2008, Serbs completely withdrew from Kosovo institutions, including the Communities Committee in Bregore/Brdašce.[134] Peacebuilders in Bregore/Brdašce thus had to focus their attention on re-establishing the Committee formally (rule 1, 2) and making it work (rule 3, 4), in addition to rendering it an effective mechanism for minority protection (rule 6, 7). They did so using the higher leverage instrument of advocacy coalitions and the lower leverage instruments of advice and capacity building.

In a first attempt at re-establishment, the OSCE advised the municipal authorities in formal and informal meetings on the importance of re-establishing the Communities Committee. The OSCE also contacted individual Committee members.[135] In a second attempt, the OSCE changed strategy and advised the Mayor to appoint new Committee members.[136] The official argument was that the law envisioned re-elections after every municipal election, but members had been the same since 2003. The unofficial reason was that the OSCE, which had not bothered about the legal situation before, hoped to install more cooperative individuals. In a third attempt at re-establishment – after the extraordinary elections in December 2010 – the OSCE Community Team and the regional office of UNMIK joined forces and formed an advocacy coalition to push the Mayor to re-establish the Committee with cooperative representatives.[137]

At first, international advice to re-establish the Committee was met with resistance from Kosovo Serbs and foot-dragging from the municipality.[138] In contrast to Zabel/Sumarak, Kosovo Serbs in Bregore/Brdašce boycotted Kosovo institutions in the first years after independence, although the new PDK-led government showed interest in setting up the Committee. The Mayor started an initiative once to set up the Committee, upon OSCE advice, but concluded that "it was really hard to bring them to one table" and stopped pursuing the project.[139] The OSCE's second attempt to re-install the Committee was also met with cooperation by the Mayor,[140] but inner-Serbian power fighting inhibited the process: While the Officer for Communities – tasked with identifying new minority representatives – supported re-establishment, the then Serbian Deputy Mayor opposed it.[141] Peacebuilders backed down from pushing further on the issue and relied on the Community Office as their main contact point for Serbian concerns. The third attempt to re-establish the Committee took place in 2011 when a new Mayor had taken office and the Serbian Deputy Mayor – the identified 'blocking factor' – had been discharged by the previous Mayor.[142] This was the chance for peacebuilders to get movement in the Committee again. Directly after the extraordinary election, UNMIK and the OSCE formed an advocacy coalition and organised a total of three meetings to make the Mayor aware of his legal obligation to establish a Communities Committee.[143] The Mayor, not yet in a position to ignore such vehement international advice, reacted with cooperation. The OSCE summarised its success as follows:

> If the OSCE as an international organisation is paying attention to one issue in particular, it is more likely that you will get attention from [the] municipality.
> (Interview with staff of the OSCE Community Team, 18/10/2012)

The Mayor justified his support of the Committee by telling his fellow politicians that the municipality had to follow the legislation (MA Bregore/Brdašce 2011a). The Mayor claimed to be interested to "hear about their [minorities] problems and find a way to help them" in order to show the Serbian community that the municipality "does not make any difference between people" and to "make municipal institutions stronger".[144] These quotes show again that the Albanian side saw the Communities Committee first and foremost as a tool to integrate Kosovo Serbs into Kosovo institutions and weaken Serbian parallel structures. In March 2011, he asked the Assembly to nominate the Albanian Committee members (MA Bregore/Brdašce 2011a). The Community Officer was then tasked with identifying the minority candidates. The OSCE Municipal Team advised the Community Officer organising public discussions with the community to identify possible candidates, but the Mayor and the Community Officer chose to personally appoint Committee members – creating the typical dependency structures prevalent in Kosovo. Mayor and Community Officer met with village leaders to identify cooperative individuals and took eight months to select Serbian participants.[145] At the end of the process, the Community Officer, upon the Mayor's consent, nominated his wife and three other candidates.[146] Committee members were thus dependent upon the consent of the Community Officer, the Mayor and Municipal Assembly – but not particularly upon the consent of their respective communities. The Committee started its work in December 2011, following a routine of monthly meetings (MLGA 2013). As the Mayor had promised the "members would get paid" (MA Bregore/Brdašce 2011a), each member received financial compensation of roughly €100 for every meeting attended, which again was an important incentive for participation. The Committee mainly dealt with topics related to socio-economic development such as garbage collection or sewage.[147] A Committee member named the most pressing topics discussed:

> The most frequent topics we discuss for Dobro Selo (the Serbian village) are water, sanitation and electricity.
> (Interview 39, Communities Committee member, Bregore/Brdašce, 01/01/2012)

The meetings were, thus, used as a forum for discussion of development concerns with the Mayor and Directors – although this did not necessarily lead to solutions to the problems discussed but often to mutual accusations.[148] The Committee also implemented development projects together with donor agencies.[149]

Peacebuilding outcome: captured implementation

The implementation of the Communities Committee reform shows a clear inclination to captured implementation in Bregore/Brdašce, transforming the Committee into a development-promoting machine for minorities but keeping out rights-related issues. It is the local population's interest in development that represents the common ground for Kosovo Albanians, Serbs and RAE in the Committee. The Communities Committee, thus, concentrated on development issues, while more politically sensitive topics such as use of language, discrimination in employment, and safety and security were left out. One Serbian participant justifies their participation as follows:

> It certainly doesn't do any damage. I think there is a use for it [the Committee] because everyone is informed about the problems we have.
> (Interview, Communities Committee member, translated from Serbian, 16/10/2012)

The above statement that minority rights provisions "don't do any damage" is a widely used justification by Serbs participating in Kosovo's institutions. There is reluctance on all sides, however, to politically engage in the work of the Committee. Albanian municipal officials had no interest in empowering Serbs and thus perceived the Communities Committee as a source of inter-ethnic tensions. At the same time, however, they were interested in Serbian participation in Kosovo institutions as a way to weaken the Serbian parallel structures and strengthen Kosovo statehood. The solution was to keep tight control over the Committee, creating the described dependency structures by appointing Committee members and offering financial compensation for their participation. Dependency structures thus minimised the risk of both Serbian empowerment and inter-ethnic tensions.[150] Minority members were aware of the Albanian municipality's grip over the Committee. In response, they chose a strategy of accommodation and avoided politically sensitive issues. The use of these strategies led to the focus on development projects. However, not all members in the Serbian community agreed with the accommodating stance of participating Serbs:

> There are people working for Kosovo institutions for whatever. I don't want this, I told the president that I want to be a partner in everything and not a servant, and that I can tell them that something is ok and something not. If something isn't ok for my community, for my family, for me, then it is not ok. And I can't say, "Okay, let's destroy our community so that it is easier for my family and me".
> (Interview, Serb, translated from Serbian, 04/10/2012)

Yet the more critical voices were not appointed to the Committee. Ultimately, peacebuilders were not successful in enforcing their vision of the Committee as a promoter of minority rights and interests in Bregore/Brdašce.

FORMAL DIMENSION

Rule 1. Community Committee established: The Communities Committee was first formally established in 2003.
Rule 2. Members of each ethnic group appointed: Three Kosovo Albanians, four Kosovo Serbs, and two Roma and Ashkali were appointed by the Municipal Assembly, upon prior identification by the Officer of Communities and approval by the Mayor (MA Bregore/Brdašce 2011a).[151]

PRACTICE DIMENSION

Rule 3. Regular meetings: The Committee held ten regular meetings in 2012 (MLGA 2013).

Rule 4. Each ethnic group participates: All minority groups attended. The Mayor also participated, whereas Municipal Assembly members did not.[152] On the one hand, the interest from the executive branch – especially the Mayor – is a positive signal, but it also further concentrates power in the executive branch, particularly in a situation where there was no communication between the Communities Committee and the Municipal Assembly.

Rule 5. Annual reports: The Communities Committee did not report to the Municipal Assembly and minority representatives were not informed of the Municipal Assembly's work.[153] There was thus no way to act as control mechanism.

CONTENT DIMENSION

Rule 6. Review municipal regulations to ensure respect for minority rights/interests: The Committee did not review municipal regulations by the Municipal Assembly with the purpose of ensuring the respect for minority rights and/or interests.[154]

Rule 7. Review municipal policies/practices with regard to minority rights/interests: Municipal policies are not reviewed with regard to minority rights but rather with regard to socio-economic development projects for minorities; for example, equal access to public services. Committee members were devoted to the improvement of the most urgent development-related problems in Serbs' and Roma's day-to-day lives: Water, sewage, garbage collection and electricity.[155]

Rule 8. Recommend measures to the Municipal Assembly to promote their ethnic identity, culture and language: No measures to protect or promote the ethnic, cultural or linguistic identity of the minority groups were recommended.

Summary: external–domestic interactions in Communities Committee reform

This section reviews the findings from the Communities Committees case studies and discusses the potential of the framework of peacebuilding interactions to explain peacebuilding outcomes. Communities Committee is a case of low international capacity invested and strong local resistance against minority rights. Advocates of the international capacity approach and advocates of the local resistance approach would both predict no implementation as the peacebuilding outcome. However, external–domestic interactions led to a captured implementation in Zabel/Šumarak as well as in Bregore/Brdašce, meaning that the Committees were more focused on development-related issues of infrastructure, access to public services and welfare, instead of on overseeing the municipalities' protection of minority rights. It is thus apparently possible to start reform implementation even in a situation of low capacity and weak domestic supports, counter to the expectations of the international capacity and local resistance arguments.

In the following paragraphs, I summarise how an analysis of external–domestic interactions can provide an explanation for the peacebuilding outcomes in Communities Committee cases. Again, the Communities Committee points to the fact that external–domestic interactions seem to be a necessary condition for the start of reform implementation. As was seen with Participatory Budget Planning, nothing happened unless peacebuilders made it happen: Although the Communities Committee law had been already adopted in 2000, the first attempts to formally establish these Committees in Zabel/Šumarak and Bregore/Brdašce took place in 2003 upon peacebuilders' initiatives. This points to serious domestic resistance and to the different set of priorities pursued by peacebuilders and domestic elites.

Peacebuilding outcomes

Communities Committees resulted in captured implementation in Zabel/ Šumarak as well as in Bregore/Brdašce. This means that peacebuilders were able to strengthen the norm of minority rights to some extent and to provide a space for inter-ethnic encounters between Kosovo Albanians and Kosovo Serbs. At the same time, domestic actors were able to use the leeway inherent in the interaction process to push the domestic priority of socio-economic development: The Communities Committee was used to take care of the development concerns of the minority population and to help in their everyday struggle for survival, dealing with infrastructure, access to public services and welfare. Yet the Committees did not function as an institutionalised control mechanism of the Municipal Government or the Assembly. My observations equal the conclusions of an OSCE report that states: "Although the multi-ethnic composition of the communities Committees is widely ensured, its performance is generally unsatisfactory, in particular regarding the frequency of the meetings and the relevance of issues dealt with" (OSCE 2009b). The OSCE found the failure of the Committees to review municipal legal drafts, plans or budgets from the municipalities "especially striking" (OSCE 2011) – meaning that Committees were far from exercising a control function over municipal institutions. The reports portray these findings as the result of 'misunderstandings', but they are in fact the result of the different priorities of the international and domestic sides and of the fact that minority rights are politically contested among Kosovo Serbs as well as Kosovo Albanians.

Prioritisation, selectivity and leverage

Peacebuilders' ad hoc tactics of prioritisation, selectivity and leverage also shaped the external–domestic interaction in the case of Communities Committee.

Table 5.4 Peacebuilding outcomes of communities committees

Communities committee outcomes

Dimension	Zabel/Šumarak	Bregore/Brdašce
Formal dimension		
1 Community Committee established	Yes	Yes
2 Members of each ethnic group appointed	Yes	Yes
Practice dimension		
3 Regular meetings (10)	In-Between	In-Between
4 All ethnic groups participate	Yes	Yes
5 Annual report	Yes	No
Content dimension		
6 Review municipal regulations/decisions to ensure respect of minority rights/interests	No	No
7 Review municipal policies, practices, activities to respect minority rights/interests	In-Between	In-Between
8 Recommend measures to promote, preserve, develop ethnic, cultural, religious, linguistic identities	In-Between	No
Outcome	Captured implementation	Captured implementation

Source: Own compilation.

Prioritisation had an important effect on the reform outcome as it made no implementation less likely. As long as 'non-compliance' with Communities Committee was not considered a security threat (2000–03) – and was thus not prioritised – peacebuilders tended to back down from their demands when resistance became evident and had little success beyond formally establishing the Committees. Peacebuilders chose to back down because they were dependent on domestic cooperation in numerous other policy fields and had little interest in spoiling relations over one issue, but also because they were aware of tense relations between the two ethnic groups. Yet when the March 2004 riots occurred, implementing the Communities Committee reform became a top priority for peacebuilders to calm the security situation. Peacebuilders were thus less inclined to tolerate Serbian resistance against the Communities Committees. The effect was an increased frequency of interaction and increased pressure to implement minimum sub-set of rules as progress had to be reported in every UN Security Council report.

Selectivity shaped the process of external–domestic interaction in that the selection of a sub-set of rules offered domestic actors the leeway to ignore remaining rules at no cost. I identified three interaction periods in which peacebuilders selected different sub-sets of rules: In the first period, international actors focused on the formal establishment of Communities Committees (rules 1, 2); then, peacebuilding attention centred on facilitating inter-ethnic dialogue and regular sessions (rules 1, 2, 3, 4); and in the third period, international actors selected a sub-set of rules emphasising the Committee's mandate to oversee minority rights (rules 1, 2, 3, 4, 6, 7). These selectivity shifts were triggered by security incidents (the March riots of 2004) and events of national importance (Kosovo independence in 2008) that led peacebuilders to change their selection of rules. The process tracing shows that domestic actors reacted with selective implementation to peacebuilders' selectivity: If formal establishment was required, nothing more than formal establishment took place; if inter-ethnic dialogue and more regular meetings were demanded, the number of meetings increased temporarily (particularly in instances when financial compensation was provided).

Leverage also had an effect on the peacebuilding outcome. When the higher leverage instruments of financial assistance or financial rewards (financial compensation for participation or funds for development projects) were provided in the second period, Kosovo Serbs, as well as Albanian municipal authorities, were more likely to drop resistance. Correspondingly, non-implementation became less likely. Leverage changed during the different interaction periods: In the first phase, peacebuilders mainly used only lower leverage instruments such as dialogue facilitation, monitoring and advice. In the second period, international actors resorted to higher leverage instruments, using financial assistance and financial rewards together with capacity building, outreach, dialogue facilitation, monitoring, reporting and advice. In the last period, domestic actors again applied the lower leverage instruments of capacity building, outreach, dialogue monitoring, reporting and advice, except in Bregore/Brdašce, where an advocacy alliance was used as a high leverage strategy.

Environment of interaction

In both municipalities, interactions took place in a rather constraining environment of interaction because of the weak domestic support for minority rights within the local population. This made full implementation a less likely outcome, as domestic actors were more likely to react with resistance, modification or foot-dragging to international demands. Rejection of the reform was especially strong within the Kosovo Serb community because of the political significance of integrating into or boycotting Kosovo institutions. The weak support for minority rights led to outright domestic resistance against reform implementation, which peacebuilders first had to overcome before starting with the 'usual program' of reform support. Even then, domestic actors tended to respond to peacebuilders' demands with a mixture of modification, foot-dragging and cooperation. Broader shifts in the Kosovo Serbian attitude regarding whether to boycott or integrate into Kosovo institutions were equally relevant for the reform process. The differences in the style of politics – cooperative in Zabel/Šumarak and competitive in Bregore/Brdašce – did lead to minor differences in domestic actors' reactions to international demands and reform implementation as a whole. In

Zabel/Šumarak, the municipality with a cooperative style of politics, account-ability rules were better respected: The Communities Committee convened with the Municipal Assembly Chairperson and reported to the Assembly. In Bregore/Brdašce, where a competitive style of politics prevailed, the Com-munities Committee convened in the presence of the Mayor, but neglected its reporting duties to the Assembly, which once more shifted the balance of power in favour of the Municipal Government. Yet peacebuilders did not pay attention to accountability rules, again leaving political dependency struc-tures untouched.

Notes

1 Several legal frameworks have regulated local governance in Kosovo since 1999: UNMIK JIAS (2000–01), UNMIK PISG (2001–08) and the Law on Local Self-Government (2008–present).
2 Interview 82 with former UNMIK Legal Officer (2005–09), headquarters, 03/10/2013. Interview 08 with International Civilian Office, Prishtina, 04/05/2012.
3 Municipalities have full financial autonomy related to capital projects, which can be financed by money allocated by the Ministry of Finance, but also through municipal revenues, grants and donations (RoK 2008b).
4 The programme name is USAID Democratic and Effective Municipalities Initi-ative (DEMI).
5 If the deadline is not met, the Municipal Assembly might be considered non-functional and possibly be dissolved (RoK 2008b). The Mayor remains un-punished.
6 The OSCE merged different regulations for public budget hearings (OSCE 2012).
7 Interview 14 with OSCE Local Governance Section, Prishtina, 08/05/2012.
8 Interview 31 with MLGA, Prishtina, 22/05/2012.
9 Evaluations found that neither citizen participation nor budget compliance had improved.
10 Interview 14 with OSCE Local Governance Section, Prishtina, 08/05/2012.
11 Peacebuilders seem to strategically include incentives as an additional motivation for participation: "Sometimes, what really draws people in, of course, is when snacks and refreshments are provided". Interview 14 with OSCE Local Govern-ance Section, Prishtina, 08/05/2012.
12 Interview 17 with OSCE, field office, Bregore/Brdašce, 10/05/2012.
13 Interview 54 with OSCE, field office, Bregore/Brdašce, 19/10/2012.
14 Ibid.
15 Interview 14 with OSCE Local Governance Section, Prishtina, 08/05/2012.
16 Ibid.
17 Interview 14 with OSCE Local Governance Section, Prishtina, 08/05/2012.
18 Interview 54 with OSCE, field office, Bregore/Brdašce, 19/10/2012 and inter-view 14 with OSCE Local Governance Section, Prishtina, 08/05/2012.
19 For example, USAID created an incentive fund, which included a category called 'Transparent Municipal Assemblies' (USAID DEMI 2011).
20 The workshop was to draft an 'Action Plan for Budget Planning' with govern-ment and Assembly members (USAID DEMI 2012b). Municipal website of Zabel/Šumarak, 25/05/2011.
21 The workshop promoted strategies to increase citizen participation, improve information materials and multiply distribution channels for outreach. Municipal website of Zabel/Šumarak, news from 19/03/2012.

22 The following conferences were organised: the 'Municipal Mid Term Budget Planning Practices' in March 2012 for ministry and municipal officials, the 'Conference on Participatory Budgeting' in May 2012 for the Municipal Assembly and the 'CSO Forum for Transparent budgeting' in June 2011 for CSOs (GFSI 2012, USAID DEMI 2012a).

23 Interview 19 with USAID, Regional Advisor, 14/05/2012.

24 Interview 57 with Municipal Assembly, Zabel/Šumarak, 29/10/2012.

25 Interview 57 with Municipal Assembly, Zabel/Šumarak, 29/10/2012 and interview 69 with Municipal Director, Zabel/Šumarak, 08/11/2012.

26 Interview 69 with Municipal Director, Zabel/Šumarak, 08/11/2012.

27 Interview 57 with Municipal Assembly, Zabel/Šumarak, 29/10/2012.

28 Outreach campaigns were started in 2009 and 2010. Interview 14 with OSCE Local Governance Section, Prishtina, 08/05/2012.

29 Interview 14 with OSCE Local Governance Section, Prishtina, 08/05/2012.

30 Disagreements between the government and the opposition, however, still existed. In 2010, for example, opposition parties lamented the low quality of infrastructure projects (MA Zabel/Šumarak 2010d). Interview 57 with Municipal Assembly, Zabel/Šumarak, 29/10/2012.

31 The budget hearing took place 30/08/2010 (Municipality Zabel/Šumarak 2011a).

32 The first public hearing was organised in 2009 via cooperation between the Mayor and Municipal Assembly (MLGA 2009). In 2010, the Municipal Assembly Chairperson organised an 'Assembly Week' to explain the Assembly work, and a public hearing on the 'Work of the Municipal Assembly between January and June'. The Mayor and the Directors also invited the public for a discussion in 2010 to present their work (2010b, Municipality Zabel/Šumarak 2010c, 2010d).

33 Interview 14 with OSCE Local Governance Section, Prishtina, 08/05/2012.

34 The OSCE financed daily radio announcements on public budget meetings, a televised debate on municipal budget preparations between the Municipal Directors of Economy and Finance, and they conducted televised street interviews with citizens on the budget (OSCE 2012).

35 Municipal website of Zabel/Šumarak, news from 05/04/2011.

36 Email exchange with USAID DEMI staff from 06/05/2012.

37 Interview 61 with Municipal Administration, Zabel/Šumarak, 31/10/2012.

38 Citizen participation in the budget process was a topic at the following events: the capacity building workshop, 'Municipal Budget Process', 2011 (Municipality Zabel/Šumarak 2011d); the workshop, 'Enhance Municipal Transparency', 2012; the USAID 'Conference on Municipal Mid-Term Budget Planning Practices', March 2012 (GFSI 2012); and the 'Conference on Participatory Budgeting', May 2012 (own observation).

39 Interview 61 with Municipal Official, Zabel/Šumarak, 31/10/2012.

40 Interviews with Municipal Assembly members from the PDK and the LDK.

41 Municipal Assembly minutes, 28/04/2011 and 29/12/2011 (MA Zabel/Šumarak 2011d).

42 One municipal official told me: "We were the ones to want those meetings, but USAID helped us with the program DEMI". Interview 61, Municipal Official, Zabel/Šumarak, 31/10/2012.

43 Two public budget hearings were organised in June for the Mid-Term Budget Framework 2011–2013 and two in July for the annual budget (Municipality Zabel/Šumarak 2011c).

44 Interview 73 with USAID, Prishtina, 19/11/2012.

45 USAID even featured an article about full legal compliance in budgeting in Zabel/Šumarak (USAID DEMI 2012c).

46 The budget was approved on 27/09/2012 with 17 yes votes and seven rejections (MA Zabel/Šumarak 2012b).

47 Some Municipal Assembly members were, however, not satisfied on the day of the budget approval. Some complained that the Mayor's village received more investments than other villages or that specific villages were not in the plans to pave roads (MA Zabel/Šumarak 2012b).

48 All actors spent a weekend in Istog/Istok. The workshop included one teaching session on the legal requirements of the budget process and one planning session, during which members of the executive and legislative branches worked on a draft budget. Interview with former Mayor (2007–2010) on 03/10/2012.

49 Ibid. and interview 40 with Municipal Assembly, Bregore/Brdašce, 02/10/2012.

50 Interview 44 with former Mayor (2007–2010), Bregore/Brdašce, 03/10/2012, interview 54 with OSCE, field office, 19/10/2012 and information from municipal website.

51 Interview 44 with former Mayor (2007–2010), Bregore/Brdašce, 03/10/2012.

52 Ibid.

53 Ibid.

54 The training covered public hearings, participation in budget planning and citizen participation in the Municipal Assembly, Assembly Committees and the Board of Directors.

55 The budget planning weekends took place in hotels in Istog/Istok and Pejë/Peć. Interview 44 with former Mayor (2007–2010), Bregore/Brdašce, 03/10/2012 and interview 54 with OSCE, Bregore/Brdašce, 19/10/2012.

56 Interview 54 with OSCE, field office, Bregore/Brdašce, 19/10/2012.

57 Political conflicts increased after the municipal elections in 2009. Although the Mayor and the majority of the Municipal Assembly were from the PDK, intra-party competition disturbed the work of the Municipal Assembly when a representative from the opposition party, the LDK, was elected Chair. Increasing intra-party competition and central-level interference provoked severe conflicts that ultimately led to the Mayor's resignation in July 2010.

58 Interview 54, OSCE, Bregore/Brdašce, 19/10/2012.

59 Ibid.; interview 44 with former Mayor (2007–2010), Bregore/Brdašce, 03/10/2012 and interview 40 with Municipal Assembly, Bregore/Brdašce, 02/10/2012.

60 Interview 54 with OSCE, field office, Bregore/Brdašce, 19/10/2012.

61 Interview 54 with OSCE, field office, Bregore/Brdašce, 19/10/2012.

62 Interview 44 with former Mayor (2007–2010), Bregore/Brdašce, 03/10/2012 and interview 54 with OSCE, field office, Bregore/Brdašce, 09/10/2012.

63 The law requires to put up public notices seven days prior to the event, at least on the municipal billboard, but does not require wider advertisement.

64 Interview 44 with former Mayor (2007–2010), Bregore/Brdašce, 03/10/2012.

65 Interview 54 with OSCE, field office, Bregore/Brdašce, 19/10/2012.

66 Email exchange with USAID DEMI staff from 06/05/2012.

67 Interview 22 with USAID Regional Advisor, Prizren region, 14/05/2012.

68 The workshop promoted strategies to increase citizen participation. Common advice given by USAID DEMI was to produce more and better information materials (website updates, posters, brochures, announcements for public events on press conferences, radio and TV). Interview with USAID DEMI staff, 14/05/2012.

69 Interview 22 with USAID Regional Advisor, 14/05/2012.

70 Interview 54 with OSCE, field office, Bregore/Brdašce, 19/10/2012.

71 The 'budget dinner' was a 'Quick Impact Initiative' of the OSCE Municipal Team in order to ensure a minimum executive-legislative dialogue on the budget. Only six people attended: Many experienced Policy and Finance

Committee members stayed away to protest the municipality's politics or because they were on holiday. Interview 54 with OSCE, 19/10/2012, two members of the Policy and Finance Committee, 03/10/2012 and 02/10/2012, and municipal website from 08/08/2012.

72 OSCE tried a half-hearted intervention with the budget dinner and advice to the Mayor.

73 In fact, USAID had already threatened to withdraw financial assistance if the municipality continued to resist the adoption of the Ahtisaari Law, even stopping financial payments for a few months. USAID was thus even less inclined to pressure the municipality for 'less important' reforms. Interview 18 with Municipal Director, Bregore/Brdašce, 11/05/2012.

74 The municipal website issued a statement saying that the budget would be harmonised with some of the propositions made at the dinner; most Municipal Assembly members claimed the meeting to have been merely a formal act. Interview 54 with OSCE, Bregore/Brdašce, 19/10/2012, two members of the Policy and Finance Committee, 03/10/2012 and 02/10/2012, and the municipal website from 08/08/2012.

75 In 2011, the budget was passed with 11 yes votes, seven abstentions and seven rejections (MA Bregore/Brdašce 2011b) and in 2012 with 18 yes votes, seven rejections and six abstentions. Own observation.

76 In fact, Municipal Assembly members were very angry about this trick. Interview 35 with Policy and Finance Committee, Bregore/Brdašce, 22/09/2012 and 54 with OSCE, 19/10/2012.

77 KFOR minutes from Directors' Meeting on 18/06/2012.

78 Particularly in 2011, but also in 2012. Interview 71 with USAID, Prishtina, 13/11/2012.

79 Interview 54 with OSCE, field office, Bregore/Brdašce, 18/10/2012.

80 Ibid.

81 Interview 22 with USAID, 14/05/2012 and 18 with Municipal Director, Bregore/Brdašce, 11/05/2012.

82 Personal observation from the Municipal Assembly session in Bregore/Brdašce, 30/09/2012.

83 Interview 54 with OSCE, Bregore/Brdašce, 19/10/2012 and two members of the Policy and Finance Committee, 03/10/2012 and 02/10/2012.

84 Municipal Assembly members were frustrated with the government's practice, as the Mayor had neither invited his party nor coalition partner. Interview 43 with Municipal Assembly, Bregore/Brdašce, 03/10/2012.

85 Municipal website of Bregore/Brdašce, 18/06/2012.

86 Interview 71 USAID, Prishtina, 13/11/2012.

87 Ibid.

88 Interview 54 with OSCE, field office, Bregore/Brdašce, 18/10/2012.

89 Interview 43 with Policy and Finance Committee member, Bregore/Brdašce, 03/10/2012.

90 International actors needed the municipalities' cooperation to pass one of the last, highly contested laws from the Ahtisaari Plan.

91 For example, OSCE national staff is often under pressure to maintain good relations with their counterparts in order to fulfil their duties successfully.

92 Other special representation provisions include the selection of a Deputy Chairperson and a Deputy Mayor for Communities for municipalities with a minority population that is greater than 10 per cent (RoK 2008b: Art. 54, 55). Non-mandatory minority protection mechanisms include the Municipal Community Office, the Municipal Returns Office and the establishment of a Municipal Working Group on Returns (OSCE 2009b).

93 Interview 55 with MLGA Monitoring Section, Prishtina, 25/10/2012 and 53 with OSCE regional office, Prizren, 18/10/2012.
94 The legal basis for this section is: UNMIK Regulation 2000/45 "On the Self-Government of Municipalities in Kosovo" (UNMIK); UNMIK Administrative Instruction 2003/02 on the "Procedural Guidance for the Work of Municipal Communities Committees" (UNMIK 2003), the Standards before Status doctrine (UN 2003) and the 2008 Law on Local Self-Government.
95 Information based on interview 54 with OSCE, Bregore/Brdašce, 19/10/2012 and interview 56 with Communities Committee, Zabel/Šumarak, 29/10/2012.
96 Interview 31 with MLGA, Prishtina, 22/05/2012.
97 Interview with former member of Communities Committee Zabel/Šumarak, 05/12/2013.
98 Between 1999 and 2002, about four dinners took place per year. Interview with former UNMIK Official of Zabel/Šumarak, and weekly reports by UNMIK Municipal Administration.
99 The Communities Committee included members from Albanian, Serb, Roma, Ashkali and Turkish ethnic groups.
100 Interview former member of Communities Committee Zabel/Šumarak, 05/12/2013.
101 Interview UNMIK staff in Zabel/Šumarak (1999–2002), 02/11/2013.
102 Ibid.
103 Interview with UNMIK staff in Zabel/Šumarak (1999–2002), 02/11/2013.
104 Please see IAN (n.a.).
105 The OSCE organised a Kosovo-wide capacity building training for all Communities Committee Chairpersons on 'Discriminatory Practices and Mediation Techniques' by the end of December and delivered the trainings for all Committee members in spring 2005 (Wyart and Simpson 2005).
106 Interview 58 with Communities Committee, Zabel/Šumarak, 29/10/2012.
107 Interview 56 with Communities Committee, Zabel/Šumarak, 29/10/2012.
108 Interview with OSCE Local Governance Section, Prishtina, 08/05/2012.
109 Interview with Serb member of Communities Committee and Serb Municipal Official in Zabel/Šumarak, 31/10/2012.
110 Nine meetings took place in 2009, whereas in 2008 – without SLS engagement – only two meetings took place (MLGA 2009).
111 Kosovo Albanian and Turkish representatives were elected from the Municipal Assembly Committees. Serbian and RAE minority representatives were proposed by the Mayor in coordination with the Community Officer, who in turn coordinated with the SLS local party branch. Interview with Serb Municipal Official in Zabel/Šumarak, 30/10/2012.
112 The 2008 Law on Local Self-Government required financial compensation for members of Standing Committees of the Municipal Assembly, such as the Communities Committee. Every municipality sets the amount of financial reward individually. Communities Committee member, 29/10/2012.
113 Several people had complained about the Chairperson being unreliable, not showing up to meetings, and not informing the ethnic group about relevant developments. Interview with Communities Committee members, 29/10/2012, 30/10/2012 and 31/10/2012.
114 Interview with Communities Committee member on 29/10/2012.
115 Interview with Serb Municipal Official and Communities Committee members, 29/10/2012, 30/10/2012 and 31/10/2012.
116 There was only one instance in which a decision of the Municipal Assembly was sent to the Communities Committee. It was directly related to the financing of the Office for Communities.

117 Interview with Communities Committee member in Zabel/Šumarak, 29/10/2012.

118 Interview 56, 58 with two Communities Committee members, Zabel/Šumarak, 29/10/2012.

119 There was only one instance in which a decision of the Municipal Assembly was sent to the Communities Committee. It was directly related to the financing of the Office for Communities.

120 Information from Annual Report of the Communities Committee Zabel/Šumarak for 2012.

121 The Committee supported a few members of extremely poor minority families in their applications for social assistance from the municipality, helped an Ashkali child to apply for financial support for school transportation and requested the provision of land for free use for a social housing project. Information from Annual Report of the Communities Committee Zabel/Šumarak for 2012 and interview with member of Communities Committee, 29/10/2012.

122 Interview with former UNMIK Official in Bregore/Brdašce, 15/09/2012.

123 Ibid.

124 Interview former Serb municipal politician in Bregore/Brdašce, 04/10/2012.

125 Interview with municipal politician of Bregore/Brdašce, 02/12/2012.

126 The Communities Committee encompassed ten members, two Albanians from the LDK, one from the PDK, one from the AAK, two Serbs from Bregore/Brdašce and two from the neighbouring Serb village, as well as two RAE representatives from Bregore/Brdašce (OSCE 2006).

127 Although Bregore/Brdašce counts as a municipality with good inter-ethnic relations and moderate Serbs (OSCE 2010), the Serb community was deeply divided over the question of whether to boycott or integrate. In general, the neighbouring Serb village proved more radical.

128 Interview 81 with former UNMIK staff, 26/09/2013.

129 The financial compensation was required by law. Interview 47, former Serb politician, Bregore/Brdašce, 04/10/2012 and UN and CCPR (2006).

130 For example, the OSCE provided financial assistance for an inter-ethnic project on freedom of movement for minorities, which had been initiated by a local NGO and supported by the Communities Committee (Wyart and Simpson 2005).

131 The NGO proposed to increase exchanges between the Communities Committee Chair, Assembly Chairperson, Office for Communities and Mediation Committee (CSSP 2007).

132 Interview 47 with former Serb politician, Bregore/Brdašce, 04/10/2012.

133 Ibid.

134 Interview 17 with OSCE field office, Bregore/Brdašce, 10/05/2012.

135 Ibid.

136 Ibid.

137 Ibid. and interview 53 with OSCE regional office, Prizren, 18/10/2012.

138 Interview 17 with OSCE, field office, Bregore/Brdašce, 10/05/2012.

139 Interview 44 with former Mayor, Bregore/Brdašce, 03/10/2012.

140 Interview 48 with Municipal Official, Bregore/Brdašce, 03/10/2012.

141 The municipality argued that the Deputy Mayor wanted to remain 'the only Serb to represent his community' and therefore opposed the re-establishment of the Committee, while the former Serbian representative argued that he wanted to keep politically experienced people in the Committee. He feared that newly elected Communities Committee members would be too accommodating because they needed to be approved by a PDK-dominated Municipal Assembly. Interview 48 with Municipal Official, Bregore/Brdašce, 05/10/2012 and interview 47 with Serb municipal politician, 04/10/2012.

142 The Mayor dismissed his Deputy Mayor for Communities on formal grounds – a Deputy Mayor for Communities was only required if the municipality had a minority population of than 10 per cent, which was not the case in Bregore/Brdašce. The unofficial reason for his dismissal was misuse of public funds. Interview with KFOR LMT, 14/05/2012.

143 Interview 17 with OSCE, field office, Bregore/Brdašce, 10/05/2012 and interview 53 with OSCE regional office, Prizren, 18/10/2012.

144 Interview 37 with Deputy Mayor, Bregore/Brdašce, 01/10/2012.

145 Interview 54 with OSCE, field office, Bregore/Brdašce, 19/10/2012 and 53 with OSCE regional office, Prizren, 18/10/2012.

146 Interview 47 with Serb municipal politician, 04/10/2012.

147 Interview 52 with Communities Committee, Bregore/Brdašce, 16/10/2012.

148 Sometimes the Mayor accused the minority representatives of being responsible for the problems because minorities did not pay their public service fees for several years.

149 In 2012, the Committee co-developed a project with a regional NGO to finance several infrastructure projects in minority areas in the Bregore/Brdašce municipality.

150 One international observer told me that he once witnessed a conflict between the Mayor and one RAE member. When the RAE member stood up to walk out the door out of protest, the Mayor threatened to withdraw his financial compensation. The RAE member then stayed.

151 Interview 48 with Office for Communities, 04/10/2012; interview 47 with Serb municipal politician, 04/10/2012 and 54 with OSCE, field office, Bregore/Brdašce, 18/10/2012.

152 The municipal officials who participated regularly were the Mayor, Deputy Mayor, Office for Returnees and Minorities and Officer for Communities. Minutes of Communities Committee meeting, 30/07/2012 and interviews with Committee members, 16/10/2012 and 01/10/2012.

153 Interview 53 with OSCE regional office, Prizren, 18/10/2012.

154 Ibid.

155 Less frequently, social issues and discrimination in employment were also discussed. Information from minutes of Communities Committee meeting on 30/07/2012 and interviews 39 and 52 with Communities Committee members, 16/10/2012 and 01/10/2012.

References

Communities Committee Zabel/Šumarak. (2011). Raport Për Punën e Komiteti Për Komunitete Për Vitin 2011 [Annual Report of Communities Committee for 2011]. Zabel/Šumarak.

CSSP. (2007). Joint Conclusions. Bregore/Brdašce.

Ebel, Robert D. and Péteri, Gábor (eds). (2007). *The Kosovo Decentralization Briefing Book*. Prishtina: Kosovo Foundation for Open Society/Local Government Initiative.

GFSI. (2012). Donor Activities [Online]. Available at: www.gfsiproject.org/node/96 [accessed 14/08/2012].

IAN. (n.a.). Bilteni [Online]. Available at: www.ian.org.rs/kosovo-info/english/bilteni/new/060/mitrovica.pdf [accessed 15/09/2012].

KFOS. (2010). *Local Reform in Kosovo*. Final Report. Prishtina.

Lane, Dennison and Brown, Keith. (2006). Who's in Charge? Reflection on the UN Administration in Kosovo. In: Brown, K. (ed.) *Transacting Transition. The Micropolitics* of *Democracy Assistance in the Former Yugoslavia*. Bloomfield, CT: Kumarian Press, 45–69.

MA Bregore/Brdašce. (2011a). Procesverbal. 14/11/2011. In: Assembly, M. (ed.). Bregore/Brdašce.

MA Bregore/Brdašce. (2011b). Procesverbal. 29/09/2011. In: Assembly, M. (ed.). Bregore/Brdašce.

MA Zabel/Šumarak. (2010a). Procesverbal. Nga mbledhja e I-rë për vitin 2010, e Kuvendit Komunal në Zabel, mbajtur më 28/01/2010 [Minutes of the 1st Meeting of 2010 of the Municipal Assembly of Zabel on 28/01/2010]. Zabel/Šumarak.

MA Zabel/Šumarak. (2010b). Procesverbal. Nga mbledhja e II-rë për vitin 2010, e Kuvendit Komunal në Zabel, mbajtur më 25/02/2010 [Minutes of the 2nd Meeting of 2010 of the Municipal Assembly of Zabel on 25/02/2010]. Zabel/Šumarak.

MA Zabel/Šumarak. (2010c). Procesverbal. Nga mbledhja e VII-rë për vitin 2010, e Kuvendit Komunal në Zabel, mbajtur më 24/06/2010 [Minutes of the 7th Meeting of 2010 of the Municipal Assembly of Zabel on 24/06/2010]. Zabel/Šumarak.

MA Zabel/Šumarak. (2010d). Procesverbal. Nga mbledhja e VIII-rë për vitin 2010, e Kuvendit Komunal në Zabel, mbajtur më 30/09/2010 [Minutes of the 8th Meeting of 2010 of the Municipal Assembly of Zabel on 30/09/2010]. Zabel/Šumarak.

MA Zabel/Šumarak. (2011a). Procesverbal. Nga mbledhja e IX-rë për vitin 2011, e Kuvendit Komunal në Zabel, mbajtur më 29/09/2011 [Minutes of the 9th Extra-ordinary Meeting of 2011 of the Municipal Assembly of Zabel on 29/09/2011]. Zabel/Šumarak.

MA Zabel/Šumarak. (2011b). Procesverbal. Nga mbledhja e V-rë për vitin 2011, e Kuvendit Komunal në Zabel, mbajtur më 26/05/2011 [Minutes of the 5th Meeting of 2011 of the Municipal Assembly of Zabel on 26/05/2011]. Vushtrri.

MA Zabel/Šumarak. (2011c). Procesverbal. Nga mbledhja e VI-rë për vitin 2011, e Kuvendit Komunal në Zabel, mbajtur më 30/06/2011 [Minutes of the 6th Meeting of 2011 of the Municipal Assembly of Zabel on 30/06/2011]. Zabel/Šumarak.

MA Zabel/Šumarak. (2011d). Procesverbal. Nga mbledhja e XII-rë për vitin 2011, e Kuvendit Komunal në Zabel, mbajtur më 29/12/2011 [Minutes of the 12th Meeting of 2011 of the Municipal Assembly of Zabel on 29/12/2011]. Zabel/Šumarak.

MA Zabel/Šumarak. (2012a). Procesverbal. Nga mbledhja e VII-rë për vitin 2012, e Kuvendit Komunal në Zabel, mbajtur më 26/07/2012 [Minutes of the 7th Meeting of 2012 of the Municipal Assembly of Zabel on 26/07/2012]. Zabel/Šumarak.

MA Zabel/Šumarak. (2012b). Procesverbal. Nga mbledhja e XIII-rë për vitin 2012, e Kuvendit Komunal në Zabel, mbajtur më 27/09/2012 [Minutes of the 8th Meeting of 2012 of the Municipal Assembly of Zabel on 27/09/2012]. Zabel/Šumarak.

MA Zabel/Šumarak. (2013). Procesverbal. Nga mbledhja e I-rë për vitin 2013, e Kuvendit Komunal në Zabel, mbajtur më 31/01/2013 [Minutes of the 1st Meeting of 2013 of the Municipal Assembly of Zabel on 31/01/2013]. Zabel/Šumarak.

MLGA. (2009). Monitoring Report of Municipalities of the Republic of Kosovo 2008. Prishtina.

MLGA. (2011). Annual Report of Monitoring of Municipalities of the Republic of Kosovo 2010. Prishtina.

MLGA. (2013). Annual Report of Monitoring of Municipalities of the Republic of Kosovo 2012. Prishtina.

Municipality Zabel/Šumarak. (2010a). Konstituohet Komiteti Per Komunitete [Online]. Available at: http://kk.rks-gov.net/vushtrri/News/Advertisement/Konstituohet-Komiteti-per-komunitete.aspx. [accessed 14/08/2013].

Municipality Zabel/Šumarak. (2010b). News from 18/03/2010 [Online]. Available at: http://kk.rks-gov.net/vushtrri/News.aspx [accessed 15/08/2012].

Municipality Zabel/Šumarak. (2010c). News from 23/06/2010 [Online]. Available at: http://kk.rks-gov.net/vushtrri/News.aspx [accessed 15/08/2012].

Municipality Zabel/Šumarak. (2010d). News from 25/06/2010 [Online]. Available at: http://kk.rks-gov.net/vushtrri/News.aspx [accessed 15/08/2012].

Municipality Zabel/Šumarak. (2011a). News from 01/08/2011 [Online]. Available at: http://kk.rks-gov.net/vushtrri/News.aspx [accessed 15/08/2012].

Municipality Zabel/Šumarak. (2011b). News from 02/06/2011 [Online]. Available at: http://kk.rks-gov.net/vushtrri/News.aspx [accessed 15/08/2012].

Municipality Zabel/Šumarak. (2011c). News from 08/07/2011 [Online]. Available at: http://kk.rks-gov.net/vushtrri/News.aspx [accessed 15/08/2012].

Municipality Zabel/Šumarak. (2011d). News from 25/05/2011 [Online]. Available at: http://kk.rks-gov.net/vushtrri/News.aspx [accessed 15/08/2012].

Municipality Zabel/Šumarak. (2012). Public Discussion/2012–08–02 [Online]. [accessed 13/09/2013].

OMIK and OSCE. (2003). Parallel Structures in Kosovo. Prishtina.

OSCE. (2003). Municipal Profile Zabel/Šumarak. Prishtina.

OSCE. (2006). Municipal Profile Bregore/Brdašce. Prishtina.

OSCE. (2009a). Municipal Profile Zabel/Šumarak. Prishtina.

OSCE. (2009b). Protection and Promotion of the Rights of Communities in Kosovo. Local Level Participation Mechanisms. Pristina.

OSCE. (2010). Kosovo Communities Profile. Prishtina.

OSCE. (2011). Municipal Responses to Security Incidents Affecting Communities in Kosovo and the Role of Municipal Community Safety Councils. Prishtina.

OSCE. (2012). 2012 Budget Development Process in Kosovo Municipalities. An Assessment. Prishtina.

RoK. (2008a). Administrative Instruction No. 2008/09 for Transparency in Municipalities. In: *Ministry of Local Government Administration* (ed.). Prishtina: Republic of Kosovo.

RoK. (2008b). Law on Local Self-Government. In: *Assembly of Republic of Kosovo* (ed.). Prishtina: Republic of Kosovo.

RoK. (2008c). Law on Public Financial Management and Accountability No. 03/L-048. In: *Assembly of Republic of Kosovo* (ed.). Prishtina: Republic of Kosovo.

UN. (2003). Standards for Kosovo. Prishtina.

UN and CCPR. (2006). Report Submitted by the United Nations Interim Administration Mission in Kosovo to the Human Rights Committee on the Human Rights Situation in Kosovo Since June 1999. In: General (ed.) 13 March 2006.

UNMIK. (2000). On Municipal Self-Government in Kosovo. In: UNMIK (ed.) UNMIK Regulation 2000/45.

UNMIK. (2003). UNMIK Administrative Direction 2003/02 on the Functioning of the Work of Community Committees. In: UNMIK PISG (ed.). Prishtina.

UNMIK. (2004). Assessment of Municipal Communities Committees. Prishtina.

USAID DEMI. (2011). USAID DEMI Incentive Fund [Online]. Available at: www.demi-ks.org/?cid=2,57 [accessed 04/11/2012].

USAID DEMI. (2012a). CSO Forum for Transparent Budgeting Held [Online]. Available at: www.demi-ks.org/?cid=2,58,227 [accessed 14/09/2013].

USAID DEMI. (2012b). Municipal Budget Hearing Details (unofficial data). Prishtina: USAID DEMI.

USAID DEMI. (2012c). Transparent Municipal Budget Process [Online]. Available at: www.demi-ks.org/?cid=2,58,101 [accessed 22/08/2013].

USAID DEMI. (2012d). USAID DEMI Incentive Fund Awarded [Online]. Available at: www.demi-ks.org/?cid=2,58,217 [accessed 15/10/2013].

USAID Kosovo. (2009). Kosovo Effective Municipality Initiative. Mid-Term Evaluation. Final Report. Prishtina.

Wyart, Virginie and Simpson, Alexandra. (2005). *Ensuring Equality in the Community*. Kosovo Focus. Prishtina.

6 Negotiating police reform

The Kosovo Police reform is a policy field in which peacebuilders invest a high level of international capacity. Police reform started with UNMIK's arrival in 1999 as part of a larger set of international activities to restore security and rule of law (Forum for Security 2013). UNMIK was tasked with the "provision of interim law enforcement services and the rapid development of a credible, professional and impartial Kosovo Police Service" (UNMIK 2003). The reform activities aim to re-structure Kosovo Police based on the international principles of democracy, minority rights, human rights and rule of law and to promote transparency, accountability and citizen participation as well as minority protection and inclusion. I trace the external–domestic interactions in two Kosovo Police reform initiatives: Municipal Communities Safety Councils (high capacity/weak resistance) and Minority Community Policing (high capacity/strong resistance). Municipal Communities Safety Councils (MCSCs) receive weak local resistance as they are connected to the generally accepted norm of democracy: they increase the accountability and transparency of the security apparatus towards the municipal authorities and rely on citizen participation. Minority Community Policing, however, receives strong resistance because it strengthens the international norm of minority rights by providing minorities with special representation forums for security matters.

In comparison to other policy fields, the international capacity invested in police reform is particularly high in Kosovo: International actors have a wide-reaching mandate with executive powers, the amount of civilian and police personnel dealing with police reform is considerable, and police reform represents one policy field with the highest financial resources invested. Internationals made a radical cut in the Kosovo Police: Right after deployment in 1999, UNMIK completely dismissed the local police corps, and UN Civilian Police (UNCIVPOL) took over all policing tasks in an attempt to restore legitimacy within the Albanian population after decades of human rights abuses from Belgrade (Bieber 2010, Heinemann-Grüder and Grebenschikow 2006). UNMIK planned to gradually build up a local police force with three successive core steps: recruitment, academy training and field training (Stodiek and Zellner 2007). UNCIVPOL took care of the field training of the new Kosovo Police officers (UNMIK 2003), while OSCE police instructors conducted basic training at the Kosovo Police Service School in Vushtrri/Vučitrn (OSCE Permanent Council 1999). In 2005, UNMIK started to gradually transfer authority to the Kosovo Police (Bieber 2010).[1] This included the transfer of policing tasks to local police, while UNCIVPOL retained supervisory powers and provided monitoring and advice.[2] After Kosovo's unilateral declaration of independence on 17 February 2008, UNMIK handed responsibility over to the EU Rule of Law Mission (EULEX). The EULEX mandate gives the mission certain executive responsibilities to deal with war crimes, terrorism, serious financial crime, organised crime, corruption and inter-ethnic crimes (CEU 2008), but the bulk of the work is accomplished through Mentoring, Monitoring and Advising (MMA) activities by international police officers chaperoning the heads of local and regional police stations. Police reform takes place in a crowded field of international actors. UNMIK, UNCIVPOL, the OSCE and EULEX have already been mentioned. In addition, there are bilateral assistance programmes such as the US Department of Justice's ICITAP or Saferworld. The number of personnel is also considerable: A contingent of 4,700 UNCIVPOL officers and 150 OSCE police instructors were responsible for police reform during UNMIK times, while EULEX police had an operational capacity of 2,569 at its peak (Bieber 2010). This tight network of international actors offers manifold opportunities for external–domestic interactions at the municipal level.

Given the high capacity employed in police reform, advocates of the international capacity explanation would expect peacebuilding success: Full implementation should be the most likely outcome, as peacebuilders have enough coercive power and resources to push for reform progress. These theoretically derived predictions are, however, not mirrored by the actual outcomes of the case studies: In the case of Municipal Communities Safety Councils (weak resistance/high capacity), the peacebuilding outcome is full implementation in Zabel/Šumarak and captured implementation in Bregore/Brdašce. In the case of Minority Community Policing (strong resistance/high capacity), the peacebuilding outcome is captured implementation in Zabel/Šumarak and even no implementation in Bregore/Brdašce. International capacity thus does not fully explain the reform outcomes.

External–domestic interactions had a decisive effect on these peacebuilding outcomes. The peacebuilders' use of the ad hoc interaction tactics of prioritisation, for example, in the Municipal Community Safety Council and Minority Community Policing in Zabel/Šumarak made no implementation a less likely outcome. As peacebuilders did not manage to pay attention to the full set of rules at once, selectivity provided domestic actors with opportunities for reform capture at no cost. The use of the high leverage instruments of coercion and financial assistance in the cases of Municipal Community Safety Council and Minority Community Policing in Zabel/Šumarak made no implementation less likely. In contrast, international capacity vested in police reform did not have a significant effect on interaction outcomes, as can be seen in the case of Minority Community Policing in Bregore/Brdašce, which resulted in no implementation. The environment of interaction influenced reform outcomes as well: An enabling environment of interaction made full implementation possible in the case of the Municipal Community Safety Council in Zabel/Šumarak, while a constraining environment made full implementation less likely in other cases due to frequent domestic resistance, modification or foot-dragging.

The two case studies follow a similar structure. First, I introduce the reform initiative, the actors involved in the interaction, and the concrete rules and regulations that are negotiated. Second, the operationalisation of the reform outcome is presented. Third, the ad hoc interaction tactics of prioritisation, selectivity and leverage are analysed. Fourth, the external–domestic interaction process in Zabel/Šumarak and Bregore/Brdašce is analysed for interaction periods, which are delineated by the particular sub-sets of rules selected by peacebuilders for negotiation.

Promoting democracy in a high capacity policy field: the Municipal Community Safety Councils

Municipal Community Safety Councils (MCSC) were introduced in 2005 (UNMIK 2005) as a reaction to the March 2004 riots. The reform had the goal of improving municipalities' response to security incidents by establishing better relations with citizens (Chavleishvili 2011). The reform serves to strengthen the norm of democracy by increasing security institutions' respect for accountability, transparency, responsiveness and citizen participation. MCSCs are a consultative body with members from the police, the municipality and citizens with the purpose of improving coordination between these actors in the area of security and safety, providing opportunities for citizen participation and building trust between the police and the population (RoK 2009). As such, MCSCs form "part of a broader programme of developing community policing across Kosovo" (EULEX 2011a), which requires Kosovo Police to "collaborate with local authorities and community leaders" (Kosovo 2008).

As the reform of Municipal Community Safety Councils is a case of high international capacity and weak local resistance, the international capacity argument and the local resistance argument alike would expect full implementation. Yet the observed outcomes do not fully conform to these expectations: The MCSC in Zabel/Šumarak results in full implementation, but the outcome in Bregore/Brdašce is only captured implementation because the domestic side used the leeway inherent in the interaction process to advance their priority of political power while disregarding rules featuring accountability mechanisms and civil society participation.

If one analyses the interaction process according to the analytical framework of peacebuilding interactions, these outcomes can be better understood: The ad hoc interaction tactic of prioritisation put MCSCs on the top of the international agenda and made no implementation less likely. Selectivity provided domestic actors in Bregore/Brdašce with leeway for reform capture to enhance their political power because of the peacebuilders' neglect of rules for accountability and citizen participation in the third interaction period. Full implementation then became less likely. Leverage influenced the peacebuilding outcome in that the use of high leverage instruments made no implementation less likely. This was the case in Bregore/Brdašce, where peacebuilders successfully used coercion to enforce a minimum sub-set of rules. The enabling environment of interaction in Zabel/Šumarak made domestic cooperation a more likely response to international reform demands, while the rather constraining environment of interaction in Bregore/Brdašce provided domestic actors with the incentive to use foot-dragging, modification and resistance to capture reform for their own priorities.

A multitude of international and domestic actors are involved in the negotiations over MCSC implementation. On the international side, UNMIK, EULEX, the OSCE and KFOR are especially involved. UNMIK offers supervision, monitoring and advice to police stations and municipal authorities until 2008. EULEX regional and local advisors support Kosovo Police Station Commanders with capacity building through monitoring, mentoring and advising. The OSCE Department for Security and Public Safety pushes reform implementation with capacity building through training sessions and workshops for police officers as well as MCSC members. The OSCE regional and field offices monitor and advise Kosovo Police and municipal authorities. KFOR usually participates in MCSC meetings with briefings on the security situation. On the domestic side, the Kosovo Police Station Commander, the Mayor and representatives from civil society – including religious institutions, NGOs and minority representatives – are involved in reform implementation. At the central level, the Kosovo Police headquarters, Ministry of Internal Affairs and Ministry of Local Government Administration monitor reform implementation in the Steering Group for Monitoring the Community Safety Strategy.[3]

To implement MCSCs, domestic actors are expected to apply the following set of rules.[4] Every municipality is required to formally establish a Municipal Community Safety Council (rule 1) (RoK 2012b). The MCSC has to be formed by the Police Station Commander, Mayor, Kosovo Security Force, Municipal Civil Emergency Directorate, Local Public Safety Committees, representatives of all religious and ethnic communities, and at least five civil society members (rule 2) (RoK 2009).[5] The appointment procedure requires that the Mayor invite all above-mentioned institutions to propose a MCSC representative (RoK 2009).[6] MCSCs need to meet regularly (rule 3). They were first required to meet at least 10 times annually (RoK), though the meetings were reduced to six in 2012 (RoK). At least 50 per cent of the members have to be present at every meeting (rule 4) (RoK). MCSC members are expected to report to the Municipal Assembly (RoK 2009) and to organise two public meetings with citizens per year (rule 5) (RoK 2009).

They are also supposed to develop an annual action plan on their activities (RoK 2009). The purpose of MCSCs is

> to develop awareness related to the nature of crime, disorder and violent behaviour in the local community, to identify the concerns regarding Security and Public Safety (rule 7) and to recommend action plans, to address those concerns through the cooperative efforts of municipal authorities, local communities and the Police (rule 8).
>
> (RoK 2012b)

In addition, MCSCs are to support awareness campaigns on security issues (rule 9) (RoK 2009).

Based on these rules, I propose the operationalisation in Table 6.1 for evaluating the peacebuilding outcome of the Municipal Community Safety Council reform.

Prioritisation, selectivity and leverage in Municipal Community Safety Councils

Unforeseen security incidents, the complex changes after Kosovo's independence and the priority shifts related to the EU dialogue all contributed to a situation in which peacebuilders were forced to resort to the ad hoc tactics of prioritisation, selectivity and leverage so that they would be capable of deciding how to react to their counterparts during the negotiation about Municipal Community Safety Councils.

Table 6.1 Outcome operationalisation – municipal community safety councils

Dimension	Period			Source
	1	*2*	*3*	
Formal dimension				
1 MCSC established	1	2	3	Law on Police Art. 7.2
2 All members appointed	–	2	3	MCSC AI Art. 5
Practice dimension				
3 Regular meetings (6–10)	–	2	3	MCSC AI Art. 7
4 All members participate (50% min)	–	2	–	MCSC AI Art. 7
5 Reporting to MA/citizens	–	–	–	MCSC AI Art. 8, Art. 11
6 Annual Action Plan	–	–	3	MCSC AI Art. 11.7
Content dimension				
7 Security issues identified	–	2	3	MCSC Art. 10.2
8 Problem-solving	–	–	3	MCSC Art. 10.2
9 Awareness raising	–	–	3	MCSC Art. 10.2

Source: Own Compilation. Abbreviations: MCSC = Municipal Community Safety Council, MCSC AI = MCSC Administrative Instruction.

Prioritisation

There was one occasion when Municipal Community Safety Councils were prioritised. This was in 2011, when MCSCs became part of the EU benchmarking catalogue in the visa liberalisation negotiations with Kosovo. The EU applied the instrument of 'policy conditionality' (Trauner 2009) to the visa liberalisation process with Kosovo and included the MCSCs in a (pre-) conditionality catalogue that Prishtina ought to fulfil in order to advance with visa liberalisation. EU conditionality led to an increased awareness of MCSCs at the central level as one OSCE employee remarks:

> They understand that MCSC functionality is a precondition for visa liberalisation. The EU says that in every report. They understand it. The Prime Minister, Minister of Internal Affairs – they always push that they should do something in this regard. So it is easy for me to work.
> (Interview 85, OSCE Department for Security and Public Safety,
> 27/11/2013)

Prioritisation meant that MCSCs figured at the top of the international agenda and that peacebuilders were under pressure to prove 'success'. Given this, peacebuilders were less tolerant with regard to domestic non-compliance; insisted on minimum sub-set of rules such as formal establishment, member appointments and regular meetings; and more frequently interacted with domestic counterparts.

Selectivity

Peacebuilders' selectivity enabled domestic actors to neglect rules at no cost in those areas where international actors did not pay attention and thus allowed domestic actors to exploit reforms for domestic priorities. From 2005 to 2007, peacebuilders focused on a sub-set of rules for formal establishment (rule 1). Then, between 2008 and 2010, the selected sub-set of rules was widened to include the *functioning* establishment of MCSCs (rules 1, 2, 3, 7). Lastly, between 2011 and 2012, peacebuilders' selectivity concentrated on a sub-set of rules for making MCSCs an effective security mechanism that showed pro-activity in problem identification and problem solving (rules 1, 2, 3, 5, 7, 8). Selectivity shifts were triggered by Kosovo's independence in 2008 and by the introduction of EU policy conditionality for visa liberalisation in 2011.

Period I (2005–07): formal establishment (rule 1)

In the beginning, peacebuilders' attention focused on a sub-set of rules that emphasised the need for the formal establishment of Municipal Community Safety Councils (1) at the local level.

Period II (2008–10): functioning establishment (rules 1, 2, 3, 7)

Peacebuilders widened the selected sub-set of rules after Kosovo independence and emphasised the necessity of the formal establishment of Municipal Community Safety Councils (1); of appointing members from the Kosovo Police, Municipal Directors and representatives from religious institutions, minority groups and civil society organisations (2); of meeting regularly (at least 10 times per year) (3); and of focusing on security and safety (7) (RoK 2009). Kosovo's independence required internationals to build up domestic institutions such as MCSCs that could serve as a 'watchdog' for the security situation since UNMIK was no longer in a position to compensate for perceived 'domestic inactivity'.

Period III (2011–12): effective security mechanism (rules 1, 2, 4, 3, 5, 7, 8)

In the third period, peacebuilders' selectivity shifted to a sub-set of rules for making MCSCs an effective security mechanism that shows pro-activity in problem identification and problem solving. Peacebuilders continued to emphasise the necessity of the formal establishment of Municipal Community Safety Councils (1); of appointing members from the Kosovo Police, Municipal Directors, institutions, minority groups and civil society organisations (2); and of meeting regularly (3) with at least one representative of each group present (4). Furthermore, they added demands to develop annual work plans (5) as well as to focus on the problem-identification of security and safety issues (7), problem-solving strategies (8) and awareness raising (9).[7] Peacebuilders left out rule 6, which required that MCSCs report to the Municipal Assembly or citizens. The reason for this comprehensive shift was the EU visa liberalisation process that included functioning MCSCs as one of the benchmarks in the conditionality catalogue (EC 2012).

Leverage

Period I (2005–08): lower leverage

In this first period, international actors used the lower leverage of capacity building, monitoring and advice to ensure the formal establishment of MCSCs in priority areas (Chavleishvili 2011).[8] Peacebuilders also use a strategy of substitution and organised parallel 'security meetings' in case domestic actors refused to establish MCSCs.

Period II (2008–10): lower leverage

In the second period, peacebuilders continued to apply the lower leverage instruments of capacity building, monitoring and advice. EULEX and the OSCE also became active in non-priority areas, where no MCSCs had been established yet.[9] The OSCE Department for Security and Public Safety started a series of capacity building workshops for MCSCs in 2010[10] and continued with capacity building trainings on community policing (including MCSCs) at the Kosovo Police School.[11] The OSCE also asked the Kosovo Police headquarters to improve their monitoring of MCSCs at municipal level[12] and to develop strategies for community safety and community policing, including MCSCs.[13]

Period III (2011–2012): higher leverage

This last phase was marked by an increase in leverage: Peacebuilders resorted to the use of conditionality (policy conditionality, pre-conditionality) in addition to capacity building, monitoring, reporting and advising. After MCSCs had been included in the EU policy conditionality catalogue, international actors became more assertive in pushing for substantive reform implementation: EULEX increased its monitoring, reporting and advice activities to help Kosovo Police use MCSCs for patrol planning and community policing (EULEX 2011a). The EU mission also sent EULEX regional advisors to MCSC meetings as part of their "strategic management development" activities, which they had not done before. EULEX regional advisors were provided with an 'MCSC inspection list', asking who amongst the Kosovo Police attended the MCSC meeting, which community policing related concerns were raised, whether the police was asked to take action, or whether the police had taken action on previously raised concerns.[14] This information was included in the quarterly reports on MCSC performance, which the EU required as part of the policy conditionality benchmarking from June 2013 on.[15] The OSCE also increased its activities: MCSCs became a monitoring priority in 2011, and an evaluation report was published in 2012 (OSCE 2011). The OSCE Department for Security and Public Safety started to schedule official meetings with Mayors twice a year to discuss the shortcomings of MCSCs.[16] The OSCE also increased awareness raising for MCSCs within their field offices[17] and started public outreach campaigns on the work done by MCSCs.[18] The field offices continuously monitored MCSC performance and provided advice to all actors.

Municipal Community Safety Council reform in Zabel/Šumarak

The external–domestic interactions over Municipal Community Safety Councils in Zabel/Šumarak resulted in captured implementation of the reform although both international capacity and local resistance advocates would have expected full implementation. Given the cooperative attitude of domestic actors to international requests, selectivity is the main reason for the reform outcome of captured implementation: Peacebuilders had not managed to tackle the total set of rules over time, particularly neglecting rule 5 throughout the entire interaction process. Yet the general pattern that only those rules selected by peacebuilders are implemented also held true in this case. Full implementation was thus not possible even in a situation where domestic actors responded cooperatively to all international demands. Of major importance for the cooperative behaviour of domestic elites was the enabling environment of interaction in Zabel/Šumarak, where there was domestic support for the promoted international norm as well as a cooperative style of politics. Such an environment made domestic actors more inclined to respond with cooperation to international demands and to sustain 'learned practices'. Domestic actors even reacted with cooperation when peacebuilders only provided advice (and thus did not employ high leverage), which at least the international capacity explanation would find counterintuitive.

In Zabel/Šumarak, the Police Commander, the Mayor, different Municipal Directors and Officers, and representatives from religious institutions, NGOs and minority communities were involved in the implementation of MSCSs. On the international side, UNMIK, the OSCE Department for Security and Public Safety, the OSCE Security Monitoring Section, and the OSCE regional teams and field teams, as well as KFOR field teams and EULEX, were engaged in reform support.

The following paragraphs trace the external–domestic interaction process over Municipal Community Safety Councils in Zabel/Šumarak and portray the peacebuilders' selected sub-set of rules in each of the three interaction periods.

Period I (2005–07): formal establishment (rule 1)

In the first phase, external actors were interested in the formal establishment of MCSCs, particularly in the priority municipality of Zabel/Šumarak, where the security situation was considered to be fragile due to its closeness to North Kosovo. The UNMIK municipal administration, KFOR field teams and OSCE municipal teams informed municipal authorities of the legal obligation to set up MCSCs. The OSCE-led Kosovo Police Service School also taught Zabel/Šumarak police officers about the legal obligation to establish MCSCs.[19] There was, however, no active promotion of MCSCs at the municipal level.[20] As long as international actors wielded supervisory powers in UNMIK, they concentrated on substitution as a strategy to improve the security situation: UNMIK regularly invited to 'security meetings', which were functionally equivalent to MCSCs but under UNMIK control. Similar to MCSCs, the 'security meetings' had the purpose of gathering information on the security situation and fostering institutional cooperation between UNMIK, KFOR, the OSCE and the local Police Station Commander, Municipal President and minority representatives (Chavleishvili 2011).

Municipal actors in Zabel/Šumarak reacted with cooperation to international demands: Having learned about the new MCSC structure, the Station Commander showed pro-active commitment to MCSC implementation, as he understood it as a tool for entering into a dialogue with the municipality and reducing inter-ethnic tensions in the area.[21] He proposed that the Municipal President establish an MCSC, and the President agreed.[22] Therefore, an MCSC was formally established as early as 2006 upon the initiative of municipal actors,[23] and "the municipality respected this regulation a lot".[24] Zabel/Šumarak thus represents one of the few cases where the mere promulgation of a law, general capacity building and occasional international advice led to the formal establishment of an MCSC.[25]

The local police and municipality also agreed to participate in the UNMIK-controlled security meetings, where the relevant security issues were discussed.[26] MCSCs and UNMIK security meetings functioned in parallel for a while. KFOR Liaison and Monitoring Teams, UNMIK and OSCE field teams regularly monitored the MCSC meetings when they took place. However, MCSCs only met on an irregular basis, the meetings were very short and minority representatives often boycotted the meetings, while civil society organisations had not been invited at all.[27] MCSC participants were not completely clear about the Council's purpose, and the topics discussed were not necessarily connected to security:[28]

> Okay, maybe at the beginning we didn't act as a Council, we didn't act as needed because we needed time to understand what the meaning, what the importance of this was.
> (Interview 67, Kosovo Police, Zabel/Šumarak, 07/11/2012)

This incomplete implementation can also be seen as a result of peacebuilders' selectivity as they had merely focused on the formal establishment of MCSCs. Lack of clear legal guidance and lack of international advice facilitated selective implementation on the domestic side.[29]

Period II (2008–10): functioning establishment (rules 1, 2, 3, 7)

As a nucleus of MCSC already existed in Zabel/Šumarak, international actors dedicated themselves to a sub-set of rules for increasing the regularity of MCSC meetings, focusing on security issues and ensuring minority participation. The selection of a wider sub-set of rules was triggered by Kosovo's independence, which made the functioning of domestic institutions more relevant for peacebuilders as they could not lead parallel institutions so easily anymore. This period was, furthermore, marked by the deployment of the EULEX field team in the local police station and by the 2009 adoption of the MCSC Administrative Instruction that provided concrete rules for the functioning of MCSCs.

KFOR, the OSCE and EULEX regularly monitored the MCSC meetings once they took place. EULEX field teams started monitoring, mentoring and advising (MMA) activities with the Station Commander on a daily basis based on EULEX 'action fiches'. EULEX's main concern about MCSCs were security-related topics and how to use information from MCSCs for patrol planning and community policing (EULEX 2009, 2011b).[30] The OSCE

Department for Security and Public Safety organised several capacity building meetings on the MCSC regulation, which Zabel/Šumarak police officials attended and also organised a capacity building workshop solely for the MCSC members of Zabel/Šumarak.[31] The OSCE's main advice was to increase the regularity of meetings, discuss security problems, take meeting minutes and increase Serbian participation.[32] Civil society participation and the problem-solving capacity of the MCSCs was less of an issue.

Police Commander and the Municipal Government showed cooperation towards the peacebuilders' demands and followed international advice. The MCSC meetings took place with increasing regularity during this time.[33] The number of participating municipal officials and minority representatives also increased, as did their participation in discussion.[34] Among the usual particip-ants were the Kosovo Police, Mayor, Directors and Officers, representatives from the Turkish, Roma and Ashkali minorities, and one or two NGOs.[35] Serbs, however, refused to participate in these meetings, with the exception of the Serbian Community Officer, who had attended the meetings since 2009.[36] Peacebuilders tolerated Serbian resistance to participation. Meetings became more formal, as reports were distributed after every meeting.[37] While the meetings in 2008 merely consisted of a brief security update by the local police and KFOR, the meetings in the following years discussed security problems more in depth.[38] Yet participants did not engage in problem solving:

> I attended two meetings in 2010. The Deputy Mayor talked for five minutes and then we went home. Definitely, it was a disaster.
> (Interview 85, OSCE Official, 27/11/2013)

This shows that peacebuilders' selectivity of a particular sub-set of rules – in this case leaving out requirements for problem-solving – significantly influ-ences the way that domestic actors implement a reform.

Period III (2011–12): effective security mechanism (rules 3, 4, 5, 7, 8, 9)

In the last phase, peacebuilders were eager to demonstrate the 'success' of their reform efforts in front of the EU and thus widened the selected sub-set of rules to make MCSCs an effective security mechanism.[39] This meant that internationals paid increasing attention to the MCSCs' performance in devel-oping a work plan, identifying and solving security and safety issues, or raising awareness for security and safety issues by, for example, issuing statements on recent security incidents. Yet they left out rule 6, which would have increased MCSCs' accountability to the Municipal Assembly and citizens. In this phase, international actors used the higher leverage instruments of conditionality (pre-conditionality, policy-conditionality) as well as capacity building, out-reach, monitoring, reporting and advice.

The inclusion of MCSCs in the EU conditionality catalogue not only led to increased interest in reform implementation by domestic elites at the national level, it first and foremost led to a sharp increase in international activities at the municipal level. EULEX increased its MMA activities with regard to MCSCs' performance and, for example, started to control whether the Station Commander followed up on MCSC issues. As of mid-2012, EULEX even accompanied the Station Commander to the MCSC meetings and regularly contacted the Mayor to discuss MCSC performance.[40] The OSCE municipal team in Zabel/Šumarak had also been increasing its monitoring and advising activities since 2011, as MCSCs had become a monitoring priority. In January 2012, OSCE headquarters published an MCSC performance report for all of Kosovo (OSCE 2011) and the OSCE regional offices organised round tables to discuss MCSC performance as a follow up.[41] The OSCE Department for Public Safety and Security started to meet twice a year with the Mayor to discuss MCSC improvements[42] and continued to provide general capacity building, including MCSCs.[43]

Domestic actors responded cooperatively to all international demands to improve the MCSC's work as an effective security mechanism. The MCSC continued to hold regular meetings during that time.[44] Kosovo Police, the Mayor, the Municipal Directors and Officers, and civil society and minority communities regularly participated.[45] The MCSC improved its safety and security related work: Kosovo Police usually gave a short briefing on the security situation that covered burglaries, traffic safety and minority safety, especially in the Serbian villages, and municipal officials raised concerns with which citizens approached them, e.g. noise from cafés or clubs.[46] The security of minorities was a recurrent concern raised by the Officer for Communities, which mostly related to a newly built bridge that connected Serbian and Albanian hamlets. The forum was also used to find solutions to the raised security problems.[47] Usually, Kosovo Police were asked to take action and to draft action plans to respond to specific problems that had been discussed. These, in turn, were reported on at the next meeting.[48] The OSCE was very satisfied with the MCSC's capacity to identify and solve problems related to security and safety in the municipality[49] although the MCSC still had not managed to draft an Annual Action Plan.[50] So far, the MCSC had engaged only to a limited extent in awareness raising activities with regard to security and safety. Yet when inter-ethnic incidents occured, the MCSC published an official condemnation on the municipal website, and further awareness raising campaigns were planned between the Kosovo Police and MCSCs.[51] However, as a result of peacebuilders' selectivity, MCSC neither reported to the Municipal Assembly nor held public meetings for citizens (rule 6).

Peacebuilding outcome: captured implementation

The outcome of captured implementation in the Municipal Community Safety Council reform in Zabel/Šumarak is particularly interesting because it is a case in which domestic actors responded with extreme cooperation to all international demands, yet the outcome did not result in full implementation.

The reason for this is peacebuilders' selectivity in relation to the set of rules demanded from domestic actors. The fact that peacebuilders never paid attention to whether MCSCs reported their work to the Municipal Assembly or to citizens allowed domestic actors to neglect rule 5 at no cost. Thus, the way that the reform was implemented weakened the accountability of the Municipal Government and Kosovo Police towards the Assembly and citizens.

FORMAL DIMENSION

Rule 1. MCSC established: The MCSC was first formally established by the Mayor and the Kosovo Police Station Commander in 2006.

Rule 2. All members appointed: The MCSC comprised members of all important groups – Kosovo Police Station Commander or his Deputy, the Mayor or his Deputy, Directors and Officers, particularly the Officer for Communities and representatives from the Serbian, Turkish, Roma and Ashkali minorities, as well as one or two NGOs.

PRACTICE DIMENSION

Rule 3. Regular meetings: The MCSC held nine meetings in 2012.

Rule 4. All members participate: Members from all groups regularly participated in the MCSC meetings.

Rule 5. Reporting to MA and to citizens: The MCSC did not report to the Municipal Assembly on its activities in 2012 and also did not organize public hearings to inform citizens about its work.

CONTENT DIMENSION

Rule 6. Security issues identified: The MCSC meetings were used to identify and discuss security problems.

Rule 7. Problem-solving: The MCSC meetings were furthermore used to develop initial problem-solving strategies for the identified security issues and Kosovo Police then continued to take care of the issue.

Rule 8. Awareness raising: The MCSC put up two public condemnations of interethnic violence on its website in 2012, but it did not organize a widespread awareness raising campaign on security-related matters.

Municipal Community Safety Council in Bregore/Brdašce

> When a person is blind with politics, you cannot talk about community safety. If you put your political problems first and then deal with community safety, it is impossible – I can tell you.
>
> (OSCE Official, Prishtina, 27/11/2013)

The negotiations over the Municipal Community Safety Council in Bregore/ Brdašce led to a captured implementation that served the Mayor's priority to increase his political power. The Mayor used the leeway inherent in the external–domestic interaction to centralise power within the executive branch and ignore accountability rules as well as requirements to include civil society. According to the reasoning of the international capacity and the local resistance explanations, full implementation should have been the peacebuilding outcome. However, high capacity and weak domestic resistance for the promoted norm do not seem to be a guarantee of full implementation. First, peacebuilders' use of ad hoc tactics shaped the reform result. Prioritisation made no implementation less likely when the MCSC reform was pushed to the top of the international agenda in January 2011: Internationals actors were less tolerant of non-compliance and insisted on the implementation of minimum sub-set of rules. Selectivity allowed domestic actors to ignore rules about accountability and civil society participation at no cost. Such leeway made full implementation less likely. In addition, the high leverage applied in the last period made no implementation less likely, as non-compliance became more costly. The rather constraining environment of interaction, characterised by a particularly competitive style of politics, also provided domestic actors with an incentive to capture reform to further their own ends: Although some of the peacebuilders' demands were met with cooperation, most were met with foot-dragging, modification or resistance, and learned practices were not sustained. Peacebuilders tolerated domestic behaviour during the first years, citing the 'chaotic political situation' as their reason for backing down.

Multiple actors were involved in reform negotiations. The domestic side was made up of the (Deputy) Police Station Commander, the Mayor, different Municipal Directors and Officers and, to limited extent, representatives from religious institutions, NGOs and minority communities. On the peacebuilding side, the KFOR Liaison Monitoring Team, UNMIK Municipal Administration, a variety of OSCE sections and EULEX were involved.

The following pages analyse the external–domestic interaction process over Municipal Community Safety Councils in Bregore/Brdašce for three interaction periods in which different sub-sets of rules were negotiated.

Period I (2005–07): formal establishment (rule 1)

At the beginning, peacebuilders used low leverage instruments such as advice and capacity building to promote formal establishment of MCSCs. But in municipalities with a stable security situation, such as Bregore/Brdašce, peacebuilders were less concerned about whether they were successful in their attempts or not. This meant that at the municipal level, neither the field offices of UNMIK and KFOR nor the OSCE actively engaged in promoting MCSCs.[52] Apparently, some peacebuilders in Bregore/Brdašce were not even aware of the existence of the legal regulation on MCSCs before 2008.[53] Instead, UNMIK started to substitute the non-functioning MCSCs by establishing monthly 'security meetings' that were under the control of UNMIK but had a similar function to MCSCs.[54] UNMIK convened these meetings with the purpose of sharing security related information and ensuring cooperation between security and civil institutions (Chavleishvili 2011). Only KFOR, UNMIK, the Kosovo Police Director, the President of the municipality, the Officer for Communities, and, if feasible, religious institutions and minority representatives were invited, but no civil society organisations.[55] To international actors, it seemed easier to ensure the functioning of an institution by keeping it under direct control, particularly in a field as vital as security.[56] Security meetings were, however, less concerned with strengthening democracy through citizen participation.[57]

> When we had security meetings, it would usually be like this: KP would brief, KFOR would also brief if they had anything to say. […] No questions.
> (Interview 54, OSCE, Bregore/Brdašce, 19/10/2012)

Domestic actors reacted cooperatively to the international invitation to attend 'security meetings'. The then Mayor remembered that he gave "a lot of importance to these meetings".[58] The local police in Bregore/Brdašce was still informed about the need to formally establish MCSCs through the OSCE's Kosovo-wide capacity building trainings for police officials. Yet neither the Kosovo Police nor the Mayor were interested in the additional obligations that MCSC meetings entailed and ignored this piece of information.[59] The 'security meetings' satisfied the local police interest in exchanging information on security issues, return or school safety and in providing grounds for institutional cooperation between the police and the municipality. A former Mayor mentioned that 'security meetings' even led to "the rebuilding of a street in the Serbian and Roma quarter",[60] which again shows the importance of socio-economic development in post-war Kosovo. Neither international nor domestic actors seemed to care that 'security meetings' did not provide for accountability or citizen participation nor did they contribute to sustainable domestic institution-building.

Period II (2008–11): functioning establishment (rules 1, 2, 3, 7)

After Kosovo independence, international actors became more interested in functioning MCSCs because domestic institutions seemed the best option for ensuring information exchange, institutional cooperation and citizen participation in the field of security. In Bregore/Brdašce, however, no MCSC had yet been established. Peacebuilders thus used lower leverage instruments such as capacity building, monitoring and advice to achieve the formal establishment of an MCSC as well as the appointment of all members, regular meetings and a focus on security issues. EULEX and the OSCE field teams were the most active international organisations in Bregore/Brdašce at that time. The OSCE field offices started to discuss the need to establish an MCSC with the Mayor, arguing that "it was a requirement under the law".[61] When the

EULEX field team arrived in January 2009, they also pointed out the need to establish an MCSC under the supervision of the local police.[62] International advice proved successful in that an MCSC was formally established in early 2009 (MLGA 2009).[63] However, the MCSC only met once. Therefore, international actors continued to resort to substituting MCSCs with 'security meetings' and neglected the build-up of domestic institutions.

The domestic side responded to international demands with a mixture of cooperation and resistance – or rather ignorance. The Mayor cooperated with international demands by formally establishing the MCSC in early 2009 (MLGA 2009). But apart from the initial meeting, no further meetings were organised (MLGA 2010), as one OSCE employee remembers:

> The law on police specifically said that the MCSCs should function, and there is a regulation, an administrative instruction … so. The earlier Mayor established it, but it was not functioning. They only met once.
> (Interview 53, OSCE field office, 19/1/2012)

There were several reasons related to the competitive style of politics in the municipality that stopped domestic actors from dedicating their time to institutionalising the work of the MCSCs: First, the Mayor's time and energy were consumed by political infighting in Bregore/Brdašce that had started after the 2009 municipal elections. As a result of this political competition, the Mayor resigned in summer 2010 and left the municipality with several months of an interim government and no time for MCSC meetings. The following extraordinary elections in the autumn of 2010 did not leave room for MCSC meetings either and the Kosovo Police were not able to implement the reform alone.[64] In response to the political dynamics, peacebuilders backed down from their demand to establish a functioning MCSC. Instead, the OSCE re-invigorated the 'security meetings'. Between 2009 and 2010, the OSCE invited KFOR, EULEX, the OSCE, the Kosovo Police, the Mayor and concerned Municipal Directors to three informal meetings.[65]

Period III (2011–12): effective security mechanism (rules 1, 2, 4, 3, 7, 8)

In the last phase, peacebuilders again insisted on the formal establishment of an MCSC in Bregore/Brdašce, mainly because MCSCs had become a priority on the international agenda as a conditionality in the EU visa liberalisation process. Peacebuilders first concentrated on formally re-establishing the MCSC in Bregore/Brdašce. To do this, the OSCE regional office and OSCE field office used coercion in form of an advocacy coalition. The two offices met together with the Mayor to lobby for MCSC establishment, arguing that MCSCs were a legal obligation to the municipality and thereby signalling to the new Mayor that this was a priority issue.[66] The strategy proved successful as the Mayor agreed to formally establish an MCSC. For the Mayor, the main motivation for setting up the Council was to "follow a legal requirement" and to "strengthen[…] the role of the municipality".[67] The Kosovo Police and the Mayor then cooperated with the peacebuilders' demands and established the MCSC in early 2011 (MLGA 2013). The Mayor appointed the MCSC members after he consulted with the municipal Directorates and offices, although his appointments took place in a rather non-transparent manner in which he chose individuals that were politically affiliated with him.[68] The Kosovo Police, municipal officials, and representatives of the Islamic community participated on a regular basis.[69] Minority representatives from the Roma and Ashkali community only showed up once in 2012, while civil society representatives, the Serbian Orthodox Church and Serbian minority representatives did not participate.[70] To compensate for the lack of minority representation, the OSCE pushed the Officer for Communities to attend MCSC meetings, whereas they did not address the lack of civil society participation.[71] The consequence was that municipal structures had the dominant presence, while minority and citizen participation remained largely inexistent. The OSCE Department for Security and Public Safety met the Mayor of Bregore/Brdašce twice to discuss how MCSC members were appointed[72] and the OSCE field teams criticised the Mayor several times.[73] Yet peacebuilders did not take action to push for more citizen participation or for respecting the accountability rules towards the Municipal Assembly or citizens:

> I did not pay attention to civil society. Maybe I'll talk to [my colleague]; we'll pay more attention next year. I agree with you, it is more important, but the OSCE, you know, we are crazy with minorities.
> (Interview 85, OSCE, 27/11/2013)

The MCSC held regular meetings throughout the year (MLGA 2013). KFOR, the OSCE and – starting in mid-2012 – EULEX regularly monitored the MCSC meetings. EULEX's main goal was to provide advice to Kosovo Police on how to identify security problems and improve their problem-solving capacity by, for example, using information from MCSCs for patrol planning and community policing (EULEX 2011a). EULEX regional advisors were sent to attend MCSC meetings, equipped with an inspection list, asking who amongst the Kosovo Police had attended the MCSC meeting, what community policing related concerns were raised and whether the local police had been asked to take action or had taken action on previously raised concerns.[74] Following international advice, the MCSC was used to discuss and solve issues of security and safety.[75] The Kosovo Police informed members of the general security situation in the municipality concerning inter-ethnic incidents, traffic safety, school problems or drugs, and other MCSC members brought up current security concerns.[76] Usually, the Kosovo Police were asked to take action and to report on the action they intended to take or had already taken. The OSCE, however, bemoaned the limited responsiveness on the side of the police.[77]

The OSCE also increased its activities to support the newly established MCSC: OSCE headquarters organised capacity building training sessions on the new Community Policing Strategy (including MCSCs) at the national level[78] and published a report on MCSC performance based on its monitoring activities in every municipality (OSCE 2011). Based on this monitoring report, OSCE regional offices organised outreach in the form of round tables to discuss possible improvements and increased personal advice to the municipality. The OSCE Department for Security and Public Safety met the Mayor of Bregore/Brdašce twice to discuss the performance of the MCSC in 2011 and proposed, for example, to provide translation for Serbian members so that they would participate.[79] The OSCE field office advised the MCSC to meet more regularly, to appoint members according to the rules, and to organise public awareness in case of security incidents.[80] In this case, the domestic side resisted international advice: No translation into Serbian was organised and there was no change in appointment of members. MCSCs also ignored the international advice to engage in awareness raising for public safety. Neither inter-ethnic incidents nor problems with drugs at school led to public awareness raising.[81]

As a result of the peacebuilders' neglect of accountability rules, the MCSC did not report about its activities in the Municipal Assembly, nor did it hold public meetings with citizens.[82] It also neglected its obligations to draft annual work plans.[83]

Peacebuilding outcome: captured implementation

In Bregore/Brdašce, the Municipal Community Safety Council reform resulted in captured implementation: The MCSC improved the cooperation between security structures and the Municipal Government, but the lack of accountability and citizen participation as well as clientelist appointment procedures distorted democracy promotion goals. Meagre citizen participation in the forum, political dependency of the MCSC participants and a lack of respect for accountability structures made the reform an instrument for the Mayor to increase his influence over security structures. International actors were well aware of the fact that the MCSC bore the potential of altered power relations in the municipality, but that police and political elites were not interested in such changes:

> If they create these [MCSCs] and the MCSCs start to function, there will be more transparency in security issues. So somehow they [the municipality and the police] still prefer the traditional ways to handle these issues.
>
> (Interview 75, OSCE Official, 20/11/2012)

One observer especially criticised the dependency of participants on the Mayor and how that influenced the work:

> In Bregore/Brdašce, I only attended [the MCSC] once.... I told the Mayor to change the list of membership because it is in principle unacceptable

– because there was a rumour that most of its members were of his party. But the MCSC is not about the party, okay? It is about the safety of the community and stakeholders of the municipality. He didn't understand, to be honest. Because he was, like, politically a very educated person.... There were some changes, but in the Bregore/Brdašce municipality, there are lots of issues that are hidden, political issues.... The members don't want to open their mouths because they will have a problem.

(Interview 85, OSCE Official, 27/11/2013)

In sum, the MCSC did little to improve citizen participation in municipal security and safety concerns and did not respect accountability rules, but it did contribute to improved cooperation between the Municipal Government and the Kosovo Police and furthermore offered the Mayor the opportunity to strengthen his political power. The rules of the reform were implemented as follows:

FORMAL DIMENSION

Rule 1. MCSC established: The MCSC was formally established by the Mayor as late as 2011 upon pressure by OSCE (MLGA 2013).
Rule 2. All members appointed: The MCSC had some members appointed, including the Kosovo Police Station Commander or his Deputy, the Mayor or his Deputy, Directors and Officers, occasionally the Officer for Communities – but civil society representatives from NGOs and minority representatives from Serbian community were not appointed.

PRACTICE DIMENSION

Rule 3. Regular meetings: The MCSC held eight meetings in 2012 (MLGA 2013).
Rule 4. All members participate: Neither civil society representatives nor minority representatives from the Serbian, Turkish, Roma and Ashkali minorities participated more than once in 2012, if at all.[84]
Rule 5. Reporting to MA and to citizens: The MCSC did not report to the Municipal Assembly on its activities in 2012 and also did not organize public hearings to inform citizens about its work.[85]
Rule 6. Annual Action Plan: There was no annual action plan developed.[86]

CONTENT DIMENSION

Rule 7. Security issues identified: The MCSC meetings were used to identify and discuss security problems.[87]
Rule 8. Problem-solving: MCSC members delegated problem-solving strategies to Kosovo Police, although some international actors were not satisfied with the level of responsiveness from the side of the police to the problems discussed.[88]
Rule 9. Awareness raising: There was no awareness raising campaign on security-related matters.[89]

Summary: external–domestic interactions in Municipal Community Safety Council reform

The Municipal Community Safety Council represents a case of high international capacity and weak resistance against democracy. In both municipalities, the result was captured implementation. The availability of major international capacity in terms of mandate, manpower or financial resources seems thus less relevant to peacebuilding success than assumed in the international capacity literature. The cooperative behaviour of municipal actors in Zabel/Šumarak, in turn, shows that international interventions do not necessarily provoke resistance as assumed in the critical peacebuilding scholarship. External–domestic interaction seems to be a necessary condition for reform implementation, as implementation was dependent upon whether peacebuilders took the initiative to push the reform or not. The case studies show that the mere adoption of the MCSC law in 2005 did not automatically lead to an onset of the reform implementation. Instead, implementation began only after peacebuilders had entered into reform negotiations with domestic actors. Once the external–domestic interaction started, however, domestic actors received considerable leeway to capture reforms for their own priorities. The following recapitulates the role of the external–domestic interaction in the case of Municipal Community Safety Councils based on the key categories of the analytical framework of peacebuilding interactions by discussing the peacebuilding outcomes, the use of ad hoc tactics of prioritisation, selectivity and leverage, as well as the environment of interaction.

Peacebuilding outcomes

The Municipal Community Safety Councils reform resulted in captured implementation in Zabel/Šumarak and Bregore/Brdašce. In Zabel/Šumarak, peacebuilders were more successful in strengthening democracy and improving cooperation and responsiveness between the police, municipality and citizens in security matters. The set of rules that had been selected by peacebuilders was fully implemented by domestic actors also in accordance with peacebuilders' intentions. The reason the reform only resulted in captured implementation lies in the peacebuilders' use of ad hoc tactics of selectivity during the negotiation process. In Bregore/Brdašce, municipal elites modified the rules promoted by peacebuilders and particularly the Mayor used the reform for his priority to broaden his political power. Although the forum proved useful for improving institutional cooperation between the police and the municipality in security and safety, it ignored the need for citizen participation as well as the requirement to be held accountable by the Municipal Assembly and citizens. In addition, the appointed MCSC members were all highly dependent on the Mayor, which made it unlikely that the work of the municipality or the police would be challenged by critical voices.

Table 6.2 Peacebuilding outcomes of municipal community safety councils

Municipal community safety council outcomes

Dimension	Zabel/Šumarak	Bregore/Brdašce
Formal dimension		
1 MCSC established	Yes	Yes
2 All members appointed	Yes	In-between
Practice dimension		
3 Regular meetings (6–10)	Yes	Yes
4 All members participate (50% min)	Yes	In-between
5 Reporting to MA/citizens	Yes (planned)	No
6 Annual action plan	In-between	No
Content dimension		
7 Security issues identified	Yes	Yes
8 Problem-solving	Yes	Yes
9 Awareness raising	Yes	No
Outcome	Full implementation	Captured implementation

Prioritisation, selectivity, leverage

Peacebuilders' ad hoc tactics of prioritisation, selectivity and leverage played an important role in the reform outcome, as they provided domestic actors with leeway to capture peacebuilding reforms for their own purposes despite the high capacity vested in police reform.

Prioritisation was an important ad hoc tactic to make no implementation less likely, particularly in Bregore/Brdašce, where municipal actors had met simple international advice with resistance. Peacebuilders prioritised MCSCs in early 2011, when MCSCs were included as a benchmark in the EU policy conditionality catalogue for visa liberalisation. The long phase of peacebuilders' tolerance for non-compliance in Bregore/Brdašce shows that peacebuilders are ready to back down from their demands unless they perceive non-compliance as threatening their core interests. Once MCSCs were moved to the top of the international agenda, peacebuilders intensified their efforts, as they saw the success of EU conditionality threatened. Interestingly, peacebuilders were more interested in demonstrating the 'success' of their reform efforts than their local counterparts: While peacebuilders heavily increased their activities to push reform implementation in municipalities, the Kosovo Police central-level coordination office was less active. This observation is somewhat counterintuitive to general assumptions in the EU conditionality literature that domestic actors increase reform activities once that reform is a condition for EU accession or, as in this case, visa liberalisation.

Selectivity also influenced reform outcomes. Peacebuilders' selectivity shifts to and from a specific sub-set of rules provided to domestic actors with the opportunity to ignore those rules not attended to by peacebuilders at no cost, using this leeway for reform capture. I identified three interaction periods: In the first period, peacebuilders paid attention to the formal establishment of MCSCs in priority areas (rule 1). Then, peacebuilders demanded the formal functioning of MCSCs (rules 1, 2, 3, 7). And lastly, international actors aimed at making MCSCs an effective security mechanism, focusing on MCSCs' capacity in drafting action plans, problem identification, problem solving and awareness raising (rules 1, 2, 3, 5, 7, 8, 9). Selectivity shifts were triggered by changes in the international agenda after Kosovo's independence (2008) and priority shifts on the international agenda due to EU policy conditionality (2011). Rule 5 was left out of all interaction periods. Given the fact that domestic actors tended to implement only those rules selected by peacebuilders, the failure of peacebuilders to tackle the total set of rules made full implementation unlikely in this case.

Leverage allowed international actors to vary the level of domestic adoption costs through their choice of high or low leverage norm promotion instruments. Different types of leverage marked each of the three periods: In the first period, peacebuilders used low leverage instruments such as capacity building, monitoring and advice. In the second, international actors again used low leverage in the form of capacity building, monitoring and advice. And in the final period, peacebuilders resorted to the higher leverage instruments of coercion and conditionality, in addition to capacity building, monitoring, reporting and advice. The fact that high leverage instruments were used in this case made a result of no implementation less likely. This is of particular importance in constraining environments of interaction such as Bregore/Brdašce, where domestic actors reacted to international demands with a mixture of resistance, foot-dragging and cooperation. There, domestic actors were more likely to respond cooperatively when international actors showed greater assertiveness with high leverage instruments. In Zabel/Šumarak, the enabling environment of interaction generally made domestic actors react to international demands cooperatively, independent of the level of leverage applied.

Environment of interaction

In an enabling environment such as in Zabel/Šumarak, domestic elites are more likely to respond with cooperation to international reform demands and less likely to react with resistance. The constraining environment in Bregore/Brdašce, on the other hand, made municipal elites in Bregore/Brdašce less inclined to cooperate with peacebuilders' demands because they feared a loss of power. They therefore were likely to react with foot-dragging and resistance, especially when faced with rules that strengthened accountability and citizen participation. However, due to the wide support for the norm of democracy within both municipalities, acts of outright resistance against reform implementation were less likely.

Promoting minority rights in a high capacity policy field: Minority Community Policing

Minority Community Policing is a crucial mechanism for promoting minority rights within the Kosovo Police at the level of the village or neighborhoods. The reform was introduced in 2005 as a response to the March 2004 riots, at a time when Kosovo institutions were in dire need of re-establishing trust amongst Kosovo Serbs (UN 2006). Minority Community Policing strengthens minority rights by establishing special representative institutions – police sub-stations and Local Public Safety Councils (LPSCs) – in minority areas. The goal is to strengthen minority protection, build trust between Kosovo Serbs and the Kosovo Police and increase local police responsiveness to minority concerns (Saferworld 2010). The police sub-stations are to be run by minority police officers to improve trust in Kosovo institutions, and the Local Public Safety Councils serve to improve citizen participation of minority communities and function as consultation mechanisms on crime prevention and community safety issues between the District Commander and the civilian side (RoK 2011).

Minority Community Policing represents a reform with high international capacity but strong resistance against the promoted international norm of minority rights. Yet I observed divergent peacebuilding outcomes in Zabel/Šumarak and Bregore/Brdašce. In the priority area Zabel/Šumarak, the outcome was captured implementation: Minority Community Policing was used for the domestic priority of socio-economic development, solving problems with illegal landfills and garbage hills piling up around the Serbian village. In Bregore/Brdašce, the outcome was no implementation, a surprising result for a reform initiative with high international capacity.

The analytical framework of peacebuilding interactions allows for a better understanding of these peacebuilding outcomes by taking into account how the ad hoc tactics of prioritisation, selectivity and leverage in combination with the environment of interaction shape peacebuilding results and offer domestic actors leeway for reform capture. Prioritisation made no implementation less likely, but only in Zabel/Šumarak, where the reform was put at the top of the local international agenda in 2011 because non-compliance with Minority Community Policing was framed as a local security threat. In Bregore/Brdašce, no prioritisation took place as non-implementation of the reform was not perceived as a security threat. Selectivity also shaped the peacebuilding outcome because internationals did not insist on security and safety problems being addressed, which offered domestic actors leeway to solve development problems instead. Leverage significantly shaped interaction dynamics, particularly in Zabel/Šumarak, where high leverage made domestic actors re-consider resistance against the reform, as the costs of non-adoption rose. A constraining environment of interaction was an important reason for the generally non-cooperative attitude and initial domestic resistance that peacebuilders had to overcome.

To be able to follow the external–domestic interaction in Minority Community Policing, one needs an overview of the various actors involved. On the international side, UNMIK, EULEX, the OSCE and KFOR were engaged in the negotiation of Minority Community Policing. UNMIK provided supervision, monitoring and advice to the Police Station Commander and police officers in their daily work until 2008. Taking over from UNMIK, EULEX engaged in supervision, monitoring, mentoring and advising to the Station Commander and other municipal police officers. The OSCE Department for Security and Public Safety provided financial assistance, extensive capacity building, monitoring and advice and was in regular contact with Station Commanders and municipal police officers through training at the national police school. The OSCE regional and field offices also regularly monitored and advised Kosovo Police as well as minority community members. KFOR monitored all security-related developments in the municipality. On the domestic side, the most frequent interaction took place with the Kosovo Police Station Commanders, sector leaders of the respective minority areas and chiefs of the Community Policing Units as well as with minority community representatives of the concerned villages and neighbourhoods (RoK 2011). At the central level, there was an inter-ministerial Working Group by the Ministry of Internal Affairs and the Kosovo Police that monitored, amongst others, Minority Community Policing. The KP headquarters' Coordinator of Safety Forums also supported the Local Public Safety Councils and police sector leaders.[90]

Minority Community Policing requires domestic actors to implement the following set of rules:[91] Local Public Safety Councils have to be established in minority areas (rule 1) (UNMIK 2005). Sub-police stations ought to be established in areas where "it is in the interests of effective policing and good relations with all Communities to do so" (rule 2) (UNMIK 2005). Kosovo Police Station Commanders must analyse the security and safety situation and identify areas in need of sub-police stations and Local Public Safety Councils to ensure good relations between the local community and the police (RoK 2008). UNMIK had already managed to set up 21 police sub-stations in identified priority areas (UN 2006, 2007). The Director of Kosovo Police officially establishes the Councils upon consultation with the local population and the Police Station Commander (RoK 2008). Local Public Safety Councils are to be convened on a regular basis by the Kosovo Police sector leader (rule 3) (RoK 2011). Participants of the Local Public Safety Councils are local governmental authorities, citizen representatives from all ethnic communities and potentially civic organizations (rule 4) (RoK 2008). The LPSC president should also join the Municipal Community Safety Council meetings (rule 5) (RoK 2012b). Police sub-stations ought to be operational in the respective area (rule 6) (RoK 2012b). The Kosovo Police are urged to use Minority Community Policing to monitor community tensions, gather community safety information (rule 7) and raise public awareness for security and safety (rule 8) (RoK 2011). Local Public Safety Councils are required to serve

Table 6.3 Outcome operationalisation – minority community policing

Dimension	Period			Source
	1	2	3	
Formal dimension				
1 LPSC established in minority area	1	2	3	Law on Police 2012 Art. 7.5
2 Police sub-station in minority area	1	2	3	Law on Police 2012 Art. 42
Practice dimension				
3 Regular meetings (at least bi-monthly)	–	2	3	Law on Police 2012 Art. 7.5
4 Participation of all members	–	–	3	MSCS AI
5 Police sub-station operational	–	2	–	Law on Police 2012 Art. 42
Content dimension				
6 Security and safety problems identified	–	–	–	Law on Police 2012 Art. 7.4
7 Problem-solving	–	–	3	Law on Police 2012 Art. 7.4
8 Awareness raising	–	–	–	Law on Police 2012 Art. 7.4

Source: Own compilation. Note on abbreviations: MCSC refers to Municipal Community Safety Council, LPSC refers to Local Public Safety Council.

"as public consultation mechanisms with the intent of reducing and/or preventing crime, increasing perceptions of safety, to address general community safety issues (rule 6) and ensure citizen willingness to cooperate with the police" (RoK 2011). Based on these rules, Table 6.3 presents the operationalisation of Minority Community Policing.

Prioritisation, selectivity and leverage in Minority Community Policing

As Minority Community Policing was regarded by peacebuilders as an accommodating strategy to stabilise the security situation in Kosovo, the external–domestic interaction was heavily influenced by the fast-changing security developments on the ground, such as local inter-ethnic incidents, the situation in North Kosovo or Kosovo independence. Peacebuilders thus often used ad hoc interaction tactics to cope with the complex post-war environment. The close connection of the reform to the security situation also led peacebuilders to differentiate between municipalities with a stable security situation, such as Bregore/Brdašce, and municipalities with a perceived unstable security situation, such as Zabel/Šumarak. Based on this, international actors defined priority areas (unstable security) and non-priority areas (stable security) for reform implementation. If UNMIK was in a priority area, they insisted on implementation, while in non-priority areas, they were more likely to step down and tolerate resistance, modification or foot-dragging.

Prioritisation

Minority Community Policing was prioritised in 2011 in response to a local security threat, but only in Zabel/Šumarak. The reason for prioritisation in Zabel/Šumarak was the finalisation of a bridge that would connect Albanian areas with a Serbian village. The international community perceived the bridge as a security threat because it would bring Albanian traffic into the Serbian village. To mitigate, peacebuilders prioritised Minority Community Policing in the hope that inter-ethnic relations would improve through the reform. In Bregore/Brdašce, no such prioritisation took place.

Selectivity

Peacebuilders performed several selectivity shifts, each time picking a different sub-set of rules from the reform to be implemented. This selectivity allowed domestic actors to ignore remaining rules from the reform without having to fear the costs. Several selectivity shifts are observed: Under UNMIK – from 2005 to 2007 – selectivity concentrated on formal establishment, particularly in priority areas (rules 1, 2). Then, between 2008 and 2010, the selected sub-set of rules required the formal establishment of Minority Community Policing structures all over Kosovo (rules 1, 2, 3). Finally, between 2011 and 2012, selectivity shifted to pro-active problem solving, promoting pro-activity, problem identification and the problem solving of community concerns (rules 1, 2, 3, 6, 7, 8).

Period I (2000–07): formal establishment (rules 1, 2)

At first, peacebuilders selected a sub-set of rules demanding the formal establishment of Minority Community Policing structures, particularly in priority areas such as Zabel/Šumarak (UN 2006), emphasising the need to establish Local Public Safety Councils (1) and police sub-stations (2).

Period II (2008–10): formal establishment (rules 1, 2, 3)

In the second period, peacebuilders' selectivity was concerned with the formal establishment of Minority Community Policing Kosovo-wide. Peacebuilders emphasised the need to establish Local Public Safety Councils (1), to police sub-stations in minority areas (2) and to hold regular meetings (3). The selectivity shift was triggered by Kosovo's independence in 2008, when UNMIK's withdrawal made functioning domestic institutions increasingly important.

Period III (2011–12): pro-active problem-solving (rules 1, 2, 3, 4, 6, 7, 8)

International actors selected a sub-set of rules related to the pro-active problem-solving capacity of Minority Community Policing structures. Peacebuilders not only emphasised the need to establish Local Public Safety

Councils (1) and police sub-stations (2) in minority areas. Once set up, they also pushed for regular meetings (3), ensured operational sub-stations (6) and focused on dealing with security and safety issues (7) and on problem-solving capacity (8). The widening of the sub-set of rules was triggered by the EU visa liberalisation dialogue, which required the adoption of the National Strategy and Action Plan for Community Safety 2011–15 and the National Strategy and Action Plan for Community Policing 2012–15, both of which included provisions for Minority Community Policing.[92]

Leverage

Period I (2005–07): higher/lower leverage

Peacebuilders used different degrees of leverage in municipalities with stable security situations than they did in municipalities with unstable security situations. In stable municipalities, peacebuilders used the lower leverage instruments of facilitation, monitoring and advice to convince domestic actors of the usefulness of the reform. In the event that international actors failed to reach an agreement, UNMIK set up its own UNMIK Community Police Offices as a substitute for domestic sub-police stations (Chavleishvili 2011).[93] In unstable areas, UNMIK additionally used executive powers to formally establish Minority Community Policing structures.

Period II (2008–10): lower leverage

In the second period, peacebuilders used the lower leverage instruments of capacity building, dialogue, monitoring and advice. EULEX and the OSCE both tried to persuade domestic actors to set up Minority Community Policing structures.[94] The OSCE also offered Kosovo-wide capacity building training for police officials, during which Minority Community Policing was discussed.[95]

Period III (2011–12): higher leverage

In 2011, the EU progress report mentioned Minority Community Policing for the first time and criticised the insufficient establishment of sub-police stations and the lack of consultation with Local Public Safety Councils (EC 2011). This led to increased international attention to the reform and the use of higher leverage instruments such as coercion or financial assistance in addition to capacity building, dialogue facilitation, monitoring, reporting or advice. EULEX increased its support of Minority Community Policing through its monitoring, mentoring and advising activities (UN 2012).[96] The OSCE made the establishment of LPSCs in minority areas a priority for 2012.[97] Particularly in unstable municipalities, the OSCE started to provide financial assistance to LPSCs for projects between €2,000 and €3,000 related to safety, security and quality of life,[98] and provided capacity building workshops specifically on the role and responsibilities of LPSCs.[99]

Minority Community Policing in Zabel/Šumarak

> KFOR construction of the Braljža/Bralje–Trepljevo bridge is potentially one of the most important projects that we have. At the same time, it will be very hard to permit Albanians a right of passage through Braljža/Bralje without being able to offer some similar freedom to the Serbs in Braljža. UNMIK has stressed to the Albanian leadership in the various affected villages that a minimum pre-condition is a meaningful dialogue.
> (UNMIK Weekly Report 16–22 June 2001 for Zabel/Šumarak Municipality)

The negotiations over Minority Community Policing in Zabel/Šumarak can only be understood in connection to local security dynamics, in which the bridge mentioned in the quote above took centre stage. The construction of the bridge between a Serbian village and several Albanian hamlets had already started in 2001 with the international support of KFOR, UNMIK and the OSCE (OSCE 2009a). The bridge construction had the high-level support of the Prime Minister, the Mayor and Kosovo Albanian municipal politicians, but Kosovo Serbs of Braljža/Bralje opposed the construction because of security concerns. Once Serbian security concerns became apparent, peacebuilders stopped the project[100] and conditioned further bridge construction on Serbian consent and the implementation of Minority Community Policing,[101] which was seen as a tool for improving inter-ethnic relations.

Minority Community Policing ultimately resulted in captured implementation, as domestic actors used the reform to solve development problems such as the irregular collection of garbage and illegal landfills. Taking external–domestic interactions into account offers an explanation for the reform outcome: Ad hoc interaction tactics impeded, on the one hand, outright resistance to the reform, but, on the other hand, left considerable leeway for reform capture. Prioritisation of the reform made no implementation less likely. Such prioritisation had been triggered in 2011, when Albanians resumed bridge construction. As peacebuilders regarded further non-compliance with Minority Community Policing a security threat, they insisted on the implementation of at least a minimum sub-set of rules. Selectivity made full implementation less likely in that rules 5 and 9 were never taken up by peacebuilders and could thus be ignored by domestic actors at no cost. High leverage made no implementation again less likely, as the use of coercion and financial assistance made non-adoption more costly for Serbs. Finally, external–domestic interactions were set in a rather constraining environment of interaction that made reform adoption more costly for domestic actors. Domestic resistance was thus the most common response to international reform proposals, especially on the side of the Kosovo Serbs.

The reform involved various actors, of which the Kosovo Police Station Commander, the Kosovo Police Section Leader, the Mayor and minority community representatives in the Serbian village were most important domestic actors. On the international side, the UNMIK Municipal Administration, KFOR Liaison Monitoring Team, EULEX and the OSCE Community Team, headquarters, and field office were involved.

The following describes the external–domestic interaction process according to the three periods of different sub-sets of rules in Minority Community Policing.

Period I (2005–07): formal establishment (rules 1, 2)

The Serbian-populated village Braljža/Braljë in Zabel/Šumarak was one of the security hot spots identified by UNMIK after the March 2004 riots (UN 2006). Relations between Kosovo Albanians and Kosovo Serbs were so tense that until 2006, UNMIK did not allow Kosovo Police to access the village.[102] The international attempt to formally establish police sub-stations and Local Crime Prevention Councils has to be seen in light of the enormous pressure on the UN mission to institute minority protection mechanisms in particularly unstable areas after March 2004 (Focus Kosovo 2005). In the first period, KFOR, UNMIK and the OSCE repeatedly facilitated informal meetings between the Station Commander, Section Leader and minority representatives of the village to gain support for minority community policing. They also advised the Kosovo Police Station Commander to build trust with the Serbian community.[103] In 2006, peacebuilders and Kosovo Police managed to improve the level of trust on the Kosovo Serbian side and local Kosovo Police was allowed to enter Serbian villages. Under pressure to produce results in the reform, UNMIK increased pressure on the Serbian community to drop resistance, identified a few Serbian individuals who were willing to participate and used its executive powers to formally establish Minority Community Policing structures (OSCE 2010):[104] A sub-station with eight Kosovo Serbs and seven Kosovo Albanian officers was established, and a Local Public Safety Council formed (OSCE 2009b, 2010). However, Kosovo Serbs used a mixture of resistance and foot-dragging strategy that rendered the peacebuilders' success at formal establishment null and void: The Local Public Safety Council never met.

> In Braljža/Braljë, one Kosovo Serbian village in Zabel/Šumarak, a Local Public Safety Committee was established in 2006. It has never functioned.
>
> (OSCE 2010)

The attitude about the reform was divided amongst domestic actors: While Kosovo Albanian actors showed themselves open to implementing Minority Community Policing, Kosovo Serbs remained opposed to the bridge and the reform. Kosovo Police and Kosovo Albanian municipal authorities cooperated with international attempts at establishing Minority Community Policing structures, and Kosovo Police in particular showed a strong commitment to improving relations with minority communities. One police officer described his approach to the Kosovo Serbian areas:

> First, we sit, we tried to show that we want to make everybody to be safe. We were trying to get people to trust in us. It was very hard for us, but I think people even have some trust in the police.[105]

Serbian representatives first reacted with resistance to international demands, but then, confronted with increasing pressure from UNMIK, moderate Serbs reluctantly consented to create Minority Community Policing institutions.[106] Yet only the formal structures were set in place because Kosovo Serbs resisted practical implementation. Peacebuilders then backed down from further demands at making the reform function.

Period II (2008–10): formal establishment (rules 1, 2, 3)

After Kosovo's independence, international actors paid growing attention to the formal establishment and regular functioning of Minority Community Policing. Yet Kosovo's independence had provoked a severe setback with regard to Minority Community Policing, as Serbs started a boycott of Kosovo institutions, including a complete withdrawal from Minority Community Policing structures: The police sub-station was closed when Serbian police officers refused to come to work, and at any rate, the Safety Council had never functioned (OSCE 2010). But independence had also brought movement into the bridge project as the municipality received a covenant from the Ministry of Urbanism to finance bridge construction in 2009.[107] From then on, the bridge was a recurrent topic in Municipal Assembly meetings,[108] and Kosovo Serbs were put under increasing pressure from the Mayor to consent to the bridge (and to Minority Community Policing)[109] – without success.

Peacebuilders cooperated closely with Kosovo Police and the Mayor to overcome Kosovo Serbian resistance against the bridge as well as Minority Community Policing. KFOR, EULEX and the OSCE used facilitation, monitoring and advice with the goal of gaining support among Serbs for the re-establishment of Minority Community Policing structures in the village.[110] EULEX closely supported the Kosovo Police's Station Commander with mentoring, monitoring and advice in its attempts to implement the reform[111] and the OSCE also provided capacity building training to police.[112]

International actors could count on the cooperation of the Kosovo Police and municipal authorities in their attempts at re-vitalising Minority Community Policing. Possibly, but not necessarily, the cooperative attitude of Kosovo Albanian actors was connected to the fact that Minority Community Policing was an international condition for the bridge construction. The

Kosovo Police Station Commander showed clear commitment and regularly conducted field visits despite the breakdown of formal structures.[113] The Mayor equally dedicated attention to the security situation in the Serbian-populated area.[114] The local sub-police station was re-established by July 2009,[115] but attempts at institutionalising the Safety Council failed. Kosovo Police organised several informal meetings with Serbian representatives, with and without international support, to increase trust within the Kosovo Serbian population.[116] Nevertheless, Kosovo Serbian resistance to the bridge and Minority Community Policing prevailed.[117]

Period III (2011–12): pro-active problem-solving (rules 1, 2, 3, 6, 7, 8)

In the third period, peacebuilders in Zabel/Šumarak continued to push for the formal establishment of Local Public Safety Councils and for the sub-set of rules promoting pro-active problem solving. Success in the formal establishment of these Councils became more and more important as the finalisation of the bridge was looming: In 2011, the Ministry of Finance announced financial grants of €450,000 for the bridge and – as an incentive for the non-cooperative Serbs – an additional €50,000 for infrastructure projects in the Serbian village.[118] One consequence of this was that the Kosovo Albanian municipality was determined to proceed with the bridge construction regardless of Serbian consent to either the bridge or Minority Community Policing mechanisms. Minority Community Policing, the peacebuilders' security guarantee for local Serbs exposed to Albanian bridge traffic, was thus at the top of the local peacebuilders' agenda.

Due to the imminent security threat, peacebuilders prioritised Minority Community Policing from 2011 on. Peacebuilders heavily increased their activities to support Minority Community Policing. EULEX engaged in regular monitoring and advice, the OSCE provided financial assistance, capacity building and outreach as well as monitoring and advice, and KFOR contributed through the facilitation of meetings. The OSCE, EULEX and KFOR facilitated informal meetings between municipal officials and Serbian representatives on different occasions.[119] International activities increased, the further the bridge construction progressed. The OSCE cooperated with Kosovo Police to organise meetings with citizens to inform them of the benefits of Minority Community Policing.[120]

> We have contacted them because sometimes the problem is that citizens don't know. Even though the OSCE spends a lot of money, they don't know much about the benefits of LPSCs. So together with the police, we organized a meeting, since Braljze had a very hot issue with the bridge.
> (Interview 75, OSCE Official, Prishtina, 20/11/2012)

Given the tense situation, EULEX, the OSCE, and KFOR decided to apply more coercive measures to pressure Serbs into dropping resistance. In spring

2012, with the finalisation of the bridge looming, the OSCE, EULEX and KFOR, together with Kosovo Police, formed an advocacy coalition to convince Serbian representatives of the need for cooperation in Minority Community Policing.[121] Yet one OSCE official rightly stated, "No matter how hard the Kosovo Police people push it, if the two communities don't support, it will fail".[122] In June 2012, the OSCE stepped up leverage by offering financial assistance for projects of the Local Public Safety Councils.[123] Braljža/Bralje was offered grants for a project to clean up an illegal landfill in the area.[124] These thematically unrelated projects aimed to institutionalise the work of LPSCs as one OSCE official explains:

> LPSCs – when they are established, they are very motivated to do something. Unless they get some support from any of the donors or the municipality, they lose their motivation, because without further support, they don't have any financial means to implement any projects, and this was somehow...
>
> (Interview 89, OSCE Department for Security and Public Safety, 06/12/2013)

Eventually, Serbs dropped their resistance and conceded to international and Albanian pressure for reform implementation, though mainly due to the €50,000 in financial assistance offered by the Ministry of Finance and to the financial assistance provided by the OSCE.[125] In April 2012, a new sub-police station was set up in a container close to the future bridge.[126] In May 2012, Serbs agreed to participate in the Local Public Safety Council.[127] Kosovo Police, in cooperation with village representatives, appointed the members of the Council from the Serbian village and the neighbouring Albanian hamlets on the other side of the river.[128] LPSC members from both sides were chosen: "They are not young people there. Village leaders in the council have 45 or 50 years or more. Most of them know each other very well".[129] The Council met regularly every second month from the time of its formation, and members of the Council participated regularly.[130] In addition, KFOR joined the meetings.[131] LPSC meetings seemed to "take place in a quiet atmosphere",[132] and international observers were content:

> I think it is a positive thing that they talk about problems and try to solve them. I think they [Serbs] understood that they have to participate. There is some pressure that they can't do otherwise because they live on Kosovo territory.
>
> (KFOR Official, Zabel/Šumarak, 26/11/2012)

Kosovo Police welcomed Minority Community Policing but also voiced reluctance for unconditional support of the reform. This might hint at the fact that part of the Albanian support for the reform was driven by an interest in building the bridge:

For us, this is a challenge. They [Serbs] are going to challenge us, because they will ask from us every time to improve security situation; they are going to watch and follow what we are doing. But it is good, because we going to follow the station better and if something happens, we can sit together and try to find a solution.

(Interview 67, Kosovo Police, Zabel/Šumarak, 07/11/2012)

The reasons for Kosovo Serbs' changing attitude also deserve discussion. Kosovo Serbs were put under enormous pressure – not only from peacebuilders' advocacy coalitions but also from the domestic side: the Serbian village received several high-level visits from the Mayor, the Minister of Urbanism and even the Prime Minister, before and during the bridge construction, with the hope of winning their support for the project.[133] Finally, Kosovo Serbs were offered considerable financial incentives: €50,000 from the Ministry of Finance if they agreed to the bridge, and further financial assistance from the OSCE for projects by the Local Public Safety Forum. Keeping in mind the poor economic conditions of the Serbian community, these incentives in and of themselves might have provoked a change of mind. This line of thinking is supported by the observation that the LPSC meetings were mainly dedicated to development problems in the villages. In fact, in Braljža/Bralje, the local safety forum concentrated on solving problems with garbage collection and illegal landfills, financed by OSCE project grants for LPSC work. One international observer told me:

We have talked about the garbage three times already – the garbage, the garbage, the garbage. Okay. But, I don't know if anyone from the community knows what to do. They write a letter that everybody signs and send that to the municipality so that they find solutions.

(Interview 79, KFOR Official, Zabel/Šumarak, 26/11/2012)

The lack of waste collection and the use of free land as a dumping ground were the most important topics during the meetings of the council.[134] Further issues were the possibility of financial compensation for members and a budget for phone and travel costs for the meetings.[135] Security and safety concerns were not part of the discussion. OSCE officials complain that there is a lack of substantial work on security and safety within Minority Community Policing structures.

It would be good if they [LPSCs] were used for security issues. Now they are mostly used for projects.

(Interview 77, OSCE Official, Prishtina, 23/11/2012)

As a consequence, the forum was limited in its original purpose of contributing to the problem solving of security or safety concerns. Yet the OSCE is 'complicit' in this accommodation strategy in Braljža/Bralje by providing financial assistance for two garbage-related projects – a 'waste management study visit' to Norway and financial support for cleaning up the waste around the village.[136] One OSCE official justifies the financing of project such as in Braljža/Bralje "because when garbage creates environmental problems and some disease, this is connected to safety and quality of life".[137] The more honest interpretation would be that OSCE openly uses financial incentives to ensure the continuous functioning of LPSCs because they feel that LPSC members are only motivated to work for the Council if they receive financial support for socio-economic development projects.[138] The OSCE's broad interpretation of projects qualifying for financial support – they have to target security, safety or quality of life – allows them to sustain the functioning of forums captured by domestic actors for development needs as much as it allows them to proclaim 'success' in Minority Community Policing.[139] The long-term sustainability of these institutions is, however, more than fragile.

Peacebuilding outcome: captured implementation

Minority Community Policing mainly served as a space for solving problems of socio-economic development in the area and the outcome is therefore judged as captured implementation. Yet the Kosovo Police considered the Local Public Safety Committee a success. Not because it helped in the identification and problem solving of security concerns, but because dealing with development issues contributed to inter-ethnic reconciliation. A Kosovo Police official described his understanding as follows:

> The idea was for those people just to sit together and just to speak. And now we can be proud because, you know, even though I am not attending this meeting, now they are speaking to each other, trying to solve the problem. They are now starting some projects together. It is something we wanted.
> (Interview 67, Kosovo Police, Zabel/Šumarak, 07/11/2012)

In the long run, these established inter-ethnic contacts might bear the potential of improving the security situation, as Kosovo Serbs now know whom to contact in the event of severe problems. However, the Council is not free from power relations between the Albanian majority and Serbian minority, and the solution to any problem will depend on the Albanians' good will. The fact that security issues are not already dealt with in the Council points to the Kosovo Serbs' low trust in the problem-solving willingness of Albanians. Focusing on the development can thus be seen as an accommodation strategy. In sum, the rules of Minority Community Policing has been implemented as follows:

FORMAL DIMENSION

Rule 1. LPSC formally established: The LPSC was first formally established in 2006, but is only functional since spring 2012.

Rule 2: Police sub-station formally established: The police sub-station was formally established already in 2006.

PRACTICE DIMENSION

Rule 3: Regular meetings at least bi-monthly: The LPSC meetings took place on a regular basis according to the municipal police.

Rule 4: Participation of all members: Members from all groups regularly participated, including the Local Sector Leader from Kosovo Police and representatives from the Albanian and the Serbian neighbourhoods.

Rule 6. Police sub-station operational: The police sub-station started to work again from mid-2009 on.

CONTENT DIMENSION

Rule 7. Security and safety problems identified: The Minority Community Policing structures, particularly LPSCs, did not identify security and safety problems, but instead dedicated meetings to socio-economic development issues.

Rule 8. Problem solving: The Minority Community Policing structures did not engage in problem solving of security and safety problems.

Rule 9. Awareness raising: There were no awareness raising campaigns on security and safety issues.

Minority Community Policing in Bregore/Brdašce

Minority Community Policing was not very popular in Bregore/Brdašce, neither amongst Kosovo Police nor the Kosovo Serbian population in the municipality. Indeed, this case is an example of how reforms can result in no implementation even in the absence of serious conflict between international and domestic actors. This result does not conform to the expectations of the high capacity argument that high capacity would support reform implementation. In fact, peacebuilders did not even utilise the high level of international capacity that was available to them in the policy field of police reform. Based on the analytical framework of peacebuilding interactions, I show how the ad hoc tactics of prioritisation, selectivity and leverage and the environment of interaction shape external–domestic interaction dynamics and reform outcomes. A constraining environment of interaction, characterised by weak domestic support for minority rights and a competitive style of politics, was the condition for reform failure because this environment created adoption costs that made it attractive for domestic actors to resist international demands. As the security situation in Bregore/Brdašce was considered stable, the municipality was not a priority area and 'non-compliance' was not a security threat; hence, no priority shift to the top of the international agenda occurred. The lack of prioritisation left no implementation as one possible outcome as peacebuilders were more inclined to tolerate 'non-compliance' in Bregore/Brdašce than in Zabel/Šumarak. Selectivity was not relevant in this case, as all international demands were met with resistance. There was no use of higher leverage in Bregore/Brdašce, either, which is why domestic actors could resist reform implementation at a low cost. This, again, made no implementation possible.

The Minority Community Policing reform in Bregore/Brdašce was negotiated mainly between the Kosovo Police Station Commander and minority community representatives in Upper Bregore/Brdašce and the neighbouring Serbian village Dobro Selo, and on the international side, the UNMIK Police, the UNMIK Municipal Administrator, EULEX regional and municipal advisors and the OSCE Department for Security and Public Safety, Community Team and field office.

The following traces the interaction process according to the sub-set of rules selected, the leverage applied and the domestic responses in each phase.

Period I: formal establishment (2005–07) (no rules for Bregore/Brdašce)

After Minority Community Policing was introduced in 2005, peacebuilders focused on priority areas to formally establish Local Public Safety Councils and police sub-stations. Bregore/Brdašce did not figure among the priority spots identified by UNMIK (UN 2006) because Kosovo Police had effectively protected Kosovo Serbs in the area during the March 2004 riots (OSCE 2006). Peacebuilders thus did not invest much time in pushing for reform implementation, but instead concentrated on setting up substitute institutions. UNMIK thus established externally controlled structures similar to those demanded by Minority Community Policing. For example, UNMIK Police maintained UNMIK Community Police Offices in the Serbian village Dobro Selo as a substitute for a domestic police sub-station[140] and convened 'security meetings', which partially substituted for the work that LPSCs were supposed to do.[141] In the absence of external demands to implement Minority Community Policing, domestic actors abstained from implementing the new rules from UNMIK legislation. This conforms to the observed pattern that domestic actors implement only those rules they are asked for by international actors, if at all. As a consequence, no sub-station was established and no Local Public Safety Council formed in Serbian minority areas of Bregore/Brdašce.[142] Municipal police, however, accepted the international substitution strategy: Kosovo Police, municipal authorities and, occasionally, minority representatives took part in the UNMIK-controlled 'security meetings' to discuss security concerns.[143] Two Serbian police officers were also working in the police station in Bregore/Brdašce.[144] For Kosovo Police officials, this seemed sufficient for improving relations between the police and Serbian minorities.[145]

Period II: formal establishment (2008–10) (rules 1, 2)

In the second period, international actors paid similarly low attention to the Minority Community Policing institutions in Bregore/Brdašce although Kosovo's independence and UNMIK's withdrawal made peacebuilders' substitution strategy impossible: Without executive powers at the municipal level, no UNMIK sub-police stations could be maintained and convening security meetings became more difficult.[146] Peacebuilders increasingly had to rely on functioning domestic institutions.

KFOR, EULEX and the OSCE did mention the need to establish Minority Community Policing structures, but did not actively promote the implementation of Minority Community Policing in this time. EULEX Municipal Advisors had other priorities than supporting the reform and focused on action fiches relating to crime investigations, patrolling and traffic security (EULEX 2009).[147] The OSCE did not engage in promoting Minority Community Policing at this point either. Apparently, peacebuilders did not seem to feel under pressure to lobby for setting up a sub-station and Local Public Safety Council in Bregore/Brdašce's minority areas: The security situation in Bregore/Brdašce municipality was deemed stable,[148] inter-ethnic relations were described as generally good by internationals and local police,[149] and there was a minimum interaction between the police and Serbian minorities because two Kosovo Serbian police officers worked at the station.[150] Peacebuilders substituted for the lack of Minority Community Policing only partially: UNMIK sub-stations in the neighbouring Serbian village were dismantled, but 'security meetings' were still convened a few times by the OSCE during this period and could partially take over the function of LPSCs.[151]

Again, the absence of external demands, beyond occasional advice, let domestic actors ignore the implementation of the reform altogether: Neither sub-stations nor Local Public Safety Councils were formed.[152] Kosovo Police and municipal authorities cooperated, however, when external actors convened the security meetings. The two Serbian police officers temporarily stopped working in 2008 to protest Kosovo's independence, but returned to duty after a few months.[153]

Period III: pro-active problem-solving (2011–12)

In the third period, peacebuilders became more attentive to having Minority Community Policing implemented in Bregore/Brdašce as international activities on that issue had increased Kosovo-wide. Peacebuilders thus focused on forming an institutional basis for Minority Community Policing and tried to formally establish sub-stations and Local Public Safety Councils. To this end, peacebuilders increased their efforts and used the lower leverage instruments of capacity building, monitoring, reporting and advice. A further possible reason for the increased international attention to reform implementation in Bregore/Brdašce was the mounting inter-ethnic tensions in the municipality that were related to international plans to establish a special protected zone in the neighbouring Serbian village to protect its rich, cultural heritage. Kosovo Albanian citizens fiercely opposed the law, which they believed would 'destroy' inter-ethnic relations, cement the 'ghettoisation' of Kosovo Serbs in the municipality, and empower Serbs, who then would be able to veto specific decisions in the municipality.[154] To pressure the municipality into accepting the law, high-ranking international actors and Kosovo central level institutions paid visits to discuss inter-ethnic relations and, on a related note, Minority Community Policing.

In the first half of 2011, Bregore/Brdašce received a range of high-ranking international and national attention: The KFOR Commander, KFOR Commander South and the OSCE Head of Regional Centre paid a visit to Bregore/Brdašce as well as national institutions such as the inter-ministerial Working Group for Monitoring the Community Safety Strategy, the Ministry of Internal Affairs' Department of Community and Safety and the Kosovo Police Coordinator of Safety Forums. The topics disscussed were connected to the special protected zone, inter-ethnic relations and minority protection mechanisms such as Communities Committees and safety forums.[155] The OSCE Department for Security and Public Safety was the first actor to advise specifically on Minority Community Policing. In early 2012, the OSCE Department for Security and Public Safety personally approached the Kosovo Police Station Commander to discuss the idea of setting up a Local Public Safety Council and opening a police sub-station in the Serbian village.[156] The OSCE field office repeated this advice in personal conversations with the municipal police in the following months.[157] The OSCE headquarters continued to provide police officials from all over Kosovo with capacity building training that tackled Minority Community Policing.

These international attempts to promote the formal setting up of Minority Community Policing structures were met with resistance on the domestic side. Kosovo Police in Bregore/Brdašce had little interest in implementing Minority Community Policing. They put forward three arguments: first, that the security situation was good; second, that the security situation and inter-ethnic relations might be aggravated by Minority Community Policing mechanisms; and third, that there was no demand from Serbs in the municipality to create such institutions.[158] Bregore/Brdašce police emphasised good relations with Serbs and pointed to the two Serbian police officers working at the station:

Concerning the Serbs, we don't have any problems. They cooperate with us, which means they work with us without problems. We have two police officers who are in contact with the Serbs 24 hours a day to solve their problems. But, I tell you, this mentality − the influence of Belgrade politics − is disturbing.

(Interview 19, Kosovo Police, 14/05/2012)[159]

The official position was that there was no need for Minority Community Policing, Local Public Safety Councils or sub-stations. The OSCE request to open a sub-station in Doblo Selo was even discussed in the Municipal Assembly but was regarded "for the moment unnecessary" thanks to the 'good security situation'.[160] As one OSCE employee explained:

> Their response was that there is nothing on going, that there were no problems, so somehow there was not any space left for us to go further. Actually it was the police's assessment that there is no need, and maybe they even thought if they established [Minority Community Policing], that the situation would reverse and create a kind of situation which is worse concerning the crime, concerning the communication between the different communities. It is not a closed story, but for the moment, there was not willingness.
>
> (Interview 75, OSCE Department for Security and Public Safety, 20/11/2012)

It is true that the security situation was considered stable, but the fact is that Kosovo Serbs in Bregore/Brdašce still felt insecure and that inter-ethnic incidents happened.[161] The main goal of peacebuilders – to improve relations between minorities and police and establish an effective mechanism for minority protection – was thus not achieved. Furthermore, the Albanian argument that Minority Community Policing might worsen the security situation seems counter-intuitive. It points to the general Kosovo Albanian perception that minority rights lead to the separation, not the integration, of Serbs and that minority rights lead to Serbian empowerment, which Albanian authorities perceive as increasing inter-ethnic tensions. Municipal authorities thus considered Local Public Safety Councils a potential challenge, as they feared the criticism of police and the public awareness of existing conflicts.[162] It is also unclear whether Kosovo Police acted against the interests of Kosovo Serbs in its decision to resist implementation. On the one hand, Serbian individuals had voiced their interest in Minority Community Policing in front of the OSCE during a headquarters field visit, but on the other hand, Kosovo Police argued that further conversations with Serbs had yielded limited interest in such a Council.[163] Considering Serbian resistance against participation in Minority Community Policing in Zabel/Šumarak, it is unclear whether Kosovo Serbs would have participated in LPSCs even if Kosovo Police had committed to the reform.

Confronted with domestic resistance, the OSCE decided to back down on its demands to implement Minority Community Policing:

> I couldn't do anything. Even if you create something, just a formal Council, it is not good, I think, to have an LPSC just formally on paper, and they are not working and not addressing issues. We don't want to establish Local Public Safety Councils just for the sake of it.
>
> (Interview 75, OSCE Department for Security and Public Safety, 20/11/2012)

The OSCE thus explained its backing down with the need for domestic support from the police – and from the community – to create functioning institutions.

Peacebuilding outcome: no implementation

The outcome of the Minority Community Policing reform in Bregore/ Brdašce is no implementation. Domestic actors successfully resisted international demands to implement the Minority Community Policing provisions.

Summary of external–domestic interactions in Minority Community Policing

The outcomes in the case of Minority Community Policing once more show that the mere availability of major international capacity is less relevant than assumed in the mainstream peacebuilding literature that discusses the need for high international investments. The local resistance explanation rightly predicts reform failure in Bregore/Brdašce, but it cannot account for the change in domestic behaviour in the case of Zabel/Šumarak, where domestic actors embraced reform after international actors increased pressure through coercion and financial incentives and local moderate Serbian forces gained strength. The case of Minority Community Policing further exemplifies that reform adoption does not guarantee reform implementation unless peacebuilders start pushing it. In this case, there was a gap of several years between law adoption in 2005 and the start of the implementation in as late as 2012 in Zabel/Šumarak, while reform implementation is still looming in Bregore/ Brdašce.

Peacebuilding outcomes

Minority Community Policing resulted in captured implementation in Zabel/ Šumarak and in no implementation in Bregore/Brdašce. In Zabel/Šumarak, Minority Community Policing was used by domestic actors to advance the domestic priority of development. Individuals involved used the Local Public Safety Council to solve development problems in the municipality such as the irregular collection of garbage and illegal landfills. In Bregore/Brdašce, however, police authorities refused to implement the reform because they were afraid that Minority Community Policing would lead to – according to them – an increase in crime and inter-ethnic tensions. A different interpretation could be that they were afraid of Serbian empowerment. Table 6.4 gives an overview of reform outcomes in both municipalities.

Table 6.4 Peacebuilding outcomes of minority community policing

Minority community policing outcomes

Dimension	Zabel/Šumarak	Bregore/Brdašce
Formal dimension		
1 LPSC established in minority area	Yes	No
2 Police sub-station in minority area	Yes	No
Practice dimension		
3 Regular meetings (at least bi-monthly)	Yes	No
4 Participation of all members	Yes	No
5 Police sub-station operational	Yes	No
Content dimension		
6 Security and safety problems identified	In-between	No
7 Problem-solving	In-between	No
8 Awareness raising	No	No
Outcome	Captured implementation	No implementation

Prioritisation, selectivity, leverage

In the case of Minority Community Policing, the external–domestic inter-action process was shaped by the ad hoc tactics of prioritisation, selectivity and leverage. These ad hoc tactics made no implementation less likely in the case of Zabel/Šumarak, but at the same time provided domestic actors with leeway to capture peacebuilding reforms for their own political agenda or to opt for non-compliance.

Prioritisation occurred only in Zabel/Šumarak because non-compliance with the reform was framed as a local security threat. The ad hoc use of pri-oritisation made no implementation a less likely outcome as peacebuilders insisted on Serbs to accept a minimum sub-set of rules. Bregore/Brdašce, on the other hand, shows that peacebuilders are inclined to tolerate resistance and back down from demands when the core international interests (stability or meeting EU conditionality benchmarks) are *not* threatened. In such situ-ations, conflict avoidance and maintaining good working relations is preferred over ensuring domestic compliance.

Selectivity in the set of rules chosen for negotiation offered domestic actors various avenues for reform capture at no cost. Peacebuilders changed the sub-set of rules three times: First, peacebuilders limited attention to the formal establishment of Minority Community Policing in priority areas (2005–07). Second, peacebuilders focused on formal establishment Kosovo-wide (2008–10). Lastly, international priority was given to improving the pro-active problem-solving capacity of LPSCs (2011–12). In Zabel/Šumarak, it was the fact that international actors were less concerned about whether the problems solved were – strictly speaking – security and safety problems, that provided an opportunity for LPSC participants to capture the reform for development concerns without incurring any costs (and even receiving financial assistance for it from OSCE).

Leverage varied over time and whether peacebuilders found themselves in a priority area or not. In priority areas, peacebuilders were more likely to step up the push for reform implementation and use higher leverage, while in non-priority areas, peacebuilders were ready to back down. The case of Zabel/Šumarak shows that the use of higher leverage instruments influences domestic calculations of adoption costs: Serbian resistance was only given up after coercion and the offer of considerable financial assistance by the OSCE and the Kosovo Government. Peacebuilders and the Kosovo Government consciously used financial dependencies and the miserable economic situation of Kosovo Serbs to buy their consent to reforms. In the case of the non-priority locale Bregore/Brdašce, the lower leverage attempts to push for the implementation of Minority Community Policing were met with resistance by Kosovo Albanian municipal and peacebuilders decided to back down from their demands.

Environment of interaction

The environment of interaction had an important influence on the external–domestic interaction dynamics in Zabel/Šumarak and Bregore/Brdašce. Interactions in Zabel/Šumarak were set in a rather constraining environment marked by a cooperative style of politics but weak support for minority rights. There, the police and municipal authorities showed themselves cooperative to international reform demands, but Serbian leaders and citizens reacted with resistance. The commitment of the police and municipality in Zabel/Šumarak might be, on the one hand, the result of the cooperative style of politics prevailing among political actors but, on the other hand, could be the result of conditioning of the bridge construction on Minority Community Policing. The external–domestic interplay in Bregore/Brdašce took place in a constraining environment marked by a competitive style of politics and weak support for minority rights. In addition to the weak support for minority rights, the prevalence of power politics in Bregore/Brdašce fostered further mistrust of potential Serbian empowerment through Minority Community Policing. This mix made resistance the most likely response to international demands for reform implementation.

Notes

1 A first step in the power transfer was the establishment of the Ministry of Internal Affairs in 2005. It received the responsibility to oversee Kosovo Police in 2006 (UNMIK 2005, 2006).
2 Interview 82 with former UNMIK staff, 03/10/2013.
3 External partners of the steering group are Saferworld, UNDP, the OSCE and International Criminal Investigative Training Assistance Program (ICITAP).

Interview 75 with the OSCE Department for Security and Public Safety, 20/11/2011.

4 MCSCs' work is regulated in several legal documents: UNMIK/REG/2005/45 On the Framework and Guiding Principles of the Kosovo Police Service (UNMIK 2005), Law on Police 2008 (RoK 2008), Law on Police 2012 (RoK 2012b) as well as the administrative instructions on MCSCs from 2009 (RoK 2009) and the revised version from September 2012 (RoK 2012a).

5 I am citing from the 2009 administrative instructions, relevant during the time investigated. The 2012 revision *additionally* includes: Chairperson of Communities Committee, Gender Equality Officer, Director of Education, Office for Communities and Return (RoK 2012a).

6 The representatives from municipal institutions select individuals proposed from minority communities and the civil society sector. If an ethnic group does not propose an MCSC member, the Mayor or Vice-Mayor appoints a representative in consultation with the Office for Community (RoK 2009). The 2012 Administrative Instruction requires approval from the Municipal Assembly for the list of MCSC members (RoK 2012a).

7 Interview 85 with OSCE Department for Security and Public Safety, Prishtina, 27/11/2013.

8 Interview 85 with OSCE Department for Security and Public Safety, Prishtina, 27/11/2013.

9 Interview 85 with OSCE Department for Security and Public Safety, Prishtina, 27/11/2013.

10 Interview 85 and 89 with OSCE Department for Security and Public Safety, Prishtina, 27/11/2013 and 06/12/2013.

11 Interview 85 with OSCE Department for Security and Public Safety, Prishtian, 27/11/2013.

12 Interview 85 with OSCE Department for Security and Public Safety, Prishtina, 27/11/2013.

13 Internationals pushed for adopting an Administrative Instruction to regulate the functioning of MCSCs in more detail. It was adopted in 2009 and revised in 2012.

14 Based on an inspection list accessed by the author.

15 Interview 85 with OSCE Department for Security and Public Safety, Prishtina, 27/11/2013.

16 Interview 85 with OSCE Department for Security and Public Safety, Prishtina, 27/11/2013.

17 Interview 85 with OSCE Department for Security and Public Safety, Prishtina, 27/11/2013.

18 The OSCE printed 70,000 leaflets and showed TV spots about MCSCs. Interview 75 with OSCE Community Policing Section, 20/11/2012.

19 Interview 67 with Kosovo Police, Zabel/Šumarak, 07/11/2012.

20 Interview 85 with the OSCE Department for Security and Public Safety, Prishtina, 27/11/2013.

21 Interview 78, KFOR, Zabel/Šumarak, 26/11/2012.

22 Interview 67 with Kosovo Police, Zabel/Šumarak, 07/11/2012 and interview 85 with OSCE Department for Security and Public Safety, Prishtina, 27/11/2013.

23 Interview 67 with Kosovo Police, Zabel/Šumarak, 07/11/2012 and 78 with OSCE regional office, Mitrovica, 26/11/2012.

24 Interview 67 with Kosovo Police, Zabel/Šumarak, 07/11/2012 and interview 78 with OSCE regional office, Mitrovica, 26/11/2012.

25 Interview 67 with Kosovo Police, Zabel/Šumarak, 07/11/2012 and interview 85 with OSCE Department for Security and Public Safety, Prishtina, 27/11/2013.

26 Participants from the municipality were usually the Police Station Commander, the Municipal President – now Mayor – and sometimes Serbian and RAE representatives. Interview 67 with Kosovo Police, Zabel/Šumarak, 07/11/2012.

27 Interview 85 with the OSCE Department for Security and Public Safety, 27/11/2013 and interview 67 with Kosovo Police, Zabel/Šumarak, 07/11/2012.

28 Interview 85 with the OSCE Department for Security and Public Safety, 27/11/2013 and interview 67 with Kosovo Police, Zabel/Šumarak, 07/11/2012.

29 The MCSCs' function was not regulated in detail in the UNMIK Regulation about Kosovo Police.

30 Interview 67 with Kosovo Police, Zabel/Šumarak, 07/11/2012 and (EULEX 2010).

31 Interview 89 with the OSCE Department for Security and Public Safety, Prishtina, 06/12/2013.

32 Interview 77 with OSCE Security Monitoring Section, Prishtina, 23/11/2012 and 85 with OSCE Department for Security and Public Safety, Prishtina, 27/11/2013.

33 While meetings took place less regularly than foreseen in 2008 and 2009 (MLGA 2010), meetings were held on a monthly basis in 2010. MLGA 2010 Municipality Monitoring January–June 2010, 53.

34 In 2008, only one NGO member and one minority representative from RAE participated, in contrast to an abundance of international organisations such as KFOR, ICO, the OSCE and UNHCR. In 2009 and 2010, there were two NGOs and representatives from the Ashkali and Turkish communities. To compensate for the lack of Serbian representatives, the Serbian Officer for Communities participated. Minutes from MCSC meeting, 01/12/2008, 06/07/2009, 01/02/2010.

35 Information from MCSC minutes from 01/12/2008, 06/07/2009.

36 No Serbs attended the meetings in 2008. Information from MCSC minutes from 01/12/2008, 06/07/2009 and interview 67 with Kosovo Police, Zabel/Šumarak, 07/11/2012.

37 Meeting minutes had existed since 2008. I was provided with the MCSC minutes from 01/12/2008, 06/07/2009 and 01/02/2010.

38 Among the topics discussed were the general security situation, traffic accidents, thefts and cooperation problems between the police and courts. Minority representatives raised recent security problems within their community. Less related to security were discussions about the provision of firewood or New Year's gifts by international organisations to the Ashkali minority, or problems with the energy provider and recent electricity cuts. Information from the MCSC minutes from 01/12/2008, 06/07/2009, 01/02/2010.

39 Interview 50 with EULEX regional office, Prizren, 10/10/2012.

40 Interview 85 with OSCE Department for Security and Public Safety, Prishtina, 27/11/2013.

41 EULEX survey about MCSC performance and interview 67 with Kosovo Police, Zabel/Šumarak, 07/11/2012.

42 EULEX survey about MCSC performance and interview 67 with Kosovo Police, Zabel/Šumarak, 07/11/2012.

43 Interview 75 with OSCE Department for Security and Public Safety, Prishtina, 20/11/2012.

44 MCSCs held 10 meetings in 2011, eight meetings in 2012 (MLGA 2011).

45 Members of the MCSC in Zabel/Šumarak were: the Kosovo Police Station Commander, Mayor, religious representatives of the Islamic community, the Kosovo Security Force and the Director for Protection and Rescue. Local Public Safety Council representatives were also invited. Minority representatives were sent from the Serbian, Turkish and Ashkali communities. NGO representatives

were appointed from the areas of youth (Youth Forum), media (local media representatives), business (Kosovo Business Alliance) and other civil societies (KAAD, NGO, THEM). In addition, the Office for Communities, Office for Returns, Office for Gender Equality, municipal spokesperson and Municipal Assembly representatives participated. Missing were representatives from the Serbian Orthodox Church. Information from MCSC minutes from 07/05/2012, 09/07/2012, 10/09/2012.

46 Information from MCSC minutes 07/05/2012, 09/07/2012 and 10/09/2012.
47 Information from MCSC minutes 07/05/2012, 09/07/2012, 10/09/2012 and interview 41 with Kosovo Police, 02/10/2012.
48 Information from MCSC minutes 07/05/2012, 09/07/2012, 10/09/2012 and interview 41 with Kosovo Police, 02/10/2012.
49 Interview 85 with OSCE Department for Safety and Community Policing, 27/11/2013 and interview 78 with OSCE Official, Mitrovica, 26/11/2012.
50 Interview 67 with Kosovo Police, Zabel/Šumarak, 07/11/2012 and interview 85 with OSCE Department for Security and Public Safety, Prishtina, 15/12/2013.
51 Statements were published on 13/03/2012, after the burning of a Serbian house in a village of the municipality and on 07/02/2011, after an attack of Serbs on Albanian youth from Zabel/Šumarak in North Mitrovica.
52 Interview 54 with OSCE, field office, Bregore/Brdašce, 19/10/2012.
53 One OSCE employee from Bregore/Brdašce told me about a change in legislation after the 2007 municipal elections and the 2008 independence that introduced MCSCs. Obviously, MCSCs had existed since 2005 but were apparently not widely known. Interview 54 with OSCE staff, Bregore/Brdašce, 19/10/2012.
54 'Security meeting' was the colloquial term used for Local Crime Prevention Councils, as Chavleishvili (2011) explains.
55 Interview 54 with OSCE, field office, Bregore/Brdašce, 19/10/2012.
56 Interview 54 with OSCE, field office, Bregore/Brdašce, 19/10/2012.
57 Interview 54 with OSCE, field office, Bregore/Brdašce, 19/10/2012 and Chavleishvili (2011).
58 Interview 44 with Municipal Official, Bregore/Brdašce, 03/10/2012.
59 Interview 67 with Kosovo Police, 07/11/2012, and interview 54 with OSCE, field office, Bregore/Brdašce, 19/10/2012.
60 Interview 44 with former Mayor, Bregore/Brdašce, 03/10/2012.
61 Interview 54 with OSCE, field office, Bregore/Brdašce, 19/10/2012 and OSCE Department for Security and Public Safety, 27/11/2013.
62 Interview 80 with EULEX, Bregore/Brdašce, 07/12/2012.
63 Interview 54 with OSCE, field office, Bregore/Brdašce, 19/10/2012.
64 Interview 42 with Kosovo Police, Bregore/Brdašce, 02/10/2012.
65 Interview 54 with OSCE, Field Team, Bregore/Brdašce, 19/10/2012. These meetings discussed security situation and property protection for minorities. EULEX remembers these meetings being very chaotic because of the amount of translation (English, Serbian, German, Albanian).
66 Interview 54 with OSCE, field office, Bregore/Brdašce, 19/10/2012.
67 Interview 68, Municipal Official, Bregore/Brdašce, 08/11/2012.
68 Interview 54 with OSCE, field office, Bregore/Brdašce, 19/10/2012.
69 Regular participants are the Kosovo Police (Police Station Commander or Deputy), municipal officials (Mayor or Deputy Mayor), the Kosovo Security Force, Officer for Minorities, Director for Emergency, Director of Administration, Head of Human Resources and Head of Commission for Returns. The OSCE, EULEX and KFOR also participated regularly. Information from MCSC minutes on 24/02/2012, 30/05/2012, 28/06/2012, 09/07/012, 30/07/2012, 02/08/2012, 10/10/2012, 21/11/2012, KFOR report on MCSC meeting on 30/07/2012.

70 In 2012, Roma and Ashkali representatives only participated once, and the only civil society representative participated only twice. Interview 35 with member of Youth Forum, 22/09/2012 and MCSC minutes on 24/02/2012, 30/05/2012, 28/06/2012, 09/07/012, 30/07/2012, 02/08/2012, 10/10/2012, 21/11/2012, KFOR report on MCSC meeting on 30/07/2012.
71 Interview 54 with OSCE, Bregore/Brdašce, 19/10/2012.
72 Interview 85 with OSCE Department for Security and Public Safety, 27/11/2013.
73 Interview 85 with OSCE Department for Security and Public Safety, 27/11/2013.
74 Based on an inspection list accessed by the author.
75 Interview 50 with EULEX regional office, Prizren, 10/10/2012.
76 Information from MCSC minutes on 24/02/2012, 30/05/2012, 28/06/2012, 09/07/012, 30/07/2012, 02/08/2012, 10/10/2012, 21/11/2012, KFOR report on MCSC meeting on 30/07/2012.
77 Interview 85 with OSCE Department for Safety and Community Policing, 27/11/2013 and interview 78, OSCE regional office, Mitrovica, 26/11/2012.
78 Interview 75 with OSCE Department for Security and Public Safety, Prishtina, 20/11/2012.
79 Interview 85 with OSCE Department for Security and Public Safety, 27/11/2013.
80 Interview 54 with OSCE, field office, Bregore/Brdašce, 19/10/2012.
81 Review of municipal website, interview with OSCE Municipal Team, analysis of MCSC minutes of 2012.
82 Interview 54 with OSCE, Bregore/Brdašce, 19/10/2012.
83 EULEX inspection list, 10/10/2012.
84 In 2012, Roma and Ashkali representatives only participated once, and the only civil society representative participated only twice. Interview 35 with member of Youth Forum, 22/09/2012 and MCSC minutes on 24/02/2012, 30/05/2012, 28/06/2012, 09/07/012, 30/07/2012, 02/08/2012, 10/10/2012, 21/11/2012, KFOR report on MCSC meeting on 30/07/2012.
85 Interview 54 with OSCE, field office, Bregore/Brdašce, 19/10/2012.
86 Interview 54 with OSCE, field office, Bregore/Brdašce, 19/10/2012.
87 Interview 50 with EULEX regional office, Prizren, 10/10/2012.
88 Interview 54 with OSCE, field office, Bregore/Brdašce, 19/10/2012.
89 Interview 54 with OSCE, field office, Bregore/Brdašce, 19/10/2012.
90 Interview 86 with Kosovo Directorate of Community Policing and Crime Prevention, Prishtina, 05/12/2013.
91 Minority Community Policing was first regulated by UNMIK Regulation 2005/45 (UNMIK 2005), then by the 2008 Law on Police and later by the 2012 Law on Police (RoK 2008, 2012b). I rely on the Law on Police 2008.
92 Interview 75 with OSCE Department for Security and Public Safety, 20/11/2012.
93 Interview 85 with OSCE Department for Security and Public Safety, 27/11/2012 and interview 54 with OSCE Official, Bregore/Brdašce, 19/10/2012.
94 Interview 50 with EULEX Official, Prizren, 10/10/2012.
95 Interview 75 with OSCE Department for Security and Public Safety, 20/11/2012.
96 Interview 50 with EULEX Official, Prizren, 10/10/2012.
97 Local Public Safety Councils are monitored either by the OSCE Regional Security Monitoring Section, the OSCE Department for Security and Public Safety or Community Teams. Interview 77 with OSCE Security Monitoring Section, Prishtina, 23/11/2012, interview 75 with OSCE Department for Security and Public Safety, Prishtina, 20/11/2012.
98 The Norwegian Embassy provides the financial assistance. Interview 89 with OSCE Department for Security and Public Safety, 06/12/2013.

99   Interview 75 and 89 with OSCE Department for Security and Public Safety, Prishtina, 20/11/2012 and 06/12/2012.
100 Municipal Assembly minutes, Zabel/Šumarak, 29/04/2010, 15.
101 Municipal Assembly minutes, Zabel/Šumarak, 29/04/2010, 15.
102 Interview 66 with Kosovo Police, Zabel/Šumarak, 07/11/2012.
103 Interview 66 with Kosovo Police, Zabel/Šumarak, 07/11/2012.
104 Interview 66 with Kosovo Police, Zabel/Šumarak, 07/11/2012.
105 Interview 67 with Kosovo Police, Zabel/Šumarak, 07/11/2012.
106 Interview 87 with former Communities Committee member, 05/12/2012.
107 Minutes, MCSC meeting, 06/07/2009.
108 Municipal Assembly minutes, Zabel/Šumarak, 29/04/2010, 09/06/2010, 29/07/2010.
109 In 2010, the Mayor's attempt to sign a memorandum of understanding with Serbian representatives failed. Municipal Assembly minutes 29/04/2010, p. 15f., 38.
110 Interview 67 with Kosovo Police, Zabel/Šumarak, 07/11/2012, interview 89 with OSCE Department for Security and Public Safety, 06/12/2013 and interview 79 with KFOR Officials, Zabel/Šumarak, 26/11/2012.
111 Interview 67 with Kosovo Police, Zabel/Šumarak, 07/11/2012.
112 Interview 89 with OSCE Department for Security and Public Safety, 06/12/2013.
113 Interview 79 with KFOR Officials, Zabel/Šumarak, 26/11/2012.
114 Interview 67 with Kosovo Police, Zabel/Šumarak, 07/11/2012.
115 Kosovo Serbian police officers had given up their boycott of Kosovo institutions by July 2009 (Beqiri 2009). One reason might be their dependency on income from Prishtina, another might be a shift in the Kosovo Serbian attitude in favour of a moderate or pragmatic stance (ICG 2012).
116 Interview 67 with Kosovo Police, 07/11/2012, interview 75 with OSCE Department for Security and Public Safety, 20/11/2012, interview 86 with Kosovo Police, Prishtina, 05/12/2013.
117 Interview 75 with OSCE Department for Security and Public Safety, 20/11/2012 and interview 86 with Kosovo Police, Prishtina, 05/12/2013.
118 Municipal website of Zabel/Šumarak, news from 15/02/2011.
119 Municipal Assembly minutes, 30/06/2011, p. 18.
120 Interview 67 with Kosovo Police, Zabel/Šumarak, 07/11/2012 and 75 with OSCE Department for Security and Public Safety, Prishtina, 20/11/2012.
121 Interview 67 with Kosovo Police, Zabel/Šumarak, 07/11/2012.
122 Interview 72 with OSCE Department for Security and Public Safety, Prishtina, 15/11/2012.
123 Financial assistance for LPSCs was possible through cooperation between the OSCE and the Norwegian Embassy, which agreed to finance these projects. The OSCE told me that the idea for the project originated from the Norwegian ambassador's visit to the LPSC in Braljža/Bralje. Interview 89 with OSCE Department for Security and Public Safety, 06/12/2013.
124 Interview with OSCE Department for Security and Public Safety, 06/12/2013.
125 Municipal website of Zabel/Šumarak, news from 15/08/2011 and Municipal Assembly minutes, 30/06/2011, 18.
126 Municipal website of Zabel/Šumarak, news from 24/04/2012.
127 Interview 67 with Kosovo Police, Zabel/Šumarak, 07/11/2012.
128 Interview 67 with Kosovo Police, Zabel/Šumarak, 07/11/2012.
129 Interview 79 with KFOR, Zabel/Šumarak, 26/11/2012.
130 Interview 79 with KFOR, Zabel/Šumarak, 26/11/2012 and conversation with Kosovo Police, Braljža/Bralje, 08/11/2012.
131 Interview 79 with KFOR, Zabel/Šumarak, 26/11/2012.

132 Interview 79 with KFOR, Zabel/Šumarak, 26/11/2012.
133 Municipal website of Zabel/Šumarak, news from 15/02/2011 and 28/08/2011.
134 Interview 79 with KFOR, Zabel/Šumarak, 26/11/2012.
135 Interview 79 with KFOR, Zabel/Šumarak, 26/11/2012.
136 Interview 89 with OSCE, 06/12/2012 and interview 79, KFOR, Zabel/ Šumarak, 26/11/2012.
137 Interview 89 with OSCE, 06/12/2012.
138 Interview 89 with OSCE, Prishtina, 06/12/2012.
139 I was told that of the 33 financial assistance projects for LPSCs, 21 are construction related projects. Interview 89 with OSCE, Prishtina, 06/12/2013.
140 The UNMIK Community Police Office in the Serbian village was closed in February 2006, which provoked strong criticism and even a petition against the closure from Serbs (OSCE 2006).
141 Interview 54 with OSCE, field office, Bregore/Brdašce, 19/10/2012.
142 Interview 19 with Kosovo Police, Bregore/Brdašce, 14/05/2012 and interview 54 with OSCE, field office, Bregore/Brdašce, 19/10/2012.
143 Kosovo Serbian minority representatives and the Orthodox Church participated until Kosovo's independence in 2008. Interview 54 with OSCE, field office, Bregore/Brdašce, 19/10/2012.
144 Interview with EULEX advisor in Bregore/Brdašce, 07/12/2012 and Kosovo Police, 14/05/2012.
145 Interview 19 with Kosovo Police, Bregore/Brdašce, 14/05/2012.
146 Interview 54 with OSCE, field office, Bregore/Brdašce, 19/10/2012.
147 Interview 80 with EULEX. Formerly Bregore/Brdašce, 07/12/2012.
148 Interview 80 with EULEX. Formerly Bregore/Brdašce, 07/12/2012.
149 Interview 80 with EULEX. Formerly Bregore/Brdašce, 07/12/2012 and interview 19, Kosovo Police, Bregore/Brdašce, 14/05/2012.
150 Interview 80 with EULEX. Formerly Bregore/Brdašce, 07/12/2012 and interview 19, Kosovo Police, Bregore/Brdašce, 14/05/2012 and OSCE (2010).
151 Interview 54 with OSCE, field office, Bregore/Brdašce, 19/10/2012, interview 44, former Municipal Official, Bregore/Brdašce, 03/10/2012, interview 80 with EULEX, formerly Bregore/Brdašce, 07/12/2012.
152 Interview 19, Kosovo Police, Bregore/Brdašce, 14/05/2012 and interview 54 with OSCE, field office, Bregore/Brdašce, 19/10/2012.
153 Interview 80 with EULEX. Formerly Bregore/Brdašce, 07/12/2012 and interview 19, Kosovo Police, Bregore/Brdašce, 14/05/2012.
154 Municipal Assembly minutes, Bregore/Brdašce, 04/07/2011, 3.
155 The KFOR Commander visited in order to inaugurate a football field next to the orthodox monastery (Municipal website, Bregore/Brdašce, 03/05/2011). The KFOR Commander South visited to discuss the security situation (Municipal website, Bregore/Brdašce, 07/02/2011), as did the head of the OSCE Regional Centre Prizren (Municipal website, Bregore/Brdašce, 16/06/2011).
156 Interview 75 with OSCE Department for Security and Public Safety, 20/11/2012, 54 with OSCE Municipal Team, 19/10/2012, 86 with Kosovo Police Department for Community Policing and Crime Prevention, 05/12/2013.
157 Interview 54 with OSCE, field office, Bregore/Brdašce, 19/10/2012.
158 Interview 86 with Kosovo Police Department for Community Policing and Crime Prevention, 05/12/2013.
159 Translation of the author from Serbian.
160 Municipal Assembly minutes, Bregore/Brdašce, 10/10/2012, 4.
161 Please see focus group discussions from 13/10/2012 and 16/10/2012.
162 Interview 67 with Kosovo Police, Zabel/Šumarak, 07/11/2012.

163 The Kosovo Police Department for Community Policing and Crime Prevention declared it would only interfere in municipal police decisions about the establishment of the reform if 10 to 15 citizens filed a request. Interview 86 with Kosovo Police, Prishtina, 05/12/2013.

References

Beqiri, Besa. (2009). Kosovo Serb Officers End Boycott. In: SEETimes, 03/07/2009.

Bieber, Florian. (2010). Policing the Peace after Yugoslavia. Police Reform between External Imposition and Domestic Reform. Tokyo.

CEU. (2008). Council Joint Action 2008/124/CFSP of 4 February 2008 on the European Union Rule of Law Mission in Kosovo. In: Council of the European Union (ed.).

Chavleishvili, Galaktion. (2011). Isomorphic Processes and Social Legitimacy of Institutionalizing Municipal Community Safety Councils (MCSCs) in Kosovo. *Journal of Public Administration and Policy Research*, 3 (3), 62–67.

EC. (2011). Kosovo 2011 Progress Report. Brussels.

EC. (2012). Visa Liberalisation with Kosovo. Roadmap. In: *European External Action Service* (ed.). Brussels: European External Action Service.

EULEX. (2009). EULEX Program Report 2009. Prishtina.

EULEX. (2010). EULEX Program Report 2010. Prishtina.

EULEX. (2011a). EULEX Program Report 2011. Prishtina.

EULEX. (2011b). EULEX Programmatic MMA Actions. Prishtina.

Focus Kosovo. (2005). No Title. Kosovo Focus. Prishtina.

Forum for Security. (2013). *The New Kosovo Security Strategy Formulation Process. Inclusiveness and Transparency*. Prishtina.

Heinemann-Grüder, Andreas and Grebenschikow, Igor. (2006). Security Governance by Internationals. The Case of Kosovo. *International Peacekeeping*, 13 (1), 43–59.

ICG. (2012). *Setting Kosovo Free. Remaining Challenges*. Prishtina.

Kosovo, Republic of. (2008). *Constitution of the Republic of Kosovo*. Prishtina: Republic of Kosovo.

MLGA. (2009). Monitoring Report of Municipalities of the Republic of Kosovo 2008. Prishtina.

MLGA. (2010). Annual Report of Monitoring of Municipalities of the Republic of Kosovo 2009. Prishtina.

MLGA. (2011). Monitoring Report of Municipalities of the Republic of Kosovo. January-June 2011. Prishtina.

MLGA. (2013). Annual Report of Monitoring of Municipalities of the Republic of Kosovo 2012. Prishtina.

OSCE. (2006). Municipal Profile Bregore/Brdašce. Prishtina.

OSCE. (2009a). CSAT. Assessing the Impact. Prishtina.

OSCE. (2009b). Municipal Profile Zabel/Šumarak. Prishtina.

OSCE. (2010). Kosovo Communities Profile. Prishtina.

OSCE. (2011). Municipal Responses to Security Incidents Affecting Communities in Kosovo and the Role of Municipal Community Safety Councils. Prishtina.

OSCE Permanent Council. (1999). Decision No. 305, PC.DEC/305, 1 July 1999.

RoK. (2008). Law on Police. In: Kosovo, A. o. R. o. (ed.). Prishtina: Republic of Kosovo.

RoK. (2009). Administrative Instruction No. 08/2009 MIA – 02/2009 MLGA for Municipal community Safety Councils. In: Ministry of Local Government Administration (ed.). Prishtina: Republic of Kosovo.

RoK. (2011). Community Policing Strategy and Action Plan 2012–2016. In: Affairs, M. o. I. (ed.). Prishtina: Republic of Kosovo.

RoK. (2012a). Administrative Instruction No. 27/2012 MIA-03/2012 MLGA for Municipal community Safety Councils. In: Republic of Kosovo (ed.). Prishtina.

RoK. (2012b). Law on Police. In: Assembly of Republic of Kosovo (ed.) 04/L-076. Prishtina: Republic of Kosovo.

Saferworld. (2010). A Matter of Trust. Public Perceptions of Safety and Security in Kosovo, 2009/2010.

Stodiek, Thorsten and Zellner, Wolfgang. (2007). *The Creation of Multi-Ethnic Police Services in the Western Balkans. A Record of Mixed Success.* Georgsmarienhütte.

Trauner, Florian. (2009). From Membership Conditionality to Policy Conditionality. EU External Governance in South Eastern Europe. *Journal of European Public Policy*, 16 (5), 774–790.

UN. (2006). Report of the Secretary-General on the United Nations Interim Administration Mission in Kosovo. In: United Nations Documents (ed.).

UN. (2007). Report of the Secretary-General on the United Nations Interim Administration Mission in Kosovo. In: United Nations Documents (ed.).

UN. (2012). Report of the Secretary-General on the United Nations Interim Administration Mission in Kosovo. In: United Nations Documents (ed.).

UNMIK. (2003). Pillar 1, Police and Justice.

UNMIK. (2005). UNMIK/REG/2005/45 On the Framework and Guiding Principles of the Kosovo Police Service. In: UNMIK (ed.). UNMIK.

UNMIK. (2006). UNMIK Press Briefing 09/08/2006. Prishtina.

7 Summary and discussion of findings

How external–domestic interactions facilitate stalled post-war transition

The analytical framework of peacebuilding interactions served as a structure for analysing and comparing the eight cases of external–domestic interaction in this book. The case studies exemplified in great detail how peacebuilding is negotiated in post-war contexts at the local level. This structured comparison offered an in-depth understanding of the logic of external–domestic interactions and allowed for the identification of non-strategic elements in the interaction process that impact post-war transitions to peace and democracy in peacebuilding contexts. The case studies are particularly helpful in understanding how interactions impact peacebuilding outcomes, how domestic priorities shape domestic practices of reform implementation, and which interaction strategies hinder and enable peacebuilders to influence domestic actors' behaviour. I studied four reform initiatives, which were selected for their variation in the standard explanations for peacebuilding success or failure, such as the level of international capacity available to peacebuilders and the level of local resistance against a promoted international norm: Participatory Budget Planning (low capacity/weak resistance), Communities Committee (low capacity/strong resistance), Municipal Community Safety Council (high capacity/weak resistance) and Minority Community Policing (high capacity/strong resistance).

The empirical findings of the case studies allow for several conclusions: First, interactions are of consequence in the outcome of peacebuilding reforms, not merely due to their strategic characteristics but due to the bounded rationality inherent in them. Second, domestic actors pursue different priorities than peacebuilders, and the way reforms are captured by domestic actors reflects these domestic priorities. Third, the case studies support the conclusion that none of the standard explanations for stalled transitions in the peacebuilding literature fully explain peacebuilding outcomes, and that interaction-based explanations can be a strong complement. After all, not even the highest level of international capacity was able to ensure full reform implementation in Kosovo, the country with one of the most intrusive peacebuilding missions in the history of UN peacekeeping.

The following section summarises the central assumptions about interactions in peacebuilding put forward in this book and recapitulates the key categories of the analytical framework of peacebuilding interactions, summing up the empirical findings from the case studies accordingly.

The scope conditions of peacebuilding

I assume that external–domestic interactions in peacebuilding are shaped by the following three scope conditions: diverging priorities, mutual dependencies and the complexity of the post-war environment. These three scope conditions shape the logic of interaction in post-war states and constrain peacebuilders' prospects of successfully negotiating peace and democracy: Diverging priorities provide domestic actors with incentives for reform capture or non-compliance, mutual dependencies foster a tendency to avoid conflict on both sides, and the complexity of the post-war environment forces peacebuilders to react ad hoc in a non-strategic manner. Studying the interactions of peacebuilding thus means accounting for the various constraints peacebuilders are confronted with when intervening in a post-war state.

The diverging priorities of peacebuilders and domestic actors make it difficult to cultivate a purely cooperative relationship between the two sides and pose a fundamental challenge for peacebuilders in Kosovo: While peacebuilders promote the international priorities of stability, democracy and minority rights, domestic elites strive to gain ground in terms of socio-economic development, political power or resolution of the Kosovo status question. While these divergent priorities are not necessarily incompatible, domestic actors have the incentive to use the leeway in the interaction process to capture reforms to further their own ends and thus tend to implement reforms in a way that satisfies the priorities on their own political agenda. In contrast to Barnett and Zürcher (2008), who identify political power as the primary goal of post-war political elites, I find that reducing domestic interests to political power seems an overly simplistic portrayal of political elites' motivations, and I therefore propose a multi-faceted view of domestic priorities. Next to political power, the quest for socio-economic development and settling the status question are strong motivations for Kosovo's political elite. I met a number of municipal politicians who had a sincere interest in socio-economic development – alleviating poverty, providing job opportunities and contributing to infrastructure development for their citizens – and Kosovo Albanians and Kosovo Serbs alike were invested in solving the Kosovo status question in their favour: Kosovo Albanians pursued independent statehood for Kosovo while Kosovo Serbs aimed for Kosovo to remain part of Serbia. Both go beyond calculations for political power: The Albanian wish is deeply rooted in the Kosovo Albanian narrative of liberation from Serbian oppression (Di Lellio and Schwandner-Sievers 2006) and Kosovo Serbs' goals are part of a strong Serbian narrative (Bieber 2002). These priorities thus exist alongside each other, acting as the powerful motor driving domestic action.

Mutual dependencies present an additional challenge for peacebuilders and domestic actors when navigating the interaction process. External–domestic interactions seldom escalate into open conflicts, even if international and domestic priorities are not aligned. This is because mutual dependencies make the maintenance of good relations so important that neither side is interested in conflict escalations, at least in the majority of situations. Peacebuilders have to choose between backing down from demands in order to ensure domestic cooperation for the realisation of peacebuilding priorities, and increasing pressure on domestic partners in order to preserve the core interests of the international agenda. Domestic actors have to choose between giving in to ensure potential financial benefits and resistance in order to preserve their top domestic priorities. External–domestic interactions are thus shaped by a tendency to avoid conflict on both sides. This conforms to Barnett and Zürcher's (2008) conjecture that peacebuilding will most likely end in a compromise.

The complexity of the post-war situation is a further constraint on peacebuilders when negotiating peacebuilding reforms. The fast-changing and overly complex environment forces international actors to reduce information overload and to prioritise and select isolated issues at a given time. This complicates a comprehensive and strategic approach to reform implementation on the ground and gives way to the non-strategic elements inherent in external–domestic interactions. Many peacebuilders I talked to complained about how difficult it was to keep track of the political developments. They were well aware of the fact that most reforms introduced by the international community were only partially implemented, but at the same time they had to decide on an ad hoc basis where to engage and where to tolerate non-compliance and reform capture.

A new analytical framework of peacebuilding interactions

How can external–domestic interactions be analysed in a systematic and comparative manner that allows conclusions to be drawn about the impact of interactions on peacebuilding? This was the initial question that led to the inductive development of the analytical framework of peacebuilding interactions. The framework consists of several categories that are relevant to an analysis of the external–domestic interaction processes in peacebuilding: (1) international ad hoc tactics, (2) domestic responses, (3) the domestic environment of interaction and (4) peacebuilding outcomes. I discuss each element below drawing on empirical findings.

Ad hoc interaction tactics of selectivity, prioritisation, leverage

The ad hoc interaction tactics are of particular importance as they show how non-strategic aspects of an interaction process can influence peacebuilding outcomes. Prioritisation refers to putting a particular reform initiative at the top of the international agenda because its implementation is important for securing international core interests. If a peacebuilding reform is not prioritised, domestic elites receive leeway for non-compliance or reform capture at a low cost. Selectivity refers to the fact that peacebuilders only select a sub-set of rules from a reform initiative to be negotiated, and they change this sub-set of rules over time. Due to selectivity, domestic actors gain leeway to ignore the non-selected rules and to capture reforms at no cost. Leverage means that international norm promotion instruments change domestic actors' calculations of (non-)adoption costs. If peacebuilders do not use high leverage instruments, it increases domestic actors' leeway to capture reform at a low cost.

If looking closely at the specific occasions that selectivity, prioritisation or leverage occurred and to what effect, the idea that international actors' decisions are long-term strategic calculations seems less plausible. Often, there seems to be no clear strategy with regard to the peacebuilding reform, unless exogenous triggers have created a certain urgency to end non-compliance. Current accounts of why interaction matters in peacebuilding (Barnett *et al.* 2014, Barnett and Zürcher 2008, Zürcher *et al.* 2013) have largely neglected the non-strategic elements of external–domestic interactions and concentrated on the strategic calculations and adoption costs.

The process tracing conducted in this book reveals valuable new insights into how external–domestic interactions work and what types of tactics exist that shape these interactions. Following external–domestic interaction processes, one can identify patterns related to when selectivity, prioritisation or leverage occur or what effect they have on the interaction. These patterns are of interest if one is to understand the logic of external–domestic interactions in post-war contexts. For example, peacebuilders only use prioritisation if they perceive domestic actors' behaviour as a threat to international core interests, such as the stability of the security situation. In most other situations, peacebuilders are inclined to back down from their demands or tolerate domestic resistance, modification or foot-dragging, as they depend on the cooperation of domestic elites in other areas or need domestic elites to control violence.

Prioritisation, selectivity and leverage do not precondition a specific peacebuilding outcome, but they make certain peacebuilding outcomes less likely. In some instances, they provide domestic actors with leeway to capture reforms for their own priorities at no or low cost. In other instances, they enable peacebuilders to push the reform process in the direction of their liking. I will summarise the findings for each interaction tactic below.

Prioritisation

The ad hoc tactic of prioritisation makes an outcome of no implementation less likely. Prioritisation refers to instances in which peacebuilders put an issue at the top of the international agenda, showing less tolerance for non-compliance and increasing the frequency of interaction for that particular reform. Prioritisation helps peacebuilders to cope with the complexity of post-war politics (Kahnemann 2011) because it allows them to focus on a few priority issues and to neglect others. The use of prioritisation is ad hoc and bound to the occurrence of certain exogenous triggers. Prioritisation was usually the strategy employed when non-compliance was interpreted as a threat to peacebuilders' core interests, such as when reform implementation was expected to stabilise the security situation (as was the case with the Communities Committee and Minority Community Policing reforms in Zabel/Šumarak) or formed part of the EU conditionality catalogue (as was the case with the Municipal Community Safety Council in Bregore/Brdašce). Triggers for prioritisation are, thus, events that threaten the core interests of peacebuilders. This means that the use of prioritisation is limited to special situations.

One effect of prioritisation is that it tends to curb leeway for non-compliance: Peacebuilders show less tolerance for non-compliance and insist on the implementation of a minimum sub-set of rules that can be easily quantified and thus is useful in proclaiming peacebuilding success in front of the donor agency, international steering committee or UN Security Council. Peacebuilders tend not to prioritise rules on more substantive matters such as compliance with formal appointment procedures in committees and councils (which were often not transparent and perpetuated political dependencies) or the purpose of the reform (which is often captured to improve development instead of rights protection or security). In this way, peacebuilders made it more risky for domestic actors to resist reform implementation in its entirety, but still left ample room for domestic actors to add, drop or modify certain rules, allowing them to capture the reform for their own priorities. The fact that prioritisation is only used following specific triggers implies that peacebuilders often choose to maintain good working relations (by tolerating domestic resistance, modification or foot-dragging, and preserving top priorities of the international agenda) over increasing pressure on domestic actors. This supports Barnett and Zürcher's (2008) core assertion that peacebuilders' first priority is stability.

Prioritisation was observed in five of the eight case studies in this book and the ensuing pattern confirms the expectation that prioritisation makes no implementation less likely: in the case of the Communities Committee in both Zabel/Šumarak and Bregore/Brdašce, in the case of the Municipal Community Safety Council in Bregore/Brdašce and in the case of Minority Community Policing in Zabel/Šumarak. In all of the cases, the reform outcome was captured implementation or full implementation, but it was never no implementation.

In all of the cases, prioritisation occurred ad hoc as a response to unforeseen events and not in a strategic manner that would have ensured the optimum reform outcome. In the case of the Communities Committee reform, international actors prioritised the reform after the March 2004 riots, when non-implementation became a major threat to stability. Peacebuilders were less inclined to tolerate non-compliance with that particular reform, insisted on a minimum sub-set of rules, such as formal establishment or Serbian participation, and interacted more frequently with municipal actors. In Bregore/Brdašce, where the work of the Communities Committee proved more unstable and suffered a complete breakdown between 2008 and 2010, international actors needed to prioritise formal re-establishment once more. In the case of the Municipal Community Safety Council, prioritisation followed the inclusion of the reform as a benchmark in the EU policy conditionality catalogue for visa liberalisation in 2011. In Bregore/Brdašce, where reform implementation had been met with resistance and foot-dragging, prioritisation led to increased pressure to formally establish a Council and hold regular meetings. In the case of the Minority Community Policing reform in Zabel/Šumarak, peacebuilders successfully prioritised the reform after non-compliance was perceived as a security threat. This meant less tolerance for non-compliance; insistence on a minimum sub-set of rules; and more frequent interactions between peacebuilders, national representatives, municipal authorities and local Serbs.

Selectivity

Selectivity makes an outcome of full implementation less likely. The ad hoc tactic of selectivity means that peacebuilders concentrate only on a particular sub-set of rules from a reform initiative when negotiating reform implementation with their domestic counterpart. This practice provides domestic actors with leeway to capture reforms for their own priorities because they can ignore non-selected rules at no cost. An emerging pattern of selectivity is that domestic actors tend to implement only the rules that peacebuilders ask for, leaving out non-selected rules that might seem counterproductive to their own priorities or that simply demand too much effort in terms of changing routines. Selectivity helps international actors cope with the complexity of post-war environments in non-strategic ways because the selective allocation of attention allows peacebuilders to reduce information overload (Kahnemann 2011) and to be "orienting and responding quickly" (Kahnemann 2011). Given the fact that peacebuilders are confronted with domestic non-compliance on numerous fronts, they have to decide which rules to focus on and where to invest human and financial resources, often in an ad hoc manner. Peacebuilders can shift to different sub-sets of rules during the course of external–domestic interactions. In some cases, this means that the total set of rules is covered over time, in some cases not. If the total set of rules is covered during the interaction, full implementation becomes possible. In the cases studied, selectivity shifts were triggered by political events of national importance such as security incidents like the riots of March 2004, the declaration of independence in 2008 or routine programme evaluations.

The case studies support the assumption that selectivity as an interaction tactic makes full implementation less likely, particularly when peacebuilders do not cover the total set of rules over time. Interestingly, in the case of Participatory Budget Planning, peacebuilders succeeded in covering the total set of rules from the start of the reform in 2007 until 2012, during which several selectivity shifts to different sub-sets of rules occurred. Full implementation thus became more likely. The process tracing showed that municipal actors tended to implement the sub-set of rules demanded by peacebuilders – with cooperation, foot-dragging or modification – but ignored all other Participatory Budget Planning rules. In an enabling environment, learned rules from previous sub-sets of rules were sustained, whereas a constraining environment of interaction motivated domestic actors to drop uncomfortable rules from previous sub-sets at no cost. This made it possible for peacebuilders to achieve full implementation in Zabel/Šumarak, but not in Bregore/Brdašce, where once-implemented rules did not prove sustainable.

In the case of the Communities Committees, selectivity shaped the entire interaction process in that peacebuilders were unable to cover the total set of rules over time. Consequently, domestic actors never implemented the non-selected rules and full implementation became less likely. This case also clearly demonstrates the typical interaction pattern of selectivity: If formal establishment was required, nothing more than formal establishment took place. If inter-ethnic dialogue through regular meetings was demanded, the number of meetings increased temporarily – usually only when financial compensation was provided. As the international norm of minority rights – which the Communities Committee reform was intended to strengthen – enjoyed only weak support among Kosovars, municipal actors tended to drop non-selected rules and modify or drag their feet on selected rules to fit their own priorities. If peacebuilders had not continually asked for the implementation of the Communities Committee reform, domestic actors most likely would have ignored it altogether.

In the case of MCSCs, peacebuilders again did not manage to cover the total set of rules between the start of the reform in 2005 and 2012. Full implementation thus became less likely, even in an enabling environment such as in Zabel/Šumarak. Here, the reform resulted in captured implementation, not because domestic actors had been foot-dragging or modifying rules, but because peacebuilders had left out some rules, which were then consequently not implemented by domestic actors. In the case of Minority Community Policing, peacebuilders consistently failed to demand the implementation of rules 7 and 9. Consequently, domestic actors Zabel/Šumarak never implemented these rules and full implementation became less likely. The prospect of full implementation was further aggravated by a constraining environment that made it more likely that domestic actors would resist, modify, or drag their feet on selected rules.

Peacebuilders often tolerated resistance, modification or foot-dragging with regard to the selected sub-set of rules, which then provided domestic elites with further leeway for reform capture at a low cost. This points to the peacebuilders' tendency to avoid conflicts with local elite, which is due to mutual dependencies and the complex post-war environment: Peacebuilders prefer to back down in order to maintain relations with their domestic counterparts and chose selective interventions in the reform process in order to navigate complexity and keep up good relations. An additional reason that peacebuilders back down from their demands is that they are aware of the difficulties of everyday life in Kosovo and as a result, are more apt to connect to and tolerate the domestic priorities.

Leverage

> FIRST TRY: Do it, because it is the right thing to do.
> DOMESTIC ACTOR: No, thank you.
> SECOND TRY: Do the right thing; you'll get votes.
> DOMESTIC ACTOR: Now you are talking my language.
> THIRD TRY: Do the right thing; we'll take you on a trip to Brussels.
> DOMESTIC ACTOR: You have to do better than that.
>   (Former UNMIK official trying to explain how he/she motivated
>   his/her counterparts to 'do the right thing', 03/10/2013)

High leverage makes an outcome of no implementation less likely. The ad hoc tactic of leverage serves peacebuilders by altering the (non-)adoption costs for domestic actors and helping overcome domestic resistance. International actors gain leverage through the use of strong norm promotion instruments such as financial assistance, conditionality and coercion. Yet this leverage is not used consistently during the interaction process – only in particular periods and in relation to particular rules. The use of instruments at the local level is often not strategically tailored to the specific situation, either, but follows protocols from standard peacebuilding programmes at the national level. In the interaction process, peacebuilders seldom take time to think strategically about which instrument would lead to their preferred outcome, but instead resort to the toolkit offered in the standard peacebuilding toolbox.

One interaction pattern I observed is that the higher leverage instrument helped peacebuilders to overcome domestic resistance against reform implementation. Domestic actors tended to drop resistance to international demands after being offered, for example, financial assistance in one form or another. Understandably, financial assistance is attractive in a context of widespread poverty, empty state treasuries and elite desires for development: In the case of the Communities Committee reform, the provision of financial compensation for Committee members presented a significant motivation for Serbs to drop their resistance against participating in the Committees. When municipalities stopped paying the members for participation, Committees met less frequently. At the same time, this proves the low sustainability of many of the peacebuilding reforms. In the case of the Minority Community Policing reform in Zabel/Šumarak, the international provision of financial assistance for community projects again presented a significant motivation for Serbs to drop their resistance.[1] In the case of budget planning, the offer of major financial assistance for infrastructure projects tied to public budget hearings significantly increased the municipalities' activities. Although domestic actors had not resisted rule implementation before, they showed greater commitment in the third period once financial incentives were used.

However, financial assistance and the dependence of domestic elites on foreign money does not necessarily lead to the full implementation of internationally pushed peacebuilding reforms. In many cases, reforms resulted in captured implementation instead. Domestic actors seem to be well aware of the minimum requirements that need to be met in order to receive financial assistance and, beyond that, use strategies of foot-dragging and modification to capture reform to further their own ends.

The high leverage instrument of coercion also helped overcome domestic resistance. Coercion was first and foremost used to push reform initiatives that promoted minority rights, as these tended to be met with more severe resistance from municipal authorities and/or Kosovo Serbs. Peacebuilders used diplomatic coercion, usually in the form of advocacy coalitions, in the cases of Albanian and Serbian resistance against the formal establishment of Communities Committee in Bregore/Brdašce and in the case of Serbian resistance against the formal establishment of Minority Community Policing in Zabel/Šumarak.[2] Advocacy coalitions signalled to municipal authorities that the reform initiative was a priority on the peacebuilders' agenda at the local level. Municipal authorities thus had to decide whether to keep up their resistance and risk a worsening of working relations or give in to international demands and commit more efforts and resources to it. In the cases studied, domestic actors decided for the latter. However, this form of diplomatic coercion again did not lead to the full implementation of peacebuilding reforms, nor were all international demands fulfilled in a coherent manner. Rather, the case studies showed that domestic actors tended to implement the minimum requirements asked for by local peacebuilders but did not engage in further efforts to implement the reform. Peacebuilders had to continue to support these newly established institutions in order to ensure their regular functioning. For example, they offered financial incentives in the form of financial compensation for Community Committee members and financial assistance for infrastructure projects for Minority Community Policing.

The environment of interaction

The outcomes of external–domestic interactions are not influenced exclusively by the international interaction strategies of selectivity, prioritisation or leverage. Whether the interaction takes place in an enabling or constraining environment of interaction also plays a role. This is a further important insight, as current studies dealing with strategic interaction in peacebuilding do not elaborate on whether and how the environment of interaction influences domestic behaviour in the external–domestic interplay. Most studies – such as those by Barnett and Zürcher (2008), Barnett *et al.* (2014), Zürcher *et al.* (2013) and Mac Ginty (2010) – assume that peacebuilders and domestic elites have different interests and that domestic elites, therefore, will tend to divert from peacebuilders' reform proposals. A constraining environment thus seems to be the rule, whereas an enabling environment that fosters cooperative behaviour by local actors is seldom considered as a possibility. The case studies, however, point to external–domestic interactions in which an enabling environment facilitates domestic cooperation with peacebuilding demands and renders external pressure obsolete. An enabling environment of interaction increases the likelihood of domestic cooperation in response to peacebuilders' demands, and a peacebuilding outcome of full implementation becomes possible. A constraining environment of interaction, however, increases the likelihood of domestic resistance, foot-dragging and modification as a response to peacebuilders' demands. A peacebuilding outcome of full implementation is then less likely.

The environment of interaction relates to the level of domestic adoption costs for a reform and is shaped by the domestic support for an international norm and the style of politics amongst the political elite. Both influence the level of the adoption costs that the political elite faces when considering whether or not to follow international demands. In an enabling environment, adoption costs are low because there is strong domestic support for an international norm *and* a cooperative style of politics at play. In such circumstances, domestic actors are more likely to respond cooperatively to international proposals; full implementation thus becomes an option. The only cases where full implementation was observed took place in an enabling environment, as was seen with the cases of Participatory Budget Planning and Municipal Community Safety Councils in Zabel/Šumarak. A constraining environment, on the other hand, means higher adoption costs for the political elite because it is marked by weak domestic support *and/or* a competitive style of politics. Here, domestic elites are more likely to use strategies of resistance, modification or foot-dragging to deal with international norm promotion efforts. The domestic response depends on the international instruments used to coerce, incentivise or persuade domestic actors to implement reforms.

The case studies reveal that if a reform promotes the international norm of democracy – a norm widely supported among Kosovars – political elites are more likely to respond with cooperation, but also possibly with foot-dragging or modification. In such cases, complete reform failure is unlikely. For example, in the democracy promoting cases of Participatory Budget Planning (with low international capacity) and Municipal Community Safety Councils (with high international capacity), domestic elites reacted to international demands with cooperation, foot-dragging or modification, but not with resistance. If the norm enjoys weak domestic support – as was the case with minority rights – domestic actors initially reacted to international demands with resistance. For example, in the minority rights promoting cases of the Communities Committee (weak support/low capacity) and Minority

Community Policing (weak support/high capacity), resistance was a recurrent reaction. Thereby, resistance was exercised by Kosovo Serbs who strove to boycott Kosovo institutions, as well as by Kosovo Albanian actors who opposed Serbian empowerment in Bregore/Brdašce. International norms might be perceived differently in post-war countries with a distinct history, social structure and geographical location. There is, thus, no general rule about which type of international norm is more likely to be supported and which one not.

The style of politics is a further factor that is relevant to the environment of interaction: A cooperative style of politics makes internationally promoted norms less costly to adopt compared to a locale where domestic elites follow a competitive style of politics. So far, peacebuilding scholarship on post-war transitions has not paid much attention to this phenomenon at the micro-level, even though studies at the macro-level have argued that institutional stability is weakened in post-war states due to the high level of polarisation (Esteban and Schneider 2008) between, for example, ethnicities (Elbadawi and Sambanis 2000) or political parties (Santiso 2002).

The influence that the style of politics has on external–domestic interactions quickly becomes apparent in the case studies: In the case of Participatory Budget Planning and Municipal Community Safety Councils, the municipality with a cooperative style of politics, Zabel/Šumarak, reacted to international demands almost exclusively with cooperation. Many experienced politicians were willing to implement democratic rules and procedures, regardless of the international norm promotion instruments applied by peacebuilders. If, occasionally, rules were not implemented exactly as intended by peacebuilders, this was related to the lack of knowledge and/or resources to do so effectively. This creates an ideal situation for successful dialogue, capacity building and financial assistance. In contrast, the municipality with a competitive style of politics, Bregore/Brdašce, was more likely to react to international demands with modification or foot-dragging. The political elite in that municipality used the leeway inherent in the external–domestic interaction process to push their own set of priorities, particularly political power. Additionally, in the case of the weakly supported minority rights reforms, differences in the style of politics led to separate courses of interactions. In the Communities Committee reform, the cooperative municipality re-established the Committee after the 2008 Serbian withdrawal by itself, whereas in the competitive municipality, heavy involvement from the local peacebuilders was needed to push re-establishment.

The empirical observations in the two municipalities suggest that the style of politics is closely connected to the level of (mis-)trust and polarisation amongst political elites. Ruggeri *et al.* (2012) similarly emphasises the impact of mistrust and commitment problems on post-war transition outcomes. The cooperative style of politics in Zabel/Šumarak is based on mutual trust between members of different parties that stems from informal friendship networks and other kinds of informal contact between members of the different parties. These types of relationships are necessary for the development of a cooperative attitude among municipal elites that makes power-sharing less costly: The Municipal Government shares information with the legislative branch, and the opposing parties are involved in decision-making processes and approve municipal acts proposed by the governing parties. Competitive politics, as seen in Bregore/Brdašce, are the result of deep mistrust and polarisation between, and within, the different Kosovo Albanian parties (Kosovo Serbian parties hardly participate in Kosovo politics). In fact, most of the other Kosovo municipalities exhibit similar practices of competitive politics and intra- and inter-party competition, which has hampered peacebuilding reform implementation in many areas (OSCE 2004). Nor is a competitive style of politics unique to Kosovo: The polarisation and competitiveness of clientelist party landscapes is seen as a stumbling block for democratisation processes in post-war states such as Bosnia and Herzegovina (Bieber 2005) or Northern Ireland (Byrne 2001). This competitive attitude turns politics into a zero-sum game: There is a low level of information and power sharing, the Municipal Government strives to concentrate political power, and opposition parties are excluded from decision-making processes whenever possible. Domestic actors thus have greater incentives not to cooperate with international reform demands, but to capture reforms to centralise power. All in all, domestic responses to international reform demands seem to differ depending on whether a cooperative or competitive style of politics prevails.

Peacebuilding outcomes of the case studies

The outcomes of these case studies offer two important insights: First, the outcomes could not be explained by current standard explanations such as international capacity or local resistance. In some cases, reforms with a low level of resistance did not result in full implementation. In other cases, reforms with strong international capacities resulted in no implementation although this went against expectations formulated by the international capacity proponents. These observations make a third interaction-based approach for the study of stalled transitions in peacebuilding even more relevant.

The second insight is that peacebuilding reforms most commonly resulted in captured implementation: rules were added, dropped or modified in a way that satisfied domestic priorities such as socio-economic development, political power or an effort to solve the Kosovo status question in their favour, even though reforms were originally supposed to improve democratic quality and/or minority rights. Domestic priorities thus significantly shaped the way peacebuilding reforms were implemented, although peacebuilders had started reform processes with a different set of priorities in mind. For example, the budget planning reform was intended to strengthen the norm of democracy. However, in Bregore/Brdašce, it was implemented in a way that reinforced the exclusionary and clientelist party network of the Mayor, who managed to turn public hearings into election campaign opportunities and excluded political rivals from the process. In the case of the Communities Committees, which were intended to strengthen minority rights, the Committee did not touch on politically sensitive areas such as language rights, protection of private property or cultural heritage. Instead, Committee members used the reform to push development-related issues such as infrastructure projects and equal access to public services. This was also true for the case of Minority Community Policing in Zabel/Šumarak, where reform implementation did not touch on politically sensitive areas of minority rights protection such as Serbs' security concerns or the various thefts in the village. Instead, the reform was used to solve issues of public waste collection. Domestic priorities such as socio-economic development, political power, or the Kosovo status question thus shaped peacebuilding outcomes. A closer look at the external–domestic interaction process can illuminate the steps to these outcomes.

The four reform initiatives resulted in the following peacebuilding outcomes: Participatory Budget Planning (low capacity/weak resistance) resulted in full implementation in Zabel/Šumarak and in captured implementation in Bregore/Brdašce. The Communities Committee reforms (low capacity/strong resistance) were judged as a captured implementation in both municipalities. Municipal Community Safety Councils (high capacity/weak resistance) resulted in captured implementation in both Zabel/Šumarak and Bregore/Brdašce. Minority Community Policing (high capacity/strong resistance) resulted in captured implementation in Zabel/Šumarak and no implementation in Bregore/Brdašce, even though high international capacity was used. Please see Table 7.1.

Peacebuilding reforms were seldom implemented unless peacebuilders actively pushed for them. So even if peacebuilders succeeded in translating international norms into the domestic legal framework – as they could easily do in Kosovo due to the supervisory powers – this did not automatically trigger implementation. Sometimes there were several years between the legal adoption of a reform and the start of its implementation, which does not conform

Table 7.1 Peacebuilding outcomes of reform initiatives

	WEAK RESISTANCE *Democracy*	STRONG RESISTANCE *Minority rights*
LOW CAPACITY *Local governance*	*Participatory Budget Planning* full (1) captured (2)	*Communities Committee* captured (1) captured (2)
HIGH CAPACITY *Police*	*Municipal Community Safety Council* captured (1) captured (2)	*Minority Community Policing* captured (1) no (2)

Note: full, captured, no refers to the level of implementation, (1) = municipality Zabel/Šumarak, (2) = municipality Bregore/Brdašce.

Table 7.2 The analytical framework of peacebuilding interactions and peacebuilding outcomes

	Environment	International ad hoc tactics			Outcome
		Prioritisation	Selectivity	Leverage	
			# rules covered over all interaction periods		
Peacebuilding reform					
Low capacity/weak resistance	Enabling (1)	No	total set	Yes	Full
Participatory budget planning	Constraining (2)	No	total set	Yes	Captured
Low capacity/strong resistance	Constraining (1)	Yes	sub-set	Yes	Captured
Communities Committee	Constraining (2)	Yes	sub-set	Yes	Captured
High capacity/weak resistance	Enabling (1)	Yes	sub-set	No	Captured
Mun. Community Safety Council	Constraining (2)	Yes	sub-set	Yes	Captured
High capacity/strong resistance	Constraining (1)	Yes	sub-set	Yes	Captured
Minority Community Policing	Constraining (2)	No	sub-set	No	No

Note
Selectivity # rules covered over all interaction periods. √ = correct prediction, x = false prediction; full, captured, no refers to the level of implementation; (1) = municipality Zabel/Šumarak, (2) = municipality Bregore/Brdašce.

to the expectations of the standard explanations. Advocates for greater international capacity would certainly have expected an earlier start to reform implementation in a high capacity policy field such as police reform. Again, this mismatch between theoretical expectations from standard explanations and empirical findings underlines the importance of alternative explanations for peacebuilding outcomes such as the external–domestic interaction process.

Table 7.2 sums up the findings of the case studies according to the analytical framework of peacebuilding interactions.

Notes

1 Financial assistance was only offered to Zabel/Šumarak and not to Bregore/ Brdašce, which might be a further reason for the failure of the reform implementation there.
2 UNMIK and the OSCE formed an advocacy coalition for the Communities Committee reform in Bregore/Brdašce in 2010, and KFOR, EULEX and the OSCE did so for the Minority Communities Policing reform in Zabel/Šumarak between 2011 and 2012.

References

Barnett, Michael, Fang, Songying and Zürcher, Christoph. (2014). Compromised Peacebuilding. *International Studies Quarterly*, Online First, 1–13.

Barnett, Michael and Zürcher, Christoph. (2008). The Peacebuilder's Contract. How External State-Building Reinforces Weak Statehood. In: Paris, R. and Sisk, T. D. (eds), *The Dilemmas of Statebuilding. Confronting the Contradictions of Postwar Peace Operations*. Abingdon: Routledge, 23–52.

Bieber, Florian. (2002). Nationalist Mobilization and Stories of Serb Suffering. The Kosovo Myth from the 600th Anniversary to the Present. *Rethinking History*, 6 (1), 95–110.

Bieber, Florian (ed.) (2005). *Power Sharing after Yugoslavia. Functionality and Dysfunctionality of Power-Sharing Institutions in Post-War Bosnia, Macedonia, and Kosovo*. Montreal: McGill-Queens University Press.

Byrne, Sean. (2001). Consociational and Civic Society Approaches to Peacebuilding in Northern Ireland. *Journal of Peace Research*, 38 (3), 327–352.

Di Lellio, Anna and Schwandner-Sievers, Stephanie. (2006). The Legendary Commander. The Construction of an Albanian Master-Narrative in Post-War Kosovo. *Nations and Nationalism*, 12 (3), 513–529.

Elbadawi, Ibrahim and Sambanis, Nicholas. (2000). Why Are There So Many Civil Wars in Africa? Understanding and Preventing Violent Conflict. *Journal of African Economies*, 9 (3), 244–269.

Esteban, Joan and Schneider, Gerald. (2008). Polarization and Conflict. Theoretical and Empirical Issues. Introduction. *Journal of Peace Research*, 45 (2), 131–141.

Kahnemann, Daniel. (2011). *Thinking, Fast and Slow*. London: Penguin Books.

Mac Ginty, Roger. (2010). Hybrid Peace. The Interaction Between Top-Down and Bottom-Up Peace. *Security Dialogue*, 41 (4), 391–412.

Ruggeri, Andrea, Gizelis, Theodora-Ismene and Dorussen, Han. (2012). Managing Mistrust. An Analysis of Cooperation with UN Peacekeeping in Africa. *Journal of Conflict Resolution*, 57 (3), 387–409.

Santiso, Carlos. (2002). Promoting Democratic Governance and Preventing the Recurrence of Conflict. The Role of the United Nations Development Programme in Post-Conflict Peace-Building. *Journal of Latin American Studies*, 34 (3), 555–586.

Zürcher, Christoph, Manning, Carrie, Evenson, Kristie D., Riese, Sarah and Roehner, Nora. (2013). *Costly Democracy. Peacebuilding and Democratization after War*. Stanford: Stanford University Press.

8 Conclusion

Assessing the impact of external–domestic interactions in peacebuilding

> What goes faster in Kosovo relative to the democratisation and the human rights, is the infrastructure, the money spend on certain needs, versus the needs for further democratisation or further human rights.
>
> *Interview 15 with OSCE regional office, Prizren, 09/05/2012*

Liberal peacebuilding is full of interactive encounters. International organisations are constantly negotiating peacebuilding with local counterparts at all stages of the intervention in regards to the terms of engagement, the content of new legislation and how it is put into practice. Peacebuilding is thus not a unidirectional, internationally controlled process, as some peacebuilding studies assume. Instead, both sides engage in multifaceted interactions against the backdrop of diverging priorities, a complex post-war environment and mutual dependencies. And these external–domestic interactions significantly influence peacebuilding results as this book shows.

This book started with a puzzle: Why do post-war states subjected to peacebuilding missions that aim to build peace and democracy so often end in a stalled transition? Not even post-war states like Kosovo that have received an enormous amount of international resources have managed the transition to peace and democracy successfully; instead, they are stuck in a mixture of clientelism and liberal and authoritarian politics. So why did one of the longest and best equipped peacebuilding enterprises fail to establish full-fledged liberal democracy in Kosovo? I propose a simple answer: The negotiation of peacebuilding between peacebuilders and domestic actors facilitates such an outcome of stalled transition. To follow this line of reasoning one has to consider that external–domestic interactions take place in complex post-war environments that peacebuilders are far from capable of controlling. They therefore react with ad hoc tactics in the interaction that offer domestic actors various opportunities to gain leeway to capture peacebuilding reforms for their own ends. A stalled transition thus becomes a more likely outcome – due to the characteristics of the external–domestic interaction process.

To come to this conclusion, this book explored the inside of peacebuilding and engaged in depth with the details of external–domestic interactions in post-war states. I was interested in what actually happens on the ground in peacebuilding and to know more about who are the protagonists of peace-building, what are their goals, and how do they act to reach their goals? My main question was how peacebuilding is negotiated between international actors and domestic agents, and how these external–domestic interactions enable domestic elites to capture the internationally dominated transition for their own priorities.

The book is based on an inductive, qualitative micro-level analysis of external–domestic interactions in post-war Kosovo. The goal was to better understand stalled transitions by taking a closer look at interactions at the micro-level. This micro-level approach had several advantages, such as the idea that tracing external–domestic interactions of peacebuilding reforms enables one to understand how domestic elites manage to capture reforms, how the environment of interaction shapes domestic adoption costs, and how peacebuilding results of captured implementation are not arbitrary, but serve to accommodate domestic priorities and interests. I traced the process of external–domestic interaction in four types of peacebuilding reforms that varied in the level of standard explanations of international capacity and local resistance: Participatory Budget Planning (low capacity/weak resistance), Communities Committee (low capacity/strong resistance), Municipal Com-munity Safety Council (high capacity/weak resistance) and Minority Com-munity Policing (high capacity/strong resistance). This allowed me to account for the explanatory power of standard theories on post-war transitions that emphasise international capacity and local resistance. The empirical data I used stemmed from semi-structured interviews with peacebuilders, domestic political elites and civil society representatives at the central, regional and municipal levels; focus group discussions with Kosovo Albanian and Kosovo Serbian citizens; primary documents (meeting minutes, monitoring reports, daily reports of international and Kosovo institutions) and secondary literature.

In order to conclude, this chapter first provides an appraisal of the inter-national intervention in Kosovo and the standard explanations for stalled transitions in the peacebuilding literature. I then summarise the argument of the book as set out in the analytical framework for peacebuilding interactions and emphasise its theoretical contribution to existing interaction-based expla-nations for post-war transitions. The last section draws conclusions beyond the case of Kosovo and proposes policy recommendations for international interventions in post-war countries.

The fate of peacebuilding in Kosovo

Kosovo has witnessed one of the most intrusive peacebuilding missions in the history of the United Nations. Indeed, international actors have seldom put as much effort into post-war reconstruction and establishing peace and demo-cracy in a war-shattered state: Peacebuilders in Kosovo took over executive, legislative and judicative authority and supervised municipal administrations; they installed an impressive amount of military and civilian personnel from top-level ministries to ethnic enclaves in remote villages; and in the past 15 years, they invested a per capita sum that has far exceeded any other peace-building mission. As a result of this strong international commitment, progress has been made towards a post-war transition to peace and democracy, but the quality of democracy has still not met the liberal international standards propagated by peacebuilders when entering the territory in 1999. The 2015 Freedom House report on Kosovo mentions a few of the problems that prevail:

> Corruption remains a serious problem. A legislative framework to combat corruption is in place, including a new four-year anticorruption strategy and action plan adopted in 2013. However, implementation has been insufficient, and graft and misconduct remain widespread across many state institutions. [...]
>
> Freedom of movement for ethnic minorities is a problem. Returning refugees face hostility and bleak economic prospects, and property reclamation by displaced persons remains problematic.
>
> (Freedom House)

The mixed peacebuilding results observed at the national level are also mirrored in the local level case studies in this book. In most cases, the peace-building reforms resulted in captured implementation, meaning that domestic actors had somehow managed to use the reform to accommodate domestic priorities through their implementation practice. Rules were added, left out or modified in a way that the domestic priorities of socio-economic development, the broadening of political power or the resolution of the Kosovo status question would be attained, rather than the peacebuilders' original goals of democracy or minority rights. In five of the eight case studies, therefore, peacebuilding reforms resulted in captured implementation (Participatory Budget Planning in Bregore/Brdašce, Municipal Community Safety Council and Communities Committees in Zabel/Šumarak and Bregore/Brdašce, and Minority Community Policing in Zabel/Šumarak), while full implementation was achieved only in the case of Participatory Budget Planning in Zabel/Šumarak, and one reform, Minority Community Policing in Bregore/Brdašce, even resulted in no implementation.

Revisiting standard explanations for post-war transitions

If one takes a closer look at the peacebuilding outcomes of the micro-level case studies, the interesting finding is that these outcomes cannot be fully explained by standard explanations in the peacebuilding literature that emphasise the importance of international capacity or local resistance for post-war transition results. The international capacity approach would expect full implementation in cases of high capacity and vice versa. The local resistance approach would predict full implementation in cases of weak local resistance and vice versa. In the case studies for this book, however, reforms with a low level of resistance did not necessarily result in full implementation. In other cases, reforms with strong international capacities resulted in no implementation although this went against expectations formulated with the international capacity argument. Standard explanations were thus often unable to explicate the outcome correctly. These observations make a third interaction-based approach to the study of stalled transitions in peacebuilding even more relevant. Before going ahead with my argument, I shortly reflect on the theoretical implications of these findings for the literature on international capacities or local resistance.

International capacities

Since Doyle and Sambanis's (2000) article was published, researchers have upheld the argument that international capacities matter for success in fostering peace and democracy and that sufficient peacebuilding capacities could level out the lack of domestic capacities or coerce 'unwilling' domestic elites into compliance (Dobbins 2007, Doyle and Sambanis 2000, Paris 2004). The findings from my case studies do not provide unanimous support for this line of thought. I measured international capacities by policy field according to mandate strength, manpower and financial assistance. Yet the policy field with high international capacities, police reform, did not yield better results than the policy field with low international capacities, local governance reform. To the contrary, the only reform initiative that was not implemented at all, the Minority Community Policing reform in Bregore/Brdašce, was part of the highly equipped policy field of police. Apparently, international capacities do not necessarily improve the peacebuilding outcome. The reason for this is that peacebuilders strive for good relationships with domestic elites and therefore do not 'activate' the capacities, even if they theoretically could. Barnett and Zürcher (2008) and Zürcher *et al.* (2013) point to similar instances where peacebuilding missions with high international capacities did not use these instruments to enforce their liberal reform package but instead tolerated domestic elite non-compliance. There are various ways that theoretically available high capacity does not take effect on the ground: For example, peacebuilders could formally have executive authority over activities of the municipal police, but de facto delegate all authority to the domestic elite. And no matter how large the number of civilian personnel deployed on the ground, as long as this personnel does not pay attention to the implementation of the reform in question, it remains ineffective. Also the amount of financial aid is useless if these financial resources are not channelled into the particular reform in a strategically clever way. The case studies thus revealed many instances, where peacebuilders chose to tolerate domestic non-compliance or reform capture and backed down from their demands, instead of using all available tools to increase pressure.

Local resistance

The close investigation of domestic responses to peacebuilding challenges the common depiction by critical peacebuilding scholars of local agency as resistance to liberal peacebuilding (Mac Ginty 2011, Richmond 2010, Richmond and Mitchell 2011): In Kosovo, resistance is only one of several types of domestic responses to international peacebuilding, and its use depends to a great extent on whether the promoted norm enjoys support in the population or not. Yet cooperation is an equally common response to international reform demands. The fact that international peacebuilding policies can actually find support within the local population is something that has been neglected in the peacebuilding literature on local resistance. Indeed, the liberal norm of democracy seems to receive widespread support within the local Kosovo population, although it might not be number one on the domestic priority list. Support exists not only because Kosovo Albanians and Kosovo Serbs strategically use it to legitimise their claims over Kosovo, but also because many appreciate the liberal elements of democracy: freedom, the right to vote for their leaders, the emphasis on accountability and transparency of institutions that would inhibit corruption, and the general promise of a better life that would lead people out of poverty. I thus found several instances of cooperation with international demands that were not the result of international pressure, but were fostered by the domestic elites' commitment to reform goals and an enabling environment.

In the end, it seems that the dismissive stance towards authoritarian means of peacebuilding has made critical peacebuilding scholarship blind to the power struggles between traditional and modern segments of post-war societies and has led many to deny the authenticity of local calls for democracy, human rights and rule of law. It seems a promising approach to draw an analytical distinction between the means used by peacebuilders and the liberal norm set promoted, and to discuss the appropriateness of each separately. In light of this, peacebuilding scholars exploring the field of local resistance could engage more deeply with the local interpretations of international norms, to identify not only the dissonance, but also the congruence with the international discourses. Given that the post-war population might potentially support liberal norms, researchers should look very closely at who these supporters are, what segment of society they represent and whose interests are served by liberal reforms.

A new approach: the analytical framework of peacebuilding interactions

Throughout the book, I have developed an argument that seeks to explain stalled post-war transitions by focusing on the external–domestic interactions in peacebuilding, particularly its non-strategic elements. I thereby build on earlier work on strategic interactions in peacebuilding by Barnett, Zürcher (2008, 2013, 2014) and others. I share the basic assumption that interaction matters and that peacebuilders and domestic elites pursue diverging goals, but at the same time are entangled in mutual dependencies, which makes a compromised outcome in the form of a stalled transition more likely. Yet existing contributions – to my opinion – put too much emphasis on the role of mutual dependencies (Barnett *et al.* 2014, Barnett and Zürcher 2008) or adoption costs (Zürcher *et al.* 2013) and in so doing, neglect the influence of bounded rationality in overly complex post-war situations. This study adds to our understanding of why interactions matter for post-war transitions by pointing to the non-strategic elements that offer opportunities for the exploitation of peacebuilding. I assume that peacebuilding negotiations usually take place in complex post-war environments that are shaped by a volatile security situation, fast-changing political developments and the need to take care of a multiplicity of tasks at once. A further complication is the fact that – no matter how much time, resources and energy peacebuilders invest in the drafting of Kosovo legislation – the actual implementation of peacebuilding reforms does not start unless international actors engage. Peacebuilders are seldom capable of keeping track of every development on the ground, and they process information in a selective, but not necessarily strategic, manner. The external–domestic interaction process is thus shaped by bounded rationality and actions are less strategically geared toward the optimum outcome than one might expect from the outset. Instead, coping strategies for dealing with overly complex situations characterise the interaction. This means that even in a highly intrusive peacebuilding intervention such as Kosovo, peacebuilders are often overwhelmed by the enormous task of social engineering entire post-war states.

This situation requires a specific analytical framework in order to be able to analyse external–domestic interactions in peacebuilding. Based on an inductive analysis, I carved out key categories of an external–domestic interaction that were of relevance for the peacebuilding reform outcome. I called this the *analytical framework of peacebuilding interactions*. Its purpose is to help in understanding the role that interactions play in peacebuilding outcomes. The key elements of the analytical framework are: (1) international ad hoc interaction tactics, (2) domestic responses, (3) the domestic environment of interaction, and (4) peacebuilding outcomes. I will briefly summarise below how the analytical framework helps to describe and analyse the influence of interactions on peacebuilding.

International ad hoc *tactics* reveal how the non-strategic aspects of an interaction process can influence peacebuilding outcomes. Prioritisation, selectivity and leverage do not precondition a specific peacebuilding outcome, but do make certain peacebuilding outcomes less likely. If careful observation is made of the specific occasions that selectivity, prioritisation or leverage occurred and to what effect, the idea that decisions are long-term strategic calculations seems less plausible. There often appears to be no clear strategy with regard to the peacebuilding reform, unless exogenous triggers create a certain urgency to end non-compliance. By following external–domestic interaction processes, one can identify patterns related to when selectivity, prioritisation or leverage occur or what effect they have on the interaction, particularly on the leeway domestic actors take to capture reforms to further their own ends.

Prioritisation refers to putting particular reform initiatives at the top of the international agenda because their implementation is important for securing international core interests such as stability or EU conditionality. Prioritisation is usually an ad hoc reaction to unexpected developments at a national or international level that require a quick re-calibration of international approaches. It cannot be considered a long-term strategic goal. If a reform becomes a priority, leeway for non-compliance tends to be curbed as peacebuilders insist on the implementation of a minimum sub-set of rules. These are usually things that are quantitative (and therefore can be used to proclaim peacebuilding success) such as formal establishment, regular meetings or minority participation. If a peacebuilding reform is not prioritised, domestic elites receive leeway for non-compliance or reform capture at a low cost. Prioritisation thus makes no implementation less likely.

There were several instances when peacebuilders used prioritisation in the external–domestic interaction to overcome domestic resistance and thus proved the pattern that prioritisation makes no implementation less likely. For instance, peacebuilders applied this tactic to the Communities Committee reform after the 2004 riots, when non-functioning committees were perceived as a security threat. Peacebuilders also used prioritisation to overcome resistance to the Minority Community Policing reform in Zabel/Šumarak, where the reform was seen as crucial to protect Serbs from security threats. Lastly, peacebuilders prioritised the Municipal Community Safety Council reform after it became a benchmark in the EU conditionality catalogue. The fact that prioritisation occurred mostly in cases of perceived security threats seems to confirm Barnett's and Zürcher's (2008: 3) notion that the peacebuilders' primary objective is stability, while democracy and minority rights are only secondary goals. The use of prioritisation always led domestic actors to drop outright resistance.

Selectivity refers to when peacebuilders select only a sub-set of rules from a reform initiative and change this sub-set of rules during the course of negotiations. Due to selectivity, domestic actors gain leeway to ignore the non-selected rules and to capture reforms at no cost. Usually, peacebuilders start an interaction by demanding the formal establishment of institutions and then shift their attention to the more practical and substantive concerns of a reform. Still, peacebuilders admit that there is no clear strategy behind the decision about which rules to select for negotiations and which not to select. Sometimes this is due to headquarters' re-framing of policies, sometimes to external shocks such as security incidents, but it is less likely to be strategically tailored to the interaction situation in a specific municipality.

Because domestic actors generally only implement those rules that peacebuilders ask them to implement, selectivity becomes a relevant factor in the course of peacebuilding reforms: If peacebuilders do not manage to cover the total set of rules during the course of an interaction, full implementation of a reform becomes nearly impossible. Selectivity thus makes full implementation less likely.

Leverage refers to international norm promotion instruments that change domestic actors' (non-)adoption costs. If peacebuilders do not use high leverage instruments, it increases domestic actors' leeway to capture reform at a low cost. Peacebuilders are able to alter adoption costs through the use of high leverage instruments such as financial assistance and diplomatic coercion. For instance, through the use of these high leverage instruments, peacebuilders succeeded in overcoming domestic resistance to unpopular and highly politicised reforms like the Communities Committee and Minority Community Policing. Leverage works because of the dependency of local actors on international resources, a fact that has already been acknowledged by existing accounts of strategic interaction in peacebuilding (Barnett *et al.*, Barnett and Zürcher 2008, Zürcher *et al.* 2013). Leverage entails a strategic element, but high leverage instruments are often used due to ad hoc decisions by peacebuilders as a response to unexpected security incidents, or due to national-wide programmes unrelated to the local situation. Leverage makes no implementation less likely.

Domestic actors were inclined to give up resistance if peacebuilders used high leverage instruments such as financial assistance or coercion. There was a clear pattern in the process tracing that showed that, if financial assistance was provided in the form of financial compensation or financial assistance for institutions or development projects, domestic actors were likely to drop resistance as well as foot-dragging strategies. The same goes for diplomatic coercion in the form of an advocacy alliance. The low leverage instruments of dialogue or capacity building did not seem to be able to overcome domestic resistance, although they certainly helped to increase the general willingness of actors to cooperate with reforms. Judging from these observations, one is led to conclude that the domestic motivation for behavioural change stems to a large extent from financial incentives and coercion, and less from being persuaded to doing the right thing. This behaviour has to be understood against the backdrop of severe poverty and scarce financial resources in Kosovo's rural areas. However, it sheds serious doubt on the sustainability of peacebuilding reforms in the long run as peacebuilders do not seem to have succeeded in shifting the priorities of the domestic agenda in a meaningful way.

Domestic responses to international interaction tactics can range from cooperation, foot-dragging and modification to outright resistance. The range of domestic responses is influenced, on the one hand, by the international tactic chosen and, on the other hand, by the environment of interaction in which negotiations take place. *Cooperation* describes domestic actors' acceptance of international demands, both in rule adoption or rule implementation. This domestic response more likely occurs in an enabling environment of interaction. *Foot-dragging* refers to activities that decelerate the reform process such as the assignment of limited priority, the use of limited effort, the allocation of limited resources and other tactics of deceleration. Foot-dragging tends to be used in any type of environment of interaction and in response to any type of international ad hoc tactic. *Modification* describes the domestic actors' substantial alteration of international demands leading to a change in the purpose of the concerned rule. As with foot-dragging, modification tends to be used in any type of environment of interaction and in response to any type of international ad hoc tactic. *Resistance* refers to the explicit rejection of international demands. It tends to be a common response in a constraining environment of interaction, unless peacebuilders resort to prioritisation or high leverage.

The *environment of interaction* is a further key element of the analytical framework of peacebuilding interactions. Interactions can take place in an enabling environment or a constraining environment. The environment of interaction describes domestic elites' adoption costs for peacebuilding reforms, which has a direct impact upon their behaviour and, in turn, the reform outcomes. Relevant factors in the calculation of adoption costs are the domestic support for international norms and the style of politics. An enabling environment is present if there is strong domestic support for an international norm *and* if there is a cooperative style of politics. Strong domestic support provides domestic elites with the incentive to cooperate with peacebuilders' demands, while weak domestic support provides domestic elites with the incentive to resist peacebuilders' demands in order to please a domestic audience. The perception of fellow politicians as being either partners or rivals also significantly influences politicians' willingness to implement peacebuilding reforms that demand power and information sharing, checks and balances and third-party inclusion in decision-making. A cooperative style of politics is based on informal networks of friendships and contacts and, possibly, mutual trust. It allows the executive branch to share power and information, and to include the opposition, minorities and/or civil society in decision-making without fearing immediate exploitation and competition. A competitive style of politics, by contrast, is based on a competitive attitude towards fellow politicians and lacks informal networks of friendships or contacts, not only with regard to relations between different parties, but also within parties. It creates an atmosphere in which those responsible for implementing reforms did so with the ultimate goal of capturing these reforms in order to broaden their individual power bases and, thus, stripped these reforms of their transformative potential to re-build relationships between former adversaries and to create a broad consensus for political decisions.

In the case studies, full implementation was only possible in an enabling environment, as was seen with the case of Participatory Budget Planning in the municipality of Zabel/Šumarak, where domestic support of promoted norms was combined with a cooperative style of politics. In a constraining environment of interaction, the peacebuilding outcome is less than full implementation and depends on the use of international ad hoc tactics. The domestic environment of interaction seems to be more relevant for peacebuilding success than the level of international capacity.

A constraining environment of interaction increases the likelihood of domestic resistance, modification or foot-dragging to international reform demands. Yet I could also observe that peacebuilders often tended to back down where they faced domestic resistance, modification or foot-dragging. Their strong interest in maintaining good relations with their local counterpart prompted international actors to disengage from a number of complicated reforms. Backing down was sometimes even an indication that peacebuilders stationed at the local level showed an understanding for domestic priorities. Having been exposed to the day-to-day constraints of municipalities, these individuals seemed more inclined to accept resistance, modification or foot-dragging than their colleagues at headquarters. The Peacebuilder's Contract (Barnett and Zürcher 2008) does refer to the possibility that peacebuilders may consciously choose to tolerate non-compliance or reform capture. My many findings of backing down might be partly due to the fact that I investigated the implementation stage of reform, while the drafting and adoption of a law tends to receive greater international attention. However, how can a law 'build peace' if it is not put into practice? The inclination of peacebuilders to back down during negotiations over reform implementation may thus be part of the explanation as to why there have been stalled transitions.

Peacebuilding outcomes in the cases studied range from full implementation, captured implementation to no implementation. *Full implementation* means that the total set of rules of a reform is implemented according to peacebuilders' intentions. *Captured implementation* means that the total set or a sub-set of rules of the reform is implemented in a way that accommodates domestic priorities of socio-economic development, political power or resolution of the Kosovo status question. *No implementation* means that the reform is not implemented at all.

The analytical framework of peacebuilding interactions reveals the specific patterns of interaction that result from the interplay of international ad hoc tactics and domestic responses in a given environment.

Generalisations beyond Kosovo

The scope of this argument is not limited to peacebuilding in Kosovo: The approach proposed in this book is valuable to understanding stalled transitions in peacebuilding contexts in many parts of the world. Certainly, the international intervention in Kosovo has been unique in several regards: The fact that Kosovo is still not recognised as an independent state by the United Nations has posed challenges that are not present in other post-war countries. Kosovo is also one of the few territories that has been fully administered by the international community, while most other peacebuilding interventions formally hold only an advisory role to the host government. Furthermore, the extent of the overhaul of domestic structures has been considerable and the amount of international resources invested in Kosovo impressive. The case of Kosovo, however, remains comparable to other post-war states, particularly because in the post-UNMIK period, the formal powers of peacebuilders have not been different from the case of Bosnia and Herzegovina, and peacebuilding practices have therefore been similar to other peacebuilding missions, in which the advisory role was filled in a more intrusive manner.

There are several reasons I assume that the analytical framework of peacebuilding interactions can be useful in understanding post-war transitions in different peacebuilding contexts. International interventions in other post-war countries are equally confronted by the scope conditions of peacebuilding, which are so fundamental to how external–domestic interactions impact peacebuilding outcomes. The diverging priorities between peacebuilders and domestic elites have been documented in numerous post-war cases. For example, Hellmüller (2013) found this to be true for the Democratic Republic of Congo, as did Kappler and Richmond (2011) for Bosnia and Herzegovina. The challenge of the over-complexity of the post-war environment and the overwhelming tasks peacebuilders set out to achieve have been discussed by Ljin (2013), who observed this in Afghanistan, and Caplan (2002: 29), who recorded similar observations in both East Timor and Kosovo. And mutual dependencies have been shown in Tajikistan and Afghanistan by Barnett and Zürcher (2008). These scope conditions limit the power of peacebuilders to enforce their vision of the post-war state upon domestic elites, a conclusion that runs like a red thread through almost all publications on hybrid peace (Mac Ginty 2011, Newman *et al.* 2009, Richmond 2009) or post-war democratization (Jarstad and Sisk 2008, Paris 2004).

Against the backdrop of the scope conditions of peacebuilding, it seems likely that external–domestic interactions are equally shaped by the international ad hoc tactics of prioritisation, selectivity and leverage and that domestic actors will use the leeway that they engender to capture reform. For example, there have been various studies that have pointed to practices of selectivity in the context of external support to democratisation (Börzel and Pamuk 2011, Carothers 2007). And increased international leverage through financial incentives – albeit with distorted consequences – has been documented in various articles on topics ranging from Europeanisation (Schimmelfennig *et al.* 2006) to democracy assistance (Knack 2004).

Domestic elites' calculation of whether or not to adopt peacebuilding reforms will most likely be influenced by the environment of interaction in other countries, too. Political elites in democratic or semi-democratic regimes are always restrained to some extent by the discourses dominating their constituencies and the level of domestic support for international norms will influence domestic elites' decisions about whether to succumb to reform demands or not. Yet the support for externally promoted norms might vary depending on the post-conflict context. I assume that norms closely related to the conflict, and therefore highly polarising, will be more likely to spark outright resistance than others. For example, in Croatia, transitional justice norms failed as long as they were depicted as contravening Croatian national identity (Freyburg and Richter 2010). In Croatia, Serbia, Cyprus and Turkey, EU reforms touching upon conflict issues failed because of their political sensitivity (Schimmelfennig 2008). Furthermore, the style of politics also poses challenges for democratisation in other post-war countries. For example, competitive politics was identified as a stumbling block for democratisation in post-war states with clientelist party systems such as in Bosnia and Herzegovina (Bieber 2005) and Northern Ireland (Byrne 2001).

Practical implications for peacebuilding

If domestic elites constantly manage to capture liberal peacebuilding to pursue their own objectives, what difference then does peacebuilding make? This question might have slipped the reader's mind while reading this book. Yet things could have fared worse. Many more Kosovo Serbs could have been killed in a majority-Albanian post-war Kosovo, many more local politicians could have been murdered in a party system infiltrated by organised crime and many more votes could have been stolen by the incumbent party if it weren't for the peacebuilders' presence. Additionally, none of the participatory and minority-empowering institutions discussed in this book would have been set up without the peacebuilders' heavy involvement in drafting Kosovo's legal framework. Even if these institutions do not fulfil their legally prescribed purpose, they do enable a dialogue between security forces, politicians, citizen representatives and minority leaders that might otherwise not have been possible. Yet it remains questionable whether these new democratic institutions will prove sustainable in the long run. This fact alone is worrisome.

It seems that peacebuilding missions will not be a 'full success' as long as peacebuilding headquarters do not engage more honestly with the scope conditions of peacebuilding. This means, first of all, to acknowledge that international and domestic priorities are not aligned and that this fact alone diminishes the prospects of success. In light of this, re-calibrating the peacebuilders' priorities enshrined in the liberal peace concept might be a necessary step. Autessere (2009, 2010) argues that peacebuilders hold on to a 'peacebuilding frame' that limits their ability to detect local conflict dynamics and limits the set of peacebuilding strategies available. It is possible that peacebuilders in Kosovo were similarly limited and did not consider alternatives beyond the liberal peace that might have contributed to reconciliation or stability. Domestic priorities seem unlikely to change even after decades of international intervention on the ground, as long as poverty powerfully shapes the everyday lives of people in post-war states, political systems incentivise power struggles over cooperation and wartime conflicts continue to dominate the political agenda and serve as mass mobilisation resources.

Why not set aside some of the grand projects of social engineering that required the complete re-writing of Kosovo's legal codes and legal framework, and instead think about how domestic priorities could be put into practice in a way that does not exacerbate existing tensions but takes domestic priorities seriously? Peacebuilders in Kosovo secretly acknowledge the pervasiveness of domestic priorities and use this insight to strategically push their liberal reform package through side payments. Yet many domestic priorities – such as socio-economic development – are not necessarily a contradiction to the core liberal foundations of the international community. Working towards a 'normal life' that offers economic opportunities, basic social services and infrastructure should be feasible in a way that contributes to relationship building between former adversaries. There are only a few programmes in the area of development geared towards re-establishing inter-ethnic relations. For example, one could devise subsidies for small businesses that hire minorities, or preferential treatment for companies with a multi-ethnic workforce. There might be greater intrinsic motivation to participate in such peacebuilding projects than sitting in a committee for two hours for small payments and little effect. Such programmes might not be sustainable without international pressure, but neither are the minority rights protecting institutions that have been established at the municipal level. Multi- or bilateral donor agencies also could be required to hire domestic companies for reconstruction efforts, instead of companies from the countries of the peacebuilders. This would provide many Kosovars with a much-needed monthly income and the state treasury with additional taxes.

Furthermore, the competitive style of politics prevalent in most Kosovo municipalities and at the national level seem seriously damaging to post-war developments. With the cooperative attitude of its political leaders, Zabel/Šumarak has been a welcome exception in this regard, and it might be an exception to learn from. So far, peacebuilding programmes do not engage intensively with political party systems and the relations between parties and politicians. If peacebuilders could influence the relations between party politicians, this might be an important way for them to proceed. An excellent example of this was given by the first UNMIK Administrator in Zabel/Šumarak, who successfully practiced informal relationship building between different parties and ethnic groups. Although it is no longer possible to trace cooperative relations between municipal politicians to UNMIK politics in the early 2000s, his approach of open doors, informal home dinners, personal engagement and constant dialogue may have left some traces on the political class of the municipality. This approach hasn't yet found its way into official peacebuilding strategy documents, but maybe some day it will.

References

Autesserre, Séverine. (2009). Hobbes and the Congo. Frames, Local Violence, and International Intervention. *International Organization*, 63 (2), 249–280.

Autesserre, Séverine. (2010). *The Trouble with the Congo. Local Violence and the Failure of International Peacebuilding*. Cambridge: Cambridge University Press.

Barnett, Michael, Fang, Songying and Zürcher, Christoph. (2014). Compromised Peacebuilding. *International Studies Quarterly*, Online First, 1–13.

Barnett, Michael and Zürcher, Christoph. (2008). The Peacebuilder's Contract. How External State-Building Reinforces Weak Statehood. In: Paris, R. and Sisk, T. D. (eds), *The Dilemmas of Statebuilding. Confronting the Contradictions of Postwar Peace Operations*. Abingdon: Routledge, 23–52.

Bieber, Florian (ed.) (2005). *Power Sharing after Yugoslavia. Functionality and Dysfunctionality of Power-Sharing Institutions in Post-War Bosnia, Macedonia, and Kosovo*. Montreal: McGill-Queens University Press.

Börzel, Tanja and Pamuk, Yasemin. (2011). *Europeanization Subverted? The European Union's Promotion of Good Governance and the Fight against Corruption in the Southern Caucasus*. Berlin.

Byrne, Sean. (2001). Consociational and Civic Society Approaches to Peacebuilding in Northern Ireland. *Journal of Peace Research*, 38 (3), 327–352.

Carothers, Thomas. (2007). The "Sequencing" Fallacy. *Journal of Democracy*, 18 (1), 12–27.

Dobbins, James. (2007). *The Beginner's Guide to Nation-Building*. Santa Monica, CA.

Doyle, Michael W. and Sambanis, Nicholas. (2000). International Peacebuilding. A Theoretical and Quantitative Analysis. *American Political Science Review*, 94 (4), 779–801.

Freedom House. (2015). Freedom in the World 2015 [Online]. Available at: http://freedomhouse.com/kosovo [accessed 04/05/2016].

Freyburg, Tina and Richter, Solveig. (2010). Identity Matters. The Limited Impact of EU Conditionality in the Western Balkans. *Journal of European Public Policy*, 17 (2), 263–281.

Hellmüller, Sara. (2013). The Power of Perceptions. Localizing International Peacebuilding Approaches. *International Peacekeeping*, 20 (2), 219–232.

Jarstad, Anna K. and Sisk, Timothy D. (eds). (2008). *From War to Democracy. Dilemmas of Peacebuilding*. Cambridge: Cambridge University Press.

Kappler, Stefanie. (2011). *Divergent Transformation and Centrifugal Peacebuilding. The EU in Bosnia-Herzegovina*. St. Andrews.

Knack, Stephen. (2004). Does Foreign Aid Promote Democracy? *International Studies Quarterly*, 48 (1), 251–266.

Mac Ginty, Roger. (2011). *International Peacebuilding and Local Resistance. Hybrid Forms of Peace*. Basingstoke: Palgrave Macmillan.

Newman, Edward, Paris, Roland and Richmond, Oliver (eds). (2009). *New Perspectives on Liberal Peacebuilding*. Tokyo: United Nations University Press.

Paris, Roland. (2004). *At War's End. Building Peace after Civil Conflict*. Cambridge: Cambridge University Press.

Richmond, Oliver. (2009). Becoming Liberal, Unbecoming Liberalism. Liberal-Local Hybridity via the Everyday as a Response to the Paradoxes of Liberal Peacebuilding. *Journal of Intervention and Statebuilding*, 3 (3), 324–344.

Richmond, Oliver. (2010). Resistance and the Post-Liberal Peace. *Millennium – Journal of International Studies*, 38 (3), 665–692.

Richmond, Oliver and Mitchell, Audra. (2011). Peacebuilding and Critical Forms of Agency. From Resistance to Subsistence. *Alternatives*, 36 (4), 326–344.

Schimmelfennig, Frank. (2008). EU Political Accession Conditionality after the 2004 Enlargement. Consistency and Effectiveness. *Journal of European Public Policy*, 15 (6), 918–937.

Schimmelfennig, Frank, Engert, Stefan and Knobel, Heiko (eds). (2006). *International Socialization in Europe. European Organizations, Political Conditionality, and Democratic Change*. Basingstoke: Palgrave Macmillan.

Zürcher, Christoph, Manning, Carrie, Evenson, Kristie D., Riese, Sarah and Roehner, Nora. (2013). *Costly Democracy. Peacebuilding and Democratization after War*. Stanford: Stanford University Press.

Appendices

Appendix 1 High, medium and low international capacity by peacebuilding intervention, 1989–2002

Post-war state	Formal powers	Material powers					
		Inhabitants p.t.	Leverage	Mission cost p.c.	Leverage	ODA p.c.	Leverage
High capacity							
Afghanistan	High	268	High	75	Low	1,139	High
Timor–Leste	High	104	High	2,838	High	1,150	High
YU – Bosnia	High	63	High	1,671	High	552	Low
YU – Kosovo	High	39	High	2,682	High	1,142	High
Medium capacity							
Cambodia	High	740	High	112	Low	446	Low
Haiti	Low	800	High	440	Low	256	Low
Liberia	Low	318	High	989	High	651	High
Sierra Leone	Low	345	High	473	Low	2,159	High
Somalia	Low	341	High	172	Low	221	Low
YU – Croatia	Low	302	High	1,155	High	507	Low
Low capacity							
Dem. Rep. Congo	Low	2,896	Low	169	Low	75	Low
El Salvador	Low	9,117	Low	17	Low	333	Low
Mozambique	Low	3,123	Low	20	Low	24	Low
Namibia	Low	388	High	159	Low	479	Low

Source: Formal powers from mission mandates, troop numbers and mission cost from UN website (www.un.org/en/peacekeeping/operations/past.shtml) or financial performance reports from UN Advisory Committee on Administrative and Budgetary Questions (www.un.org/ga/acabq/subject.asp?desc=pki) or SIPRI yearbook, number of inhabitants and ODA for first 10 years after conflict end from World Bank (http://data.worldbank.org/country).

Appendix 2 International capacity per policy field in Kosovo

Policy field	Formal powers					Total	ODA total (million U.S. dollar)	Material powers Total
	exec.	judic.	legis.	admin.				
Security	Yes	n/a	Veto	Yes		High	367,770	Above average
Rule of law	Yes	Yes	Veto	Yes		High	237,187	Below average
Democratic governance	No	n/a	Veto	No		Low	558,405	Above average
Democratic liberties, elections, institution-building							407,202	Above average
Public administration							150,865	Below average
Local governance and decentralisation	No	n/a	Veto	No		Low	338	Below average
Socio-economic development	No	n/a	Veto	No		Low	3,518,321	Above average
Political community	No	n/a	Veto	No		Low	57,873	Below average
Humanitarian assistance	No	n/a	Veto	No		Low	76,622	Below average

Source: Formal powers from mission mandates of EULEX, ICO, OSCE, KFOR, ODA from 1999 to 2011 from the Annual Report on Donor Activities by the Government of Kosovo (1999–2011), which sorts ODA contributions according to OECD DAC sectors.

Note
Average of total ODA: 4887039.

Appendix 3 Level of resistance for democracy and minority rights

Citizen statements	Weak resistance	Strong resistance
	Democracy	Minority rights
Zabel/Šumarak	positive: 55 (A)/7 (S) negative: 0 (A)/0 (S)	positive: 8 (A)/2 (S) negative: 31 (A)/0 (S)
Bregore/Brdašce	positive: 19 (A)/11 (S) negative: 0 (A)/0 (S)	positive: 9 (A)/0 (S) negative: 15 (A)/18 (S)

Note
Number of positive and negative statements made by Kosovo citizens with regard to democracy and minority rights during focus group discussions. (A) = Albanian, (S) = Serbian. See also Appendix.

Index